Published Annually Since 1905

LLEWELLYN'S 2023
MOON SIGN BOOK

P9-DMO-122

PLAN YOUR LIFE
by the CYCLES of the MOON

Llewellyn's 2023 Moon Sign Book®

ISBN 978-0-7387-6397-2

Cover design by Kevin R. Brown
Editing by Hanna Grimson
Stock photography models used for illustrative purposes only and may not endorse or represent the book's subject.
Typography owned by Llewellyn Worldwide Ltd.

Weekly tips by Penny Kelly, Lupa, and Shelby Deering.

Any internet references contained in this work are current at publication time, but the publisher cannot guarantee that a specific location will continue to be maintained.

A special thanks to Beth Rosato for astrological proofreading.

Astrological data compiled and programmed by Rique Pottenger. Based on the earlier work of Neil F. Michelsen.

You can order Llewellyn annuals and books from *New Worlds*, Llewellyn's catalog. To request a free copy of the catalog, call toll-free 1-877-NEW-WRLD or visit our website at www.llewellyn.com.

Llewellyn Publications is a registered trademark of Llewellyn Worldwide Ltd.
2143 Wooddale Drive, Woodbury, MN 55125-2989 USA
Moon Sign Book® is registered in U.S. Patent and Trademark Office.
Moon Sign Book is a trademark of Llewellyn Worldwide Ltd. (Canada).

Llewellyn Publications
A Division of Llewellyn Worldwide Ltd.
2143 Wooddale Drive
Woodbury, MN 55125-2989
www.llewellyn.com

Printed in the United States of America

Table of Contents

The Methods of the *Moon Sign Book*

Whether we live in simple, primitive times or a time of high technology and mass communication, we need our connection to Mother Nature and an understanding of how all of her systems work together—soil, sun, wind, water, plants, animals, people, and planets.

The connections among elements of nature become especially relevant when we recognize that many energies—both subtle and obvious—flow through our world and affect all things. Ancient civilizations knew about these changing energies and were much more attuned to the subtle effects that they had on us.

In the world of unseen energies, it has long been accepted in many quarters that the position of the planets makes a difference in the energy flowing around planet Earth. Those who question these energy flows are often sadly divorced from nature.

Imagine placing a large rock in the waters of a flowing stream or creek. Immediately you would notice numerous changes in the flow of the water moving over, around, and past the rock.

It is no different with our solar system. We live on a planet that floats in a solar sea of energies and frequency waves. As the planets move around the sun, the currents of energy flowing through the solar sea change in the same way that flowing water changes around the rock placed in a creek or stream…and we are affected by those changes at every level—physically, mentally, emotionally, and spiritually.

The ability to detect these changes and their effect on us has long been organized into knowledge systems, and the *Moon Sign Book* has always been a stable anchor in maintaining this knowledge and recognizing its importance. We call these organized methods of gaining knowledge *astrology*, and ancient cultures around the globe used this as their science. It was how they found and maintained a sense of prediction, control, and security, something we are still striving for even today as we try to anticipate the cycles and events of our daily lives.

Although there are several ways of organizing and assessing these energy flows based on planetary positions, the *Moon Sign Book* uses the tropical system, which says that spring officially begins when the Sun is directly over the equator at noon, something that occurs around March 20 to 21 every year. Once that moment has been determined, the rest of the zodiac calendar is laid out at thirty-degree intervals. This allows us to be precise, but also flex with the changing nature of all things, including our solar system. We support a knowledge base that upholds the ancient wisdom and teaches it to all who are interested. We invite you to read what we have written here and to celebrate the interactions of these energies with the plants, animals, earth, and stars that share this time and space with us.

Weekly Almanac

Your Guide to
Lunar Gardening
& Good Timing for Activities

♉ January

January 1–7

If Winter comes, can Spring be far behind?
~Percy Bysshe Shelley

Date	Qtr.	Sign	Activity
Jan. 6, 6:08 pm– Jan. 7, 9:40 pm	3rd	Cancer	Plant biennials, perennials, bulbs and roots. Prune. Irrigate. Fertilize (organic).
Jan. 7, 9:40 pm– Jan. 10, 10:15 am	3rd	Leo	Cultivate. Destroy weeds and pests. Harvest fruits and root crops for food. Trim to retard growth.

Commit one year to creating excellent health. Learn to prepare vegetables and salads that are delicious, exercise briefly but regularly, take a full-range amino acid capsule and a multimineral-multivitamin capsule, drink plenty of water, and get enough sleep. At the end of the year, reflect on what you think needs to be changed in our world in order for us to be healthy.

_____

_____

_____

_____

○
January 6
6:08 pm EST

JANUARY

S	M	T	W	T	F	S
1	2	3	4	5	6	7
8	9	10	11	12	13	14
15	16	17	18	19	20	21
22	23	24	25	26	27	28
29	30	31				

January 8–14 ♉

Music has healing power. It has the ability to take people out
of themselves for a few hours.   ~ELTON JOHN

Date	Qtr.	Sign	Activity
Jan. 10, 10:15 am– Jan. 12, 9:56 pm	3rd	Virgo	Cultivate, especially medicinal plants. Destroy weeds and pests. Trim to retard growth.

If you feel your mood dip in the wintertime or on a cloudy day, consider turning to energizing, mood-lifting light therapy, purchased online or through health stores. Sit a couple feet away from the lamp—placed at an angle on a nightstand, desk, or table—for at least 30 minutes. Aim for first thing in the morning—if you do it in the afternoon or too close to bedtime, you may be awake all night.

January 14
9:10 pm EST

JANUARY

S	M	T	W	T	F	S
	1	2	3	4	5	6	7
8	9	10	11	12	13	14
15	16	17	18	19	20	21
22	23	24	25	26	27	28
29	30	31				

January 15–21

That's what winter is: an exercise in remembering how to still yourself then how to come pliantly back to life again.

~ALI SMITH

Date	Qtr.	Sign	Activity
Jan. 15, 7:08 am– Jan. 17, 12:33 pm	4th	Scorpio	Plant biennials, perennials, bulbs and roots. Prune. Irrigate. Fertilize (organic).
Jan. 17, 12:33 pm– Jan. 19, 2:11 pm	4th	Sagittarius	Cultivate. Destroy weeds and pests. Harvest fruits and root crops for food. Trim to retard growth.
Jan. 19, 2:11 pm– Jan. 21, 1:29 pm	4th	Capricorn	Plant potatoes and tubers. Trim to retard growth.
Jan. 21, 1:29 pm– Jan. 21, 3:53 pm	4th	Aquarius	Cultivate. Destroy weeds and pests. Harvest fruits and root crops for food. Trim to retard growth.

Make friends and family feel right at home in your guest room. Before their arrival, set out a tray with all the comforts they could need during their stay: fresh washcloths, miniature guest soaps, tea bags, linen spray for their bed, new eye masks, and for a pretty touch, a small vase of flowers picked right from your garden.

_____

_____

_____

January 21
3:53 pm EST

JANUARY

S	M	T	W	T	F	S
1	2	3	4	5	6	7
8	9	10	11	12	13	14
15	16	17	18	19	20	21
22	23	24	25	26	27	28
29	30	31				

January 22–28 ～～

The ability to read awoke inside of me some long dormant
craving to be mentally alive.   ~MALCOLM X

Date	Qtr.	Sign	Activity
Jan. 23, 12:36 pm– Jan. 25, 1:48 pm	1st	Pisces	Plant grains, leafy annuals. Fertilize (chemical). Graft or bud plants. Irrigate. Trim to increase growth.
Jan. 27, 6:42 pm– Jan. 28, 10:19 am	1st	Taurus	Plant annuals for hardiness. Trim to increase growth.
Jan. 28, 10:19 am– Jan. 30, 3:35 am	2nd	Taurus	Plant annuals for hardiness. Trim to increase growth.

At the beginning of the year, get a journal you can write in. Each evening, sit down and reflect on your day, assessing what you learned, noting what you observed, recording what you felt, or putting down on paper whatever thoughts come to you about that day. Write the date on each entry and make each entry no more than 1–3 sentences. At the end of the year, you will have created a daybook of thoughts and will be surprised at the power of what you've written.

_____

_____

_____

_____

January 28
10:19 am EST

JANUARY

S	M	T	W	T	F	S
1	2	3	4	5	6	7
8	9	10	11	12	13	14
15	16	17	18	19	20	21
22	23	24	25	26	27	28
29	30	31				

≋ February

January 29– February 4

Anything that's human is mentionable, and anything that is
mentionable can be more manageable.   ∼FRED ROGERS

Date	Qtr.	Sign	Activity
Feb. 1, 3:11 pm– Feb. 4, 3:48 am	2nd	Cancer	Plant grains, leafy annuals. Fertilize (chemical). Graft or bud plants. Irrigate. Trim to increase growth.

Throw a grownup tea party for you and your closest friends. Purchase an antique teacup and saucer for each guest that they can take home, punctuate a table with a colorful vintage tablecloth and fresh flowers, and wear the biggest hats you can find. Serve up other beverages, too, like lemonade or a spot of coffee if that's what your gang prefers.

_____

_____

_____

_____

FEBRUARY

S	M	T	W	T	F	S
			1	2	3	4
5	6	7	8	9	10	11
12	13	14	15	16	17	18
19	20	21	22	23	24	25
26	27	28				

February 5–11 ≈≈

*What you do makes a difference, and you have to decide what
kind of difference you want to make.*   ~JANE GOODALL

Date	Qtr.	Sign	Activity
Feb. 5, 1:29 pm– Feb. 6, 4:14 pm	3rd	Leo	Cultivate. Destroy weeds and pests. Harvest fruits and root crops for food. Trim to retard growth.
Feb. 6, 4:14 pm– Feb. 9, 3:47 am	3rd	Virgo	Cultivate, especially medicinal plants. Destroy weeds and pests. Trim to retard growth.
Feb. 11, 1:34 pm– Feb. 13, 11:01 am	3rd	Scorpio	Plant biennials, perennials, bulbs and roots. Prune. Irrigate. Fertilize (organic).

If you don't have a diffuser, you can still enjoy the smell of lavender or lemon essential oils by putting 2 cups of water in a small saucepan, sprinkling 6–8 drops of essential oil on the water, then simmering at a very low temperature for an hour. The whole house smells wonderful.

○
February 5
1:29 pm EST

FEBRUARY

S	M	T	W	T	F	S
			1	2	3	4
5	6	7	8	9	10	11
12	13	14	15	16	17	18
19	20	21	22	23	24	25
26	27	28				

≈≈≈ February 12–18

*I am who I am, doing what I came to do, acting upon you
like a drug or a chisel to remind you of your me-ness, as I
discover you in myself.*   ~AUDRE LORDE

Date	Qtr.	Sign	Activity
Feb. 13, 11:01 am– Feb. 13, 8:31 pm	4th	Scorpio	Plant biennials, perennials, bulbs and roots. Prune. Irrigate. Fertilize (organic).
Feb. 13, 8:31 pm– Feb. 16, 12:00 am	4th	Sagittarius	Cultivate. Destroy weeds and pests. Harvest fruits and root crops for food. Trim to retard growth.
Feb. 16, 12:00 am– Feb. 18, 12:35 am	4th	Capricorn	Plant potatoes and tubers. Trim to retard growth.
Feb. 18, 12:35 am– Feb. 19, 11:56 pm	4th	Aquarius	Cultivate. Destroy weeds and pests. Harvest fruits and root crops for food. Trim to retard growth.

I f your world has been consumed by videos and podcasts and you've run out of new and informative things to watch or listen to, get a book on an interesting topic and read for 15–20 minutes each morning; then think deeply about what you read and what that information means in today's world.

_____

_____

_____

_____

February 13
11:01 am EST

FEBRUARY

S	M	T	W	T	F	S
			1	2	3	4
5	6	7	8	9	10	11
12	13	14	15	16	17	18
19	20	21	22	23	24	25
26	27	28				

February 19–25

Growth is uncomfortable; you have to embrace the discomfort
if you want to expand.   ~JONATHAN MAJORS

Date	Qtr.	Sign	Activity
Feb. 19, 11:56 pm– Feb. 20, 2:06 am	4th	Pisces	Plant biennials, perennials, bulbs and roots. Prune. Irrigate. Fertilize (organic).
Feb. 20, 2:06 am– Feb. 22, 12:14 am	1st	Pisces	Plant grains, leafy annuals. Fertilize (chemical). Graft or bud plants. Irrigate. Trim to increase growth.
Feb. 24, 3:29 am– Feb. 26, 10:48 am	1st	Taurus	Plant annuals for hardiness. Trim to increase growth.

Studies have proven that pets can lower blood pressure and help manage depression and loneliness. If you don't have a pet of your own, ask a friend if you can cat-sit. Volunteer as a dog walker at the local shelter or work at an adoption fair. Or simply sit in a park and ask passersby if you can pet their pooches.

February 20
2:06 am EST

FEBRUARY

S	M	T	W	T	F	S
			1	2	3	4
5	6	7	8	9	10	11
12	13	14	15	16	17	18
19	20	21	22	23	24	25
26	27	28				

♓ March

February 26–March 4

You cannot protect yourself from sadness without protecting yourself from happiness.   ∼JONATHAN SAFRAN FOER

Date	Qtr.	Sign	Activity
Feb. 28, 9:40 pm– Mar. 3, 10:16 am	2nd	Cancer	Plant grains, leafy annuals. Fertilize (chemical). Graft or bud plants. Irrigate. Trim to increase growth.

Drinking enough water is critical for health. To make water more interesting, fill your water bottle with clean water from a trusted source, then add 1–2 drops of peppermint essential oil and 8–10 drops of liquid trace minerals. The peppermint oil keeps your brain and breath fresh, and keeps flies, gnats, and other insects away. The trace minerals are excellent for stimulating many nutritional transactions in the body.

_____

_____

_____

_____

◐
February 27
3:06 am EST

MARCH

S	M	T	W	T	F	S
			1	2	3	4
5	6	7	8	9	10	11
12	13	14	15	16	17	18
19	20	21	22	23	24	25
26	27	28	29	30	31	

March 5–11

You know, you can always begin anywhere.

~JOHN CAGE

Date	Qtr.	Sign	Activity
Mar. 7, 7:40 am– Mar. 8, 9:44 am	3rd	Virgo	Cultivate, especially medicinal plants. Destroy weeds and pests. Trim to retard growth.
Mar. 10, 7:06 pm– Mar. 13, 3:21 am	3rd	Scorpio	Plant biennials, perennials, bulbs and roots. Prune. Irrigate. Fertilize (organic).

S pend a nostalgic afternoon listening to old records, whether you dust them off from a long-ago collection or purchase some at a flea market. To keep them looking and sounding their best, store the records in a wooden crate away from direct sunlight. If they happen to have some small scratches here and there, that's okay—it only adds to their character.

March 7
7:40 am EST

MARCH

S	M	T	W	T	F	S
			1	2	3	4
5	6	7	8	9	10	11
12	13	14	15	16	17	18
19	20	21	22	23	24	25
26	27	28	29	30	31	

March 12–18

You can't rely on how you look to sustain you. What actually sustains us, what is fundamentally beautiful, is compassion for yourself and for those around you.   ~LUPITA NYONG'O

Date	Qtr.	Sign	Activity
Mar. 13, 3:21 am– Mar. 14, 10:08 pm	3rd	Sagittarius	Cultivate. Destroy weeds and pests. Harvest fruits and root crops for food. Trim to retard growth.
Mar. 14, 10:08 pm– Mar. 15, 8:06 am	4th	Sagittarius	Cultivate. Destroy weeds and pests. Harvest fruits and root crops for food. Trim to retard growth.
Mar. 15, 8:06 am– Mar. 17, 10:25 am	4th	Capricorn	Plant potatoes and tubers. Trim to retard growth.
Mar. 17, 10:25 am– Mar. 19, 11:12 am	4th	Aquarius	Cultivate. Destroy weeds and pests. Harvest fruits and root crops for food. Trim to retard growth.

Plant some catnip and lemon balm in separate containers. Harvest the leaves by cutting back stems before the plants flower. Make a cup of catnip tea or lemon balm tea in the evening before bedtime and you will find yourself naturally going to bed without having to push yourself to turn off the computer and call it a day. You'll also sleep better and deeper than you usually do.

_____

_____

_____

Daylight Saving Time begins March 12, 2:00 am

March 14 10:08 pm EDT

MARCH

S	M	T	W	T	F	S
			1	2	3	4
5	6	7	8	9	10	11
12	13	14	15	16	17	18
19	20	21	22	23	24	25
26	27	28	29	30	31	

March 19–25

Music is life itself. ~LOUIS ARMSTRONG

Date	Qtr.	Sign	Activity
Mar. 19, 11:12 am– Mar. 21, 12:01 pm	4th	Pisces	Plant biennials, perennials, bulbs and roots. Prune. Irrigate. Fertilize (organic).
Mar. 21, 12:01 pm– Mar. 21, 1:23 pm	4th	Aries	Cultivate. Destroy weeds and pests. Harvest fruits and root crops for food. Trim to retard growth.
Mar. 23, 2:42 pm– Mar. 25, 8:42 pm	1st	Taurus	Plant annuals for hardiness. Trim to increase growth.

Although the planters you buy from the garden supply store are fine and dandy, why not give them a dose of character? Starting with plain planters, work your DIY magic by coating them in metallic spray paint, creating your own designs with weather-resistant acrylic paint, covering them in cane for a bohemian feel, or wrapping them in glued-on rope to make them look oh so rustic.

March 21
1:23 pm EDT

MARCH

S	M	T	W	T	F	S
			1	2	3	4
5	6	7	8	9	10	11
12	13	14	15	16	17	18
19	20	21	22	23	24	25
26	27	28	29	30	31	

♈ April

March 26–April 1

Start by doing what's necessary; then do what's possible; and suddenly you are doing the impossible.   ∼St. Francis

Date	Qtr.	Sign	Activity
Mar. 28, 6:22 am– Mar. 28, 10:32 pm	1st	Cancer	Plant grains, leafy annuals. Fertilize (chemical). Graft or bud plants. Irrigate. Trim to increase growth.
Mar. 28, 10:32 pm– Mar. 30, 6:31 pm	2nd	Cancer	Plant grains, leafy annuals. Fertilize (chemical). Graft or bud plants. Irrigate. Trim to increase growth.

Got dandelions? All parts except the stems are edible! Leaves are great in salad when young; when older, they can be blended with other greens to make pesto. Raw or roasted dandelion roots are often made into tea. Yellow dandelion flowers with the green parts removed can be dredged in pancake batter, fried in a neutral oil, and served with a drizzle of honey.

_____

_____

_____

March 28
10:32 pm EDT

April

S	M	T	W	T	F	S
						1
2	3	4	5	6	7	8
9	10	11	12	13	14	15
16	17	18	19	20	21	22
23	24	25	26	27	28	29
30						

April 2–8 ♈

If you have friends, you have family.

~JEFF WINGER, *COMMUNITY*

Date	Qtr.	Sign	Activity
Apr. 4, 5:51 pm– Apr. 6, 12:34 am	2nd	Libra	Plant annuals for fragrance and beauty. Trim to increase growth.
Apr. 7, 2:29 am– Apr. 9, 8:57 am	3rd	Scorpio	Plant biennials, perennials, bulbs and roots. Prune. Irrigate. Fertilize (organic).

If you do not have a food dryer but want to dry some herbs, find some old window screens, spread the herbs on the screens, and cover with brown paper grocery bags that have been cut open and laid on top. Suspend the screen between two chairs in a dim or dark room. The screens allow good air circulation, and the brown paper keeps light from reacting with the oils in the herbs. When dry, store in glass canning jars with tight lids out of the sunlight.

○
April 6
12:34 am EDT

APRIL

S	M	T	W	T	F	S
						1
2	3	4	5	6	7	8
9	10	11	12	13	14	15
16	17	18	19	20	21	22
23	24	25	26	27	28	29
30						

April 9–15

Celebrate the idea that you don't fit in. Find your own fit.
Stay unique.   ~BETSEY JOHNSON

Date	Qtr.	Sign	Activity
Apr. 9, 8:57 am– Apr. 11, 1:33 pm	3rd	Sagittarius	Cultivate. Destroy weeds and pests. Harvest fruits and root crops for food. Trim to retard growth.
Apr. 11, 1:33 pm– Apr. 13, 5:11 am	3rd	Capricorn	Plant potatoes and tubers. Trim to retard growth.
Apr. 13, 5:11 am– Apr. 13, 4:42 pm	4th	Capricorn	Plant potatoes and tubers. Trim to retard growth.
Apr. 13, 4:42 pm– Apr. 15, 6:57 pm	4th	Aquarius	Cultivate. Destroy weeds and pests. Harvest fruits and root crops for food. Trim to retard growth.
Apr. 15, 6:57 pm– Apr. 17, 9:09 pm	4th	Pisces	Plant biennials, perennials, bulbs and roots. Prune. Irrigate. Fertilize (organic).

Get your camera and go on a snapshot excursion. Take photos of the familiar things in your house, your yard, your town, and life in general. Put the photos away and don't look at them for a few months. Then get them out and look at them with a detached eye. Ask yourself, "What do these photos say about my life?"

_____

_____

_____

_____

April 13
5:11 am EDT

APRIL

S	M	T	W	T	F	S
						1
2	3	4	5	6	7	8
9	10	11	12	13	14	15
16	17	18	19	20	21	22
23	24	25	26	27	28	29
30						

April 16–22

There are a thousand reasons to live this life, every one of them is sufficient. ~MARILYNNE ROBINSON

Date	Qtr.	Sign	Activity
Apr. 17, 9:09 pm– Apr. 20, 12:13 am	4th	Aries	Cultivate. Destroy weeds and pests. Harvest fruits and root crops for food. Trim to retard growth.
Apr. 20, 12:30 am– Apr. 22, 6:11 am	1st	Taurus	Plant annuals for hardiness. Trim to increase growth.

While you can certainly harvest plenty of goodies from your garden, have you considered also supporting local farms with a CSA? Standing for "community-supported agriculture," many farms offer these veggie and fruit-filled boxes once a week or biweekly to nearby customers. It's a great way to back your community and enjoy fresh produce to boot.

April 20
12:13 am EDT

APRIL

S	M	T	W	T	F	S
						1
2	3	4	5	6	7	8
9	10	11	12	13	14	15
16	17	18	19	20	21	22
23	24	25	26	27	28	29
30						

April 23–29

A good book is an event in my life.   ∼STENDHAL

Date	Qtr.	Sign	Activity
Apr. 24, 2:58 pm– Apr. 27, 2:30 am	1st	Cancer	Plant grains, leafy annuals. Fertilize (chemical). Graft or bud plants. Irrigate. Trim to increase growth.

Chop up ¼–½ of a cucumber and put it in a blender. Add 1 tablespoon of plain yogurt or heavy whipping cream, and 1 tablespoon of honey. Blend to a smooth consistency. Fill a basin with hot water. Tie back your hair, lay on a towel, and put a thick layer of this on your face and neck and cover lightly with a washcloth dipped in the hot water and squeezed out. After 15 minutes, add more cucumber mixture. Leave on another 15 minutes, then wipe away with warm water and washcloth. Your skin will be radiant and beautiful.

_____

_____

_____

_____

April 27
5:20 pm EDT

APRIL

S	M	T	W	T	F	S
						1
2	3	4	5	6	7	8
9	10	11	12	13	14	15
16	17	18	19	20	21	22
23	24	25	26	27	28	29
30						

May ♉

April 30–May 6

I have learned not to allow rejection to move me.

~CICELY TYSON

Date	Qtr.	Sign	Activity
May 2, 2:09 am– May 4, 10:32 am	2nd	Libra	Plant annuals for fragrance and beauty. Trim to increase growth.
May 4, 10:32 am– May 5, 1:34 pm	2nd	Scorpio	Plant grains, leafy annuals. Fertilize (chemical). Graft or bud plants. Irrigate. Trim to increase growth.
May 5, 1:34 pm– May 6, 4:04 pm	3rd	Scorpio	Plant biennials, perennials, bulbs and roots. Prune. Irrigate. Fertilize (organic).
May 6, 4:04 pm– May 8, 7:33 pm	3rd	Sagittarius	Cultivate. Destroy weeds and pests. Harvest fruits and root crops for food. Trim to retard growth.

If you see spiders or snakes around your home, leave them be! These animals have scary reputations, but most of them are harmless to humans. Letting them hang out means you're less likely to have more harmful animals like roaches or rats, and giving them some space will keep everyone safe!

○
May 5
1:34 pm EDT

MAY

S	M	T	W	T	F	S
	1	2	3	4	5	6
7	8	9	10	11	12	13
14	15	16	17	18	19	20
21	22	23	24	25	26	27
28	29	30	31			

May 7–13

Be so good they can't ignore you.

~STEVE MARTIN

Date	Qtr.	Sign	Activity
May 8, 7:33 pm– May 10, 10:05 pm	3rd	Capricorn	Plant potatoes and tubers. Trim to retard growth.
May 10, 10:05 pm– May 12, 10:28 am	3rd	Aquarius	Cultivate. Destroy weeds and pests. Harvest fruits and root crops for food. Trim to retard growth.
May 12, 10:28 am– May 13, 12:39 am	4th	Aquarius	Cultivate. Destroy weeds and pests. Harvest fruits and root crops for food. Trim to retard growth.
May 13, 12:39 am– May 15, 3:56 am	4th	Pisces	Plant biennials, perennials, bulbs and roots. Prune. Irrigate. Fertilize (organic).

If you've found a baby bird on the ground, it's important to determine whether it actually needs help. If it is naked and its eyes are closed, put it back in its nest if you can, or hang or nail a butter container lined with soft grass as close to the old nest as possible. If it has feathers and is hopping around, it is a fledging and the parents are likely nearby watching it.

May 12
10:28 am EDT

MAY

S	M	T	W	T	F	S
	1	2	3	4	5	6
7	8	9	10	11	12	13
14	15	16	17	18	19	20
21	22	23	24	25	26	27
28	29	30	31			

May 14–20

There's nothing like a really loyal, dependable, good friend.
Nothing.   ~JENNIFER ANISTON

Date	Qtr.	Sign	Activity
May 15, 3:56 am– May 17, 8:28 am	4th	Aries	Cultivate. Destroy weeds and pests. Harvest fruits and root crops for food. Trim to retard growth.
May 17, 8:28 am– May 19, 11:53 am	4th	Taurus	Plant potatoes and tubers. Trim to retard growth.
May 19, 11:53 am– May 19, 2:48 pm	1st	Taurus	Plant annuals for hardiness. Trim to increase growth.

Before you reach for the aspirin, consider trying a natural headache aid instead. Peppermint and lavender, two pain relievers that may be found in your herb garden, have aromatherapeutic properties that ease headaches when inhaled. Dry the herbs and, either separately or together, place them in a sachet for aromatherapy whenever you need it. Or purchase either scent in the form of essential oils to mix with a carrier oil (like almond oil) and dot on your pulse points.

May 19
11:53 am EDT

MAY

S	M	T	W	T	F	S
	1	2	3	4	5	6
7	8	9	10	11	12	13
14	15	16	17	18	19	20
21	22	23	24	25	26	27
28	29	30	31			

May 21–27

All my life through, the new sights of Nature made me rejoice like a child.   ~Marie Curie

Date	Qtr.	Sign	Activity
May 21, 11:28 pm– May 24, 10:35 am	1st	Cancer	Plant grains, leafy annuals. Fertilize (chemical). Graft or bud plants. Irrigate. Trim to increase growth.

As the popular saying goes, "One man's trash is another man's treasure"—something you can think about if you spot a piece of furniture on a curb. If it's in reasonably good, clean condition, take home that piece destinated for the landfill and give it a new lease on life with a fresh coat of paint, wood glue, or even a douse with a pressure washer. It's eco-friendly and you can infuse it with your personality.

May 27
11:22 am EDT

			MAY			
S	M	T	W	T	F	S
	1	2	3	4	5	6
7	8	9	10	11	12	13
14	15	16	17	18	19	20
21	22	23	24	25	26	27
28	29	30	31			

June ♊

May 28–June 3

*If I wait for someone to validate my existence, it will mean
that I'm shortchanging myself.*   ~Zanele Muholi

Date	Qtr.	Sign	Activity
May 29, 10:51 am– May 31, 7:45 pm	2nd	Libra	Plant annuals for fragrance and beauty. Trim to increase growth.
May 31, 7:45 pm– Jun. 3, 1:03 am ·	2nd	Scorpio	Plant grains, leafy annuals. Fertilize (chemical). Graft or bud plants. Irrigate. Trim to increase growth.
Jun. 3, 11:42 pm– Jun. 5, 3:31 am	3rd	Sagittarius	Cultivate. Destroy weeds and pests. Harvest fruits and root crops for food. Trim to retard growth.

Get a planter from your local hardware store that is 3 feet long, 8–10 inches wide, and 8–10 inches deep. Put it on your porch or balcony, fill with potting soil, and plant thyme, basil, and parsley, or perhaps marjoram, cilantro, and oregano. These herbs don't mind living in a container and there is nothing as wonderful as fresh herbs in your salad!

○
June 3
11:42 pm EDT

June

S	M	T	W	T	F	S
				1	2	3
4	5	6	7	8	9	10
11	12	13	14	15	16	17
18	19	20	21	22	23	24
25	26	27	28	29	30	

June 4–10

*Preserve and cherish the pale blue dot, the only home we've
ever known.* ∼CARL SAGAN

Date	Qtr.	Sign	Activity
Jun. 5, 3:31 am– Jun. 7, 4:42 am	3rd	Capricorn	Plant potatoes and tubers. Trim to retard growth.
Jun. 7, 4:42 am– Jun. 9, 6:14 am	3rd	Aquarius	Cultivate. Destroy weeds and pests. Harvest fruits and root crops for food. Trim to retard growth.
Jun. 9, 6:14 am– Jun. 10, 3:31 pm	3rd	Pisces	Plant biennials, perennials, bulbs and roots. Prune. Irrigate. Fertilize (organic).
Jun. 10, 3:31 pm– Jun. 11, 9:20 am	4th	Pisces	Plant biennials, perennials, bulbs and roots. Prune. Irrigate. Fertilize (organic).

If you lose a family member, plant an apple tree in their memory and join the ranks of those who think about long-term food supply. Pay attention to which varieties will do well in your region and consider an heirloom variety. Also think about tree height and the need for trimming, whether the apples come early or late, and what kind of soil amendments it may need.

_____

_____

_____

_____

June 10
3:31 pm EDT

JUNE

S	M	T	W	T	F	S
					1	2	3
4	5	6	7	8	9	10
11	12	13	14	15	16	17
18	19	20	21	22	23	24
25	26	27	28	29	30	

June 11–17

Let us be grateful to people who make us happy; they are the charming gardeners who make our souls blossom.

~MARCEL PROUST

Date	Qtr.	Sign	Activity
Jun. 11, 9:20 am– Jun. 13, 2:31 pm	4th	Aries	Cultivate. Destroy weeds and pests. Harvest fruits and root crops for food. Trim to retard growth.
Jun. 13, 2:31 pm– Jun. 15, 9:46 pm	4th	Taurus	Plant potatoes and tubers. Trim to retard growth.
Jun. 15, 9:46 pm– Jun. 18, 12:37 am	4th	Gemini	Cultivate. Destroy weeds and pests. Harvest fruits and root crops for food. Trim to retard growth.

You can invite pollinators to cozy up to your backyard with an "insect hotel." Featuring holes, nooks, and crannies where bees, ladybugs, and beetles can rest and raise their young, you can either buy one ready-made or make a DIY version using twigs, hollow reeds, bricks with holes, and cardboard tubing, all contained in a wooden house. It looks surprisingly pretty and it's good for the environment too.

			JUNE			
S	M	T	W	T	F	S
				1	2	3
4	5	6	7	8	9	10
11	12	13	14	15	16	17
18	19	20	21	22	23	24
25	26	27	28	29	30	

June 18–24

We all live with the objective of being happy; our lives are all different and yet the same.   ~ANNE FRANK

Date	Qtr.	Sign	Activity
Jun. 18, 6:58 am–Jun. 20, 6:04 pm	1st	Cancer	Plant grains, leafy annuals. Fertilize (chemical). Graft or bud plants. Irrigate. Trim to increase growth.

Save time and soil health by practicing no-till/low-till gardening! Instead of turning over your soil every year, which disturbs the delicate layers of fungus, beneficial bacteria, and other parts of the soil microbiome, no-till/low-till techniques preserve this ecosystem and improve your soil. Better yet, you save some time and energy, and you also have an easy way to make use of your compost each fall, too!

_____

_____

_____

_____

June 18
12:37 am EDT

JUNE

S	M	T	W	T	F	S
				1	2	3
4	5	6	7	8	9	10
11	12	13	14	15	16	17
18	19	20	21	22	23	24
25	26	27	28	29	30	

July

June 25–July 1

Let me tell you the secret that has led me to my goals: my
strength lies solely in my tenacity.   ～Louis Pasteur

Date	Qtr.	Sign	Activity
Jun. 25, 6:57 pm– Jun. 26, 3:50 am	1st	Libra	Plant annuals for fragrance and beauty. Trim to increase growth.
Jun. 26, 3:50 am– Jun. 28, 4:55 am	2nd	Libra	Plant annuals for fragrance and beauty. Trim to increase growth.
Jun. 28, 4:55 am– Jun. 30, 10:59 am	2nd	Scorpio	Plant grains, leafy annuals. Fertilize (chemical). Graft or bud plants. Irrigate. Trim to increase growth.

One of life's great pleasures is the taste of shortcake made with strawberries, peaches, blueberries, raspberries, or other berries. Over the summer, enjoy a shortcake breakfast of berries, biscuit, and cream. The berries are excellent nutrition, the biscuit replaces toast, and the cream provides a dose of healthy fat so necessary for brain function.

June 26
3:50 am EDT

July

S	M	T	W	T	F	S
						1
2	3	4	5	6	7	8
9	10	11	12	13	14	15
16	17	18	19	20	21	22
23	24	25	26	27	28	29
30	31					

July 2–8

Summer afternoon—summer afternoon; to me those have always been the two most beautiful words in the English language.
~ HENRY JAMES

Date	Qtr.	Sign	Activity
Jul. 2, 1:20 pm– Jul. 3, 7:39 am	2nd	Capricorn	Graft or bud plants. Trim to increase growth.
Jul. 3, 7:39 am– Jul. 4, 1:30 pm	3rd	Capricorn	Plant potatoes and tubers. Trim to retard growth.
Jul. 4, 1:30 pm– Jul. 6, 1:33 pm	3rd	Aquarius	Cultivate. Destroy weeds and pests. Harvest fruits and root crops for food. Trim to retard growth.
Jul. 6, 1:33 pm– Jul. 8, 3:19 pm	3rd	Pisces	Plant biennials, perennials, bulbs and roots. Prune. Irrigate. Fertilize (organic).
Jul. 8, 3:19 pm– Jul. 9, 9:48 pm	3rd	Aries	Cultivate. Destroy weeds and pests. Harvest fruits and root crops for food. Trim to retard growth.

If you can't get out for a hike or walk in a park, you can do some birdwatching from your own backyard. Set up lots of bird feeders and complete the area with a nearby birdbath. Use a guidebook or the internet to identify visiting birds.

_____

_____

_____

○
July 3
7:39 am EDT

JULY

S	M	T	W	T	F	S
						1
2	3	4	5	6	7	8
9	10	11	12	13	14	15
16	17	18	19	20	21	22
23	24	25	26	27	28	29
30	31					

July 9–15

*Embrace your vulnerability and celebrate your flaws; it will
let you appreciate the world around you and make you more
compassionate.*   ~MASABA GUPTA

Date	Qtr.	Sign	Activity
Jul. 9, 9:48 pm– Jul. 10, 7:55 pm	4th	Aries	Cultivate. Destroy weeds and pests. Harvest fruits and root crops for food. Trim to retard growth.
Jul. 10, 7:55 pm– Jul. 13, 3:26 am	4th	Taurus	Plant potatoes and tubers. Trim to retard growth.
Jul. 13, 3:26 am– Jul. 15, 1:13 pm	4th	Gemini	Cultivate. Destroy weeds and pests. Harvest fruits and root crops for food. Trim to retard growth.
Jul. 15, 1:13 pm– Jul. 17, 2:32 pm	4th	Cancer	Plant biennials, perennials, bulbs and roots. Prune. Irrigate. Fertilize (organic).

In summer, drag your houseplants onto a shady porch along with a couple of wicker chairs, a small table, and some colorful outdoor pillows. Hang an outdoor sculpture on the wall, plant some flowers in decorative pots, and voilà—you have created a small but inviting retreat center for yourself.

July 9
9:48 pm EDT

JULY

S	M	T	W	T	F	S
						1
2	3	4	5	6	7	8
9	10	11	12	13	14	15
16	17	18	19	20	21	22
23	24	25	26	27	28	29
30	31					

July 16–22

*Love takes off the masks that we fear we cannot live without
and know we cannot live within.*   ∼JAMES BALDWIN

Date	Qtr.	Sign	Activity
Jul. 17, 2:32 pm– Jul. 18, 12:39 am	1st	Cancer	Plant grains, leafy annuals. Fertilize (chemical). Graft or bud plants. Irrigate. Trim to increase growth.

If a day at the beach or in the garden produces a bad sunburn on your back or legs, fill a bathtub with tepid water, add 2–3 cups of apple cider vinegar, and soak in the tub for 30 minutes. If your neck and face are burned, fill a basin with 1 gallon of tepid water and add ½ cup of apple cider vinegar. Soak a washcloth in the vinegar water and lay the cloth over your face and neck. When finished, apply aloe or calendula cream for quick healing.

_____

_____

_____

_____

July 17
2:32 pm EDT

JULY

S	M	T	W	T	F	S
						1
2	3	4	5	6	7	8
9	10	11	12	13	14	15
16	17	18	19	20	21	22
23	24	25	26	27	28	29
30	31					

July 23–29

Everything in nature invites us constantly to be what we are.
~GRETEL EHRLICH

Date	Qtr.	Sign	Activity
Jul. 23, 1:54 am– Jul. 25, 12:55 pm	1st	Libra	Plant annuals for fragrance and beauty. Trim to increase growth.
Jul. 25, 12:55 pm– Jul. 25, 6:07 pm	1st	Scorpio	Plant grains, leafy annuals. Fertilize (chemical). Graft or bud plants. Irrigate. Trim to increase growth.
Jul. 25, 6:07 pm– Jul. 27, 8:24 pm	2nd	Scorpio	Plant grains, leafy annuals. Fertilize (chemical). Graft or bud plants. Irrigate. Trim to increase growth.
Jul. 29, 11:44 pm– Jul. 31, 11:58 pm	2nd	Capricorn	Graft or bud plants. Trim to increase growth.

Go outside on a calm, warm summer night and look up at the sky. Let yourself feel the huge expanse of the universe you are part of and become aware of the great wisdom underlying this beautiful place you live in. Be aware that this wisdom lives also in you.

July 25
6:07 pm EDT

JULY

S	M	T	W	T	F	S
						1
2	3	4	5	6	7	8
9	10	11	12	13	14	15
16	17	18	19	20	21	22
23	24	25	26	27	28	29
30	31					

♌ August

July 30–August 5

Rare as is true love, true friendship is rarer.

~Jean de La Fontaine

Date	Qtr.	Sign	Activity
Aug. 1, 2:32 pm– Aug. 2, 11:05 pm	3rd	Aquarius	Cultivate. Destroy weeds and pests. Harvest fruits and root crops for food. Trim to retard growth.
Aug. 2, 11:05 pm– Aug. 4, 11:19 pm	3rd	Pisces	Plant biennials, perennials, bulbs and roots. Prune. Irrigate. Fertilize (organic).
Aug. 4, 11:19 pm– Aug. 7, 2:25 am	3rd	Aries	Cultivate. Destroy weeds and pests. Harvest fruits and root crops for food. Trim to retard growth.

Many common weeds, like dandelions, broadleaf plantain, and purslane, are edible. Research the weeds that are common in your garden and (untreated) yard, and then try them in salads and other recipes. Only eat a small amount of each new species the first time, to make sure you don't have any allergic or other reactions. Then load up your plate!

_____

_____

_____

_____

○
August 1
2:32 pm EDT

AUGUST						
S	M	T	W	T	F	S
		1	2	3	4	5
6	7	8	9	10	11	12
13	14	15	16	17	18	19
20	21	22	23	24	25	26
27	28	29	30	31		

August 6–12

*A classic is a book which with each rereading offers as much
of a sense of discovery as the first reading.*

~ITALO CALVINO

Date	Qtr.	Sign	Activity
Aug. 7, 2:25 am– Aug. 8, 6:28 am	3rd	Taurus	Plant potatoes and tubers. Trim to retard growth.
Aug. 8, 6:28 am– Aug. 9, 9:05 am	4th	Taurus	Plant potatoes and tubers. Trim to retard growth.
Aug. 9, 9:05 am– Aug. 11, 6:52 pm	4th	Gemini	Cultivate. Destroy weeds and pests. Harvest fruits and root crops for food. Trim to retard growth.
Aug. 11, 6:52 pm– Aug. 14, 6:36 am	4th	Cancer	Plant biennials, perennials, bulbs and roots. Prune. Irrigate. Fertilize (organic).

When life becomes problematic or overwhelming, sit under the nearest tree with your back against it. Within a short time, you will feel the gentle upward movement of electricity through the tree. Let it heal and reassure you that in nature, things remain calm and steady. Remember—you are part of nature.

August 8
6:28 am EDT

AUGUST

S	M	T	W	T	F	S
		1	2	3	4	5
6	7	8	9	10	11	12
13	14	15	16	17	18	19
20	21	22	23	24	25	26
27	28	29	30	31		

August 13–19

What we have to do…is to find a way to celebrate our diversity and debate our differences without fracturing our communities. ~HILLARY CLINTON

Date	Qtr.	Sign	Activity
Aug. 14, 6:36 am– Aug. 16, 5:38 am	4th	Leo	Cultivate. Destroy weeds and pests. Harvest fruits and root crops for food. Trim to retard growth.
Aug. 19, 7:53 am– Aug. 21, 7:22 pm	1st	Libra	Plant annuals for fragrance and beauty. Trim to increase growth.

Indulge your love of flowers by creating a container garden of nothing but bright blooms. Fill old whiskey half barrels, 5-gallon buckets, or any large pots with good soil, then plant everything from sunflowers and lavender to petunias, marigolds, Shirley poppies, and zinnias. Keep color, heights, and seasonal timing in mind. You will be rewarded with riots of color and visits by birds, butterflies, bees, and all sorts of flying friends.

_____

_____

_____

_____

August 16
5:38 am EDT

AUGUST

S	M	T	W	T	F	S
		1	2	3	4	5
6	7	8	9	10	11	12
13	14	15	16	17	18	19
20	21	22	23	24	25	26
27	28	29	30	31		

August 20–26

Understanding the difference between healthy striving and perfectionism is critical to laying down the shield and picking up your life.   ~Brené Brown

Date	Qtr.	Sign	Activity
Aug. 21, 7:22 pm–Aug. 24, 4:07 am	1st	Scorpio	Plant grains, leafy annuals. Fertilize (chemical). Graft or bud plants. Irrigate. Trim to increase growth.
Aug. 26, 9:05 am–Aug. 28, 10:32 am	2nd	Capricorn	Graft or bud plants. Trim to increase growth.

Set up an outdoor picnic to enjoy with a partner, friends, or family. Don't forget an old-school picnic basket (vintage varieties are the most adorable), a checkered blanket, melamine plates and cutlery, and foods that pack easily and can be set out stylishly, such as cheese and fruit for a charcuterie board or supplies to build your own sandwiches. Bring along a little vase of wildflowers for ambiance.

August 24
5:57 am EDT

August

S	M	T	W	T	F	S
		1	2	3	4	5
6	7	8	9	10	11	12
13	14	15	16	17	18	19
20	21	22	23	24	25	26
27	28	29	30	31		

♍ September

August 27–September 2

I know that to give the best of me, I have to take care of myself and listen to my body. ~BEYONCÉ

Date	Qtr.	Sign	Activity
Aug. 30, 9:56 am– Aug. 30, 9:36 pm	2nd	Pisces	Plant grains, leafy annuals. Fertilize (chemical). Graft or bud plants. Irrigate. Trim to increase growth.
Aug. 30, 9:36 pm– Sep. 1, 9:25 am	3rd	Pisces	Plant biennials, perennials, bulbs and roots. Prune. Irrigate. Fertilize (organic).
Sep. 1, 9:25 am– Sep. 3, 11:00 am	3rd	Aries	Cultivate. Destroy weeds and pests. Harvest fruits and root crops for food. Trim to retard growth.

If your dog or cat is shedding and you brush them out to help get rid of their old coat, you can give it to birds for their nests! Do not put out any hair that has come into direct contact with topical medications or that has soap residues from recent baths; the rest should be fine as long as it's clean. You can put it in a box or an old suet feeder or even in piles on the ground.

_____

_____

_____

_____

○
August 30
9:36 pm EDT

SEPTEMBER

S	M	T	W	T	F	S
					1	2
3	4	5	6	7	8	9
10	11	12	13	14	15	16
17	18	19	20	21	22	23
24	25	26	27	28	29	30

September 3–9 ♍

Men argue. Nature acts.   ∼VOLTAIRE

Date	Qtr.	Sign	Activity
Sep. 3, 11:00 am– Sep. 5, 4:07 pm	3rd	Taurus	Plant potatoes and tubers. Trim to retard growth.
Sep. 5, 4:07 pm– Sep. 6, 6:21 pm	3rd	Gemini	Cultivate. Destroy weeds and pests. Harvest fruits and root crops for food. Trim to retard growth.
Sep. 6, 6:21 pm– Sep. 8, 1:00 am	4th	Gemini	Cultivate. Destroy weeds and pests. Harvest fruits and root crops for food. Trim to retard growth.
Sep. 8, 1:00 am– Sep. 10, 12:36 pm	4th	Cancer	Plant biennials, perennials, bulbs and roots. Prune. Irrigate. Fertilize (organic).

If you aren't going to garden over the winter, plant a cover crop in the fall. Red clover and rye grass are both popular choices, but there are many great plants that fix nitrogen and protect the soil from weeds. You don't have to till them in the spring, either. Just mow them short a few times early in spring, and then plant in the soil beneath the cuttings, which act as a convenient mulch.

September 6
6:21 pm EDT

SEPTEMBER

S	M	T	W	T	F	S
					1	2
3	4	5	6	7	8	9
10	11	12	13	14	15	16
17	18	19	20	21	22	23
24	25	26	27	28	29	30

♍ September 10–16

The thinker sees his own actions as experiments and questions, as seeking explanations of something: to him, success and failure are primarily answers.

~FRIEDRICH NIETZSCHE

Date	Qtr.	Sign	Activity
Sep. 10, 12:36 pm– Sep. 13, 1:18 am	4th	Leo	Cultivate. Destroy weeds and pests. Harvest fruits and root crops for food. Trim to retard growth.
Sep. 13, 1:18 am– Sep. 14, 9:40 pm	4th	Virgo	Cultivate, especially medicinal plants. Destroy weeds and pests. Trim to retard growth.
Sep. 15, 1:44 pm– Sep. 18, 12:58 am	1st	Libra	Plant annuals for fragrance and beauty. Trim to increase growth.

Plan an entire day of perusing garage sales. Look them up in your local paper or online, map out a route, and come with a list in hand. Are you after vintage glassware? A midcentury dresser? Some offbeat tchotchkes for a shelf? Don't forget to put towels in your car if you're moving a large furniture piece and wear comfortable shoes so you can cover entire neighborhoods.

_____

_____

_____

_____

September 14
9:40 pm EDT

SEPTEMBER

S	M	T	W	T	F	S
					1	2
3	4	5	6	7	8	9
10	11	12	13	14	15	16
17	18	19	20	21	22	23
24	25	26	27	28	29	30

September 17–23 ♍

Music is healing. …Music holds things together. ∼PRINCE

Date	Qtr.	Sign	Activity
Sep. 18, 12:58 am– Sep. 20, 10:06 am	1st	Scorpio	Plant grains, leafy annuals. Fertilize (chemical). Graft or bud plants. Irrigate. Trim to increase growth.
Sep. 22, 4:20 pm– Sep. 24, 7:29 pm	2nd	Capricorn	Graft or bud plants. Trim to increase growth.

Sleep experts say that having a bedtime ritual each night can help you snooze even better. Make it a routine that emphasizes self-care, with lavender-scented lotions and dimly lit candles or lights. Power down your devices at least an hour before bed. Take care with your skin, with face creams and serums that make you feel good and help you wake up looking well-rested. Play soft, calming music to set the scene.

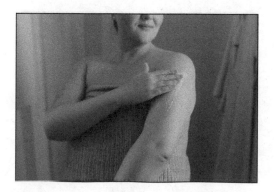

September 22
3:32 pm EDT

SEPTEMBER

S	M	T	W	T	F	S
					1	2
3	4	5	6	7	8	9
10	11	12	13	14	15	16
17	18	19	20	21	22	23
24	25	26	27	28	29	30

♎ September 24–30

For in the end, freedom is a personal and lonely battle, and one faces down fears of today so that those of tomorrow might be engaged.   ~ALICE WALKER

Date	Qtr.	Sign	Activity
Sep. 26, 8:18 pm– Sep. 28, 8:17 pm	2nd	Pisces	Plant grains, leafy annuals. Fertilize (chemical). Graft or bud plants. Irrigate. Trim to increase growth.
Sep. 29, 5:58 am– Sep. 30, 9:18 pm	3rd	Aries	Cultivate. Destroy weeds and pests. Harvest fruits and root crops for food. Trim to retard growth.
Sep. 30, 9:18 pm– Oct. 3, 1:03 am	3rd	Taurus	Plant potatoes and tubers. Trim to retard growth.

If your cat has escaped outdoors, put their litter box, bed, and a bowl of water on the porch. No food, as this can attract wildlife or other cats that can scare your cat away. Most lost cats don't go far, so ask your neighbors to check their garages, shrubbery, and other hiding places. Try calling your cat while shaking a container of food or treats. Hopefully your kitty will be home in no time!

_____

_____

_____

_____

○
September 29
5:58 am EDT

SEPTEMBER

S	M	T	W	T	F	S
					1	2
3	4	5	6	7	8	9
10	11	12	13	14	15	16
17	18	19	20	21	22	23
24	25	26	27	28	29	30

October ♎
October 1–7

The ridiculous events in everyday life are often overlooked—people don't recognise it as potentially cinematic.
                                    ~TAIKA WAITITI

Date	Qtr.	Sign	Activity
Oct. 3, 1:03 am– Oct. 5, 8:32 am	3rd	Gemini	Cultivate. Destroy weeds and pests. Harvest fruits and root crops for food. Trim to retard growth.
Oct. 5, 8:32 am– Oct. 6, 9:48 am	3rd	Cancer	Plant biennials, perennials, bulbs and roots. Prune. Irrigate. Fertilize (organic).
Oct. 6, 9:48 am– Oct. 7, 7:24 pm	4th	Cancer	Plant biennials, perennials, bulbs and roots. Prune. Irrigate. Fertilize (organic).
Oct. 7, 7:24 pm– Oct. 10, 8:02 am	4th	Leo	Cultivate. Destroy weeds and pests. Harvest fruits and root crops for food. Trim to retard growth.

Bird baths are good, but have you tried a bird fountain? Get a small decorative fountain with multiple tiers and set it up near your feeders. Watch as the birds enjoy the new bath!

_____

_____

_____

_____

October 6
9:48 am EDT

OCTOBER

S	M	T	W	T	F	S
1	2	3	4	5	6	7
8	9	10	11	12	13	14
15	16	17	18	19	20	21
22	23	24	25	26	27	28
29	30	31				

♎ October 8–14

Love demands expression. It will not stay still, stay silent, be good, be modest, be seen and not heard, no. It will break out in tongues of praise, the high note that smashes the glass and spills the liquid.   ~JEANETTE WINTERSON

Date	Qtr.	Sign	Activity
Oct. 10, 8:02 am– Oct. 12, 8:22 pm	4th	Virgo	Cultivate, especially medicinal plants. Destroy weeds and pests. Trim to retard growth.
Oct. 14, 1:55 pm– Oct. 15, 7:04 am	1st	Libra	Plant annuals for fragrance and beauty. Trim to increase growth.

In the fall, spread four bags of compost over a sunny, 12 foot × 15 foot area in your yard, then rototill or turn over that soil. In the spring, plant one tomato plant, one zucchini, one cucumber, two cabbages, four green beans, six peas, four lettuces, a row of carrots, a few beets, a row of corn, two parsley, and one basil. You will be amazed at how much food this small garden will produce.

October 14
1:55 pm EDT

OCTOBER

S	M	T	W	T	F	S
1	2	3	4	5	6	7
8	9	10	11	12	13	14
15	16	17	18	19	20	21
22	23	24	25	26	27	28
29	30	31				

October 15–21

*Nature never repeats herself, and the possibility of one
human soul will never be found in another.*

~ELIZABETH CADY STANTON

Date	Qtr.	Sign	Activity
Oct. 15, 7:04 am– Oct. 17, 3:36 pm	1st	Scorpio	Plant grains, leafy annuals. Fertilize (chemical). Graft or bud plants. Irrigate. Trim to increase growth.
Oct. 19, 9:55 pm– Oct. 21, 11:29 pm	1st	Capricorn	Graft or bud plants. Trim to increase growth.
Oct. 21, 11:29 pm– Oct. 22, 2:06 am	2nd	Capricorn	Graft or bud plants. Trim to increase growth.

Got a kitchen knife that needs sharpening, but no sharpener? Grab a ceramic coffee mug and turn it over. Holding the edge of the blade at about a fifteen to twenty degree angle from the bottom of the mug, run the blade lengthwise across the unglazed ring around the edge ten times on each side. Check the sharpness, and then repeat if needed.

October 21
11:29 pm EDT

OCTOBER

S	M	T	W	T	F	S
1	2	3	4	5	6	7
8	9	10	11	12	13	14
15	16	17	18	19	20	21
22	23	24	25	26	27	28
29	30	31				

♎ October 22–28

Music…can name the unnamable, and communicate the
unknowable.   ~LEONARD BERNSTEIN

Date	Qtr.	Sign	Activity
Oct. 24, 4:33 am– Oct. 26, 6:02 am	2nd	Pisces	Plant grains, leafy annuals. Fertilize (chemical). Graft or bud plants. Irrigate. Trim to increase growth.
Oct. 28, 7:44 am– Oct. 28, 4:24 pm	2nd	Taurus	Plant annuals for hardiness. Trim to increase growth.
Oct. 28, 4:24 pm– Oct. 30, 11:08 am	3rd	Taurus	Plant potatoes and tubers. Trim to retard growth.

Paint-by-number paintings are having a resurgence once again. First popular in the 1950s, you can now easily purchase your own kit, found through online marketplaces. Search for ones geared toward adults and create a masterpiece featuring sunflowers, mountain vistas, or colorful butterflies. After all, studies have shown that expressing yourself through art can lower anxiety and depression.

○
October 28
4:24 pm EDT

OCTOBER

S	M	T	W	T	F	S
1	2	3	4	5	6	7
8	9	10	11	12	13	14
15	16	17	18	19	20	21
22	23	24	25	26	27	28
29	30	31				

November ♏

October 29–November 4

Each of us must confront our own fears, must come face to face with them. How we handle our fears will determine where we go with the rest of our lives. ~JUDY BLUME

Date	Qtr.	Sign	Activity
Oct. 30, 11:08 am–Nov. 1, 5:30 pm	3rd	Gemini	Cultivate. Destroy weeds and pests. Harvest fruits and root crops for food. Trim to retard growth.
Nov. 1, 5:30 pm–Nov. 4, 3:21 am	3rd	Cancer	Plant biennials, perennials, bulbs and roots. Prune. Irrigate. Fertilize (organic).
Nov. 4, 3:21 am–Nov. 5, 3:37 am	3rd	Leo	Cultivate. Destroy weeds and pests. Harvest fruits and root crops for food. Trim to retard growth.

It can be surprisingly tricky to decorate the area above one's bed. Above a headboard, hang up artwork or framed photos to create a small gallery, or include a floating shelf filled with verdant houseplants. Or skip the headboard altogether and "make" one using large, layered wall baskets or floral vintage fans.

NOVEMBER

S	M	T	W	T	F	S
				1	2	3	4
5	6	7	8	9	10	11
12	13	14	15	16	17	18
19	20	21	22	23	24	25
26	27	28	29	30		

♏ November 5–11

Believe that anything is possible when you have the right
people there to support you.   ~MISTY COPELAND

Date	Qtr.	Sign	Activity
Nov. 5, 3:37 am– Nov. 6, 2:39 pm	4th	Leo	Cultivate. Destroy weeds and pests. Harvest fruits and root crops for food. Trim to retard growth.
Nov. 6, 2:39 pm– Nov. 9, 3:08 am	4th	Virgo	Cultivate, especially medicinal plants. Destroy weeds and pests. Trim to retard growth.
Nov. 11, 1:39 pm– Nov. 13, 4:27 am	4th	Scorpio	Plant biennials, perennials, bulbs and roots. Prune. Irrigate. Fertilize (organic).

Have you thought about starting a vintage collection? Pick a shelf in your home that could use some bygone vibes and choose something specific to be on the lookout for at flea markets and secondhand stores. Consider: souvenir plates featuring states or favorite locales, miniature painted portraits, bingo cards, milk glass, or trophies. As you arrange your collection, try tucking in faux or live houseplants as a visually pleasing touch.

―――――――――――――――――

―――――――――――――――――

―――――――――――――――――

―――――――――――――――――

Daylight Saving Time
ends November 5, 2:00 am

November 5
3:37 am EST

NOVEMBER

S	M	T	W	T	F	S
			1	2	3	4
5	6	7	8	9	10	11
12	13	14	15	16	17	18
19	20	21	22	23	24	25
26	27	28	29	30		

November 12–18 ♏

*At this season of the year, darkness is a more insistent thing
than cold. The days are short as any dream.*

~E. B. WHITE

Date	Qtr.	Sign	Activity
Nov. 13, 4:27 am– Nov. 13, 9:23 pm	1st	Scorpio	Plant grains, leafy annuals. Fertilize (chemical). Graft or bud plants. Irrigate. Trim to increase growth.
Nov. 16, 2:41 am– Nov. 18, 6:28 am	1st	Capricorn	Graft or bud plants. Trim to increase growth.

If you have boxes or envelopes of old photos in your closet or basement, sort them into periods or subject matter, then buy a photo album and put the photos in the album. Put the album on your bookshelf or coffee table and look at it from time to time as a reminder of how much everything in this world changes. Learn to anticipate and roll with the changes.

_____

_____

_____

_____

November 13
4:27 am EST

NOVEMBER

S	M	T	W	T	F	S
			1	2	3	4
5	6	7	8	9	10	11
12	13	14	15	16	17	18
19	20	21	22	23	24	25
26	27	28	29	30		

♏ November 19–25

Accepting oneself does not preclude an attempt to become
better.   ~FLANNERY O'CONNOR

Date	Qtr.	Sign	Activity
Nov. 20, 9:29 am– Nov. 22, 12:19 pm	2nd	Pisces	Plant grains, leafy annuals. Fertilize (chemical). Graft or bud plants, Irrigate. Trim to increase growth.
Nov. 24, 3:29 pm– Nov. 26, 7:40 pm	2nd	Taurus	Plant annuals for hardiness. Trim to increase growth.

Vintage magazines are a treat for the eyes, and you may even
pick up some tips as you flip through them—or ones that
you may snicker at! While you may not be cooking a chicken
that promises an engagement from your partner, you might have
fun whipping up an old-school punch recipe for a party or cutting out pictures to add to an inspiration board. Pick some up at
garage sales and flea markets.

_____

_____

_____

_____

November 20
5:50 am EST

NOVEMBER

S	M	T	W	T	F	S
			1	2	3	4
5	6	7	8	9	10	11
12	13	14	15	16	17	18
19	20	21	22	23	24	25
26	27	28	29	30		

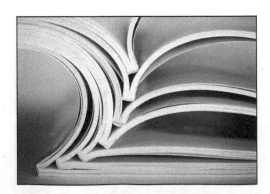

December ♐

November 26–December 2

We should indeed keep calm in the face of difference, and live our lives in a state of inclusion and wonder at the diversity of humanity. ~GEORGE TAKEI

Date	Qtr.	Sign	Activity
Nov. 27, 4:16 am– Nov. 29, 1:54 am	3rd	Gemini	Cultivate. Destroy weeds and pests. Harvest fruits and root crops for food. Trim to retard growth.
Nov. 29, 1:54 am– Dec. 1, 11:00 am	3rd	Cancer	Plant biennials, perennials, bulbs and roots. Prune. Irrigate. Fertilize (organic).
Dec. 1, 11:00 am– Dec. 3, 10:50 pm	3rd	Leo	Cultivate. Destroy weeds and pests. Harvest fruits and root crops for food. Trim to retard growth.

Write a letter to each of your children or special people, telling them on paper what you like about them, why you love them, and why they're special.

_____

_____

_____

_____

November 27
4:16 am EST

DECEMBER

S	M	T	W	T	F	S
					1	2
3	4	5	6	7	8	9
10	11	12	13	14	15	16
17	18	19	20	21	22	23
24	25	26	27	28	29	30
31						

December 3–9

It is hard to fail, but it is worse never to have tried to succeed.
~THEODORE ROOSEVELT

Date	Qtr.	Sign	Activity
Dec. 3, 10:50 pm– Dec. 5, 12:49 am	3rd	Virgo	Cultivate, especially medicinal plants. Destroy weeds and pests. Trim to retard growth.
Dec. 5, 12:49 am– Dec. 6, 11:35 am	4th	Virgo	Cultivate, especially medicinal plants. Destroy weeds and pests. Trim to retard growth.
Dec. 8, 10:35 pm– Dec. 11, 6:11 am	4th	Scorpio	Plant biennials, perennials, bulbs and roots. Prune. Irrigate. Fertilize (organic).

Keep up with your times. Listen to music by singers you have never heard of. Watch a few of the current movies to see what "movie messages" are being presented. Get familiar with blockchain or other technology. Read a Pulitzer Prize–winning book just to see what is considered good reading these days. Listen to intelligent and informative discussions about artificial intelligence or economics.

December 5
12:49 am EST

DECEMBER

S	M	T	W	T	F	S
					1	2
3	4	5	6	7	8	9
10	11	12	13	14	15	16
17	18	19	20	21	22	23
24	25	26	27	28	29	30
31						

December 10–16

There's always an excuse to celebrate someone you love.

~Cynthia Rowley

Date	Qtr.	Sign	Activity
Dec. 11, 6:11 am– Dec. 12, 6:32 pm	4th	Sagittarius	Cultivate. Destroy weeds and pests. Harvest fruits and root crops for food. Trim to retard growth.
Dec. 13, 10:31 am– Dec. 15, 12:56 pm	1st	Capricorn	Graft or bud plants. Trim to increase growth.

Do yourself a favor and try a social media detox for a day, week, or even a month. Experts say that spending too much time on social media can be detrimental to one's mental health and prevents a person from fully enjoying the present. Instead, read books, catch up with friends in person or over the phone, and practice meditation to stay in the moment.

_____

_____

_____

_____

December 12
6:32 pm EST

DECEMBER

S	M	T	W	T	F	S
					1	2
3	4	5	6	7	8	9
10	11	12	13	14	15	16
17	18	19	20	21	22	23
24	25	26	27	28	29	30
31						

December 17–23

You mustn't confuse single failure with a final defeat.

~F. Scott Fitzgerald

Date	Qtr.	Sign	Activity
Dec. 17, 2:58 pm– Dec. 19, 1:39 pm	1st	Pisces	Plant grains, leafy annuals. Fertilize (chemical). Graft or bud plants. Irrigate. Trim to increase growth.
Dec. 19, 1:39 pm– Dec. 19, 5:47 pm	2nd	Pisces	Plant grains, leafy annuals. Fertilize (chemical). Graft or bud plants. Irrigate. Trim to increase growth.
Dec. 21, 9:50 pm– Dec. 24, 3:15 am	2nd	Taurus	Plant annuals for hardiness. Trim to increase growth.

Over the dry winter months, treat yourself to a "spa day." Put a heavy duty conditioner on your hair and cover with a plastic cap. Get a piece of 400-grit sandpaper and lightly sand the dry skin from arms and legs. Soak in a tub of very warm water and Epsom salts for half an hour. Groom your feet, cut toenails, rub a good moisturizer into your skin; then wash your hair, let it dry naturally, and feel totally renewed!

_____

_____

_____

_____

December 19
1:39 pm EST

DECEMBER

S	M	T	W	T	F	S
					1	2
3	4	5	6	7	8	9
10	11	12	13	14	15	16
17	18	19	20	21	22	23
24	25	26	27	28	29	30
31						

December 24–30

I say that the most liberating thing about beauty is realizing that you are the beholder. This empowers us to find beauty in places where others have not dared to look including in nature or even inside ourselves.   ~SALMA HAYEK

Date	Qtr.	Sign	Activity
Dec. 26, 10:15 am– Dec. 26, 7:33 pm	2nd	Cancer	Plant grains, leafy annuals. Fertilize (chemical). Graft or bud plants. Irrigate. Trim to increase growth.
Dec. 26, 7:33 pm– Dec. 28, 7:23 pm	3rd	Cancer	Plant biennials, perennials, bulbs and roots. Prune. Irrigate. Fertilize (organic).
Dec. 28, 7:23 pm– Dec. 31, 6:53 am	3rd	Leo	Cultivate. Destroy weeds and pests. Harvest fruits and root crops for food. Trim to retard growth.

If you've always wanted to sew, knit, crochet, build, weld, wire an old lamp, or read classic literature, give yourself the Christmas gift of subscribing to an online group that is involved in teaching and learning what you would love to be able to do. Start small and keep at it. Good skills are essential in this world.

○

December 26
7:33 pm EST

DECEMBER

S	M	T	W	T	F	S
					1	2
3	4	5	6	7	8	9
10	11	12	13	14	15	16
17	18	19	20	21	22	23
24	25	26	27	28	29	30
31						

December 31–January 6

*If more of us valued food and cheer and song above hoarded
gold, it would be a merrier world.*

~J. R. R. TOLKIEN

Date	Qtr.	Sign	Activity
Jan. 5, 7:39 am– Jan. 7, 4:08 pm	4th	Scorpio	Plant biennials, perennials, bulbs and roots. Prune. Irrigate. Fertilize (organic).

Get off the beaten path and locate some quirky museums
around your area that you've never visited before. For
example, Le Roy, New York, has the Jell-O Museum, Middleton,
Wisconsin, has the National Mustard Museum, and Gatlinburg,
Tennessee, has the Salt and Pepper Shaker Museum.

_____

_____

_____

_____

◐

January 3
10:30 pm EST

DECEMBER

S	M	T	W	T	F	S
					1	2
3	4	5	6	7	8	9
10	11	12	13	14	15	16
17	18	19	20	21	22	23
24	25	26	27	28	29	30
31						

Gardening by the Moon

Welcome to the world of gardening by the Moon! Unlike most gardening advice, this article is not about how to garden, it's about when to garden. Timing is everything; if you know how to use the Moon, you'll not only be in sync with nature but you can sit back and watch your garden grow beyond your wildest dreams.

Gardening by the Moon is nothing new. It's been around since ancient times when people used both the Sun and the Moon to predict the tides, as well as fertility and growth cycles for plants and animals.

Lunar gardening is simple and the results are immediate. It doesn't matter whether you're a beginner gardener with a single pot or an old hand with years of master gardening experience—your garden will grow bigger and better if you follow the cycles of the Moon and match up the right time with the right garden activity. When the temperature has dropped and the sun is low on the horizon, you can apply what you've learned to your indoor plants as well.

The sky is a celestial clock, with the Sun and the Moon as the "hands" that tell the time. The Sun tells the season, and the light and location of the Moon tell the best times for birth, growth, and death in the garden. The Moon doesn't generate any light by itself, but as it circles the Earth it reflects the light of the Sun, which makes the Moon look like it's getting bigger and smaller. The cyclical increases and decreases in the light of the Moon are phases and tell times of growth.

Moon Phases

The theory behind gardening by the Moon is "as the Moon goes, so goes the garden." The Earth circles around the Sun once a year, but the Moon has a much shorter "life span" of twenty-eight to thirty days. Every month, as the light of the Moon increases and decreases, it mirrors the cycle of birth, growth, and death in the garden. After adjusting your garden activities to the light of the Moon, you'll be amazed to see how well your garden grows.

The **waxing phase** is the growth cycle in the garden. It begins with the New Moon and lasts for two weeks. Each month the Moon is "born" at the New Moon (day one) and grows bigger and brighter until it reaches maturity at the Full Moon (day fourteen). When the light of the Moon is increasing, it's the best time of the month to sow seeds, plant leafy annuals, and cut back or prune plants to encourage bigger growth.

The **waning phase** is the declining cycle in the garden. It begins with the Full Moon (day fourteen) and lasts for two weeks. The Moon grows older after the Full Moon as the light begins to decrease, until it disappears or "dies" at day twenty-eight. The decreasing light of the Moon is the time to plant bulbs, root vegetables, and perennials that store their energy underground. The waning Moon phase is also a good time for garden maintenance, including weeding, raking, deadheading, mowing, working the soil, destroying insects, and burning brush.

How can you tell if the Moon is waxing or waning?

Cup your right hand into a C shape and look up into the sky. If the crescent Moon fits into the closed part of your right hand, it's a waxing Moon.

Cup your left hand into a C shape and look up into the sky. If the crescent Moon fits into the closed part of your left hand, it's a waning Moon.

New Moon and Full Moon

Every month, the Moon takes one day off. This time-out between waning and waxing is called the New Moon. The time-out between waxing and waning is called the Full Moon. When the Moon reaches either of these stopping points, it's time for you to follow its example and take a one-day break from the garden.

Moon Signs

Once you know the Moon phases, the next step is to locate where the Moon is in the zodiac. The Moon hangs out in each of the zodiac signs for two to three days per month.

There's no such thing as a "bad" time in the garden, but there are Moon signs that are better for growth and others that are better for digging and weeding. Growth times alternate every two to three days with maintenance times. The trick is knowing which one is which.

The grow signs are Taurus, Cancer, Libra, Scorpio, Capricorn, and Pisces. When the Moon is in these signs, it's time to seed and plant.

The no-grow/maintenance signs are Aries, Gemini, Leo, Virgo, Sagittarius, and Aquarius. When the Moon is in these signs, it's time for digging, weeding, mowing, and pruning.

Remember: It's always a good time to garden something!

Putting It All Together

In order to get started, you'll need three tools: a calendar with New and Full Moons, the Moon tables (pg. 136), and the Moon phases and signs below.

Then follow these simple steps:

1. Mark your calendar with your time frame for gardening.
2. Figure out when the Moon is waxing (1st and 2nd quarters) and waning (3rd and 4th quarters). Use the tables in the Weekly Almanac section.
3. Locate the Moon by zodiac sign.
4. Check out the gardening advice below, which takes into account the Moon's phase and sign.

Moon Phases and Signs

Note: Can be applied to any calendar year.

Waxing Aries Moon (October–April)

Aries is one of the three fire signs that is hot and barren. Seeds planted under a waxing Aries Moon tend to be bitter or bolt quickly, but if you're feeling lucky, you could try your hand at hot and spicy peppers or herbs that thrive in dry heat.

Waning Aries Moon (April–October)

The decreasing light of the waning Aries Moon makes these two to three days a good time to focus on harvesting, cutting back, mowing the lawn, and getting rid of pests.

Waxing Taurus Moon (November–May)

Taurus is one of the three semi-fruitful earth signs. These days are perfect ones to establish your garden by planting or fertilizing annuals. Annuals with outside seeds like lettuces, cabbage, corn, and broccoli grow faster when planted under a waxing Taurus Moon that is one to seven days old. Vegetables with inside seeds like cucumbers, melons, squash, tomatoes, and beans should be planted when the Moon is seven to twelve days old. Annual flowers can be planted any time during this two-week phase.

Waning Taurus Moon (May–November)
The decreasing light of this semi-fruitful waning Taurus Moon gives you a perfect two- or three-day window for planting perennials or digging in root vegetables and flower bulbs.

Waxing Gemini Moon (December–June)
Gemini is one of the three dry and barren signs. But with the light of the Moon increasing, you can use these two to three days to prune or cut back plants you want to flourish and grow bigger.

Waning Gemini Moon (June–December)
Gemini can be all over the place, so use these couple of dry and barren days when the light is decreasing to weed invasive plants that are out of control.

Waxing Cancer Moon (January–July)
Cancer is one of the three wet and fruitful signs, so when the Moon is waxing in Cancer it's the perfect time to plant seeds or set out seedlings and annual flowers that live for only one season. Annuals with outside seeds grow faster when planted under a Moon that is one to seven days old. Vegetables with inside seeds should be planted when the Moon is seven to twelve days old. Annual flowers can be planted any time during these two weeks.

Waning Cancer Moon (July–January)
Plant perennials, root vegetables, and bulbs to your heart's content under the decreasing light of this fruitful Moon.

Waxing Leo Moon (February–August)
The light of the Moon is increasing, but Leo is one of the three hot and barren fire signs. Use the two or three days of this waxing Leo Moon to cut and prune the plants and shrubs you want to be the king or queen of your garden.

Waning Leo Moon (August–February)

With the light of the Moon decreasing, this Leo Moon is a good period to dig the soil, destroy pests and insects, and burn brush.

Waxing Virgo Moon (March–September)

Virgo is a semi-barren sign, which is good for fertilizing (Virgo is a "greenie" type that loves organics) and for planting woody vines and hardy herbs.

Waning Virgo Moon (September–March)

With the light of this semi-barren Moon decreasing for a couple of days, plan to hoe those rows and get rid of your weeds. Harvest Moon in September.

Waxing Libra Moon (October–April)

Libra is a semi-fruitful sign focused on beauty. Because the Moon is growing brighter in Libra, these two to three days are a great time to give your flower garden some heavy-duty TLC.

Waning Libra Moon (April–October)

If you want to encourage re-blooming, try deadheading your vegetables and flowers under the light of this decreasing Libra Moon. Harvest your flowers.

Waxing Scorpio Moon (November–May)

Scorpio is one of the three wet and fruitful signs. When the Moon is waxing in Scorpio, it's the perfect time for planting annuals that have a bite, like arugula and hot peppers. Annuals with outside seeds grow faster when planted under a Moon that is one to seven days old. Vegetables with inside seeds should be planted when the Moon is seven to twelve days old. Annual flowers can be planted anytime during this two-week phase.

Waning Scorpio Moon (May–November)

With the light of the Moon decreasing in Scorpio, a sign that likes strong and intense flavors, this is the perfect period to plant hardy perennials, garlic bulbs, and onion sets.

Waxing Sagittarius Moon (June–December)
Sagittarius is one of the three hot and barren signs. Because Sagittarius prefers roaming to staying still, this waxing Moon is not a good time for planting. But you can encourage growth during the two or three days when the light is increasing by cutting back, mowing, and pruning.

Waning Sagittarius Moon (December–June)
It's time to discourage growth during the days when the light of the Moon is decreasing in Sagittarius. Cut back, mow the lawn, prune, and destroy pests and insects you never want to darken your garden again.

Waxing Capricorn Moon (July–January)
Capricorn is a semi-fruitful earth sign. The couple of days when the light of the Moon is increasing in Capricorn are good for getting the garden into shape, setting out plants and transplants, and fertilizing.

Waning Capricorn Moon (January–July)
The decreasing light of this fruitful Capricorn Moon is the perfect window for digging and dividing bulbs and pinching back suckers to encourage bigger blooms on your flowers and vegetables.

Waxing Aquarius Moon (August–February)
Aquarius is a dry and barren sign. However, the increasing light of the Aquarian Moon makes this a good opportunity to experiment by pruning or cutting back plants you want to flourish.

Waning Aquarius Moon (February–August)
The light of the Moon is decreasing. Use this time to harvest or to weed, cut back, and prune the shrubs and plants that you want to banish forever from your garden. Harvest vegetables.

Waxing Pisces Moon (September–March)
When the Moon is increasing in fruitful Pisces, it's a perfect period for planting seeds and annuals. Annuals with outside seeds grow faster when planted under a Moon that is one to seven days old.

Vegetables with inside seeds should be planted when the Moon is seven to twelve days old. Annual flowers can be planted any time during these two weeks.

Waning Pisces Moon (March–September)

With the light of the Moon decreasing, it's time to plant all perennials, bulbs, and root vegetables except potatoes. Garden lore has it that potatoes planted under a Pisces Moon tend to grow bumps or "toes" because Pisces is associated with the feet.

Here's hoping that this has inspired you to give gardening by the Moon a try. Not only is it the secret ingredient that will make your garden more abundant, but you can use it as long as the Sun is in the sky and the Moon circles the Earth!

A Guide to Planting

Plant	Quarter	Sign
Annuals	1st or 2nd	
Apple tree	2nd or 3rd	Cancer, Pisces, Virgo
Artichoke	1st	Cancer, Pisces
Asparagus	1st	Cancer, Scorpio, Pisces
Aster	1st or 2nd	Virgo, Libra
Barley	1st or 2nd	Cancer, Pisces, Libra, Capricorn, Virgo
Beans (bush & pole)	2nd	Cancer, Taurus, Pisces, Libra
Beans (kidney, white & navy)	1st or 2nd	Cancer, Pisces
Beech tree	2nd or 3rd	Virgo, Taurus
Beets	3rd	Cancer, Capricorn, Pisces, Libra
Biennials	3rd or 4th	
Broccoli	1st	Cancer, Scorpio, Pisces, Libra
Brussels sprouts	1st	Cancer, Scorpio, Pisces, Libra
Buckwheat	1st or 2nd	Capricorn
Bulbs	3rd	Cancer, Scorpio, Pisces
Bulbs for seed	2nd or 3rd	
Cabbage	1st	Cancer, Scorpio, Pisces, Taurus, Libra
Canes (raspberry, blackberry & gooseberry)	2nd	Cancer, Scorpio, Pisces
Cantaloupe	1st or 2nd	Cancer, Scorpio, Pisces, Taurus, Libra
Carrots	3rd	Cancer, Scorpio, Pisces, Taurus, Libra
Cauliflower	1st	Cancer, Scorpio, Pisces, Libra
Celeriac	3rd	Cancer, Scorpio, Pisces
Celery	1st	Cancer, Scorpio, Pisces
Cereals	1st or 2nd	Cancer, Scorpio, Pisces, Libra
Chard	1st or 2nd	Cancer, Scorpio, Pisces
Chicory	2nd or 3rd	Cancer, Scorpio, Pisces
Chrysanthemum	1st or 2nd	Virgo
Clover	1st or 2nd	Cancer, Scorpio, Pisces

Plant	Quarter	Sign
Coreopsis	2nd or 3rd	Libra
Corn	1st	Cancer, Scorpio, Pisces
Corn for fodder	1st or 2nd	Libra
Cosmos	2nd or 3rd	Libra
Cress	1st	Cancer, Scorpio, Pisces
Crocus	1st or 2nd	Virgo
Cucumber	1st	Cancer, Scorpio, Pisces
Daffodil	1st or 2nd	Libra, Virgo
Dahlia	1st or 2nd	Libra, Virgo
Deciduous trees	2nd or 3rd	Cancer, Scorpio, Pisces, Virgo, Libra
Eggplant	2nd	Cancer, Scorpio, Pisces, Libra
Endive	1st	Cancer, Scorpio, Pisces, Libra
Flowers	1st	Cancer, Scorpio, Pisces, Libra, Taurus, Virgo
Garlic	3rd	Libra, Taurus, Pisces
Gladiola	1st or 2nd	Libra, Virgo
Gourds	1st or 2nd	Cancer, Scorpio, Pisces, Libra
Grapes	2nd or 3rd	Cancer, Scorpio, Pisces, Virgo
Hay	1st or 2nd	Cancer, Scorpio, Pisces, Libra, Taurus
Herbs	1st or 2nd	Cancer, Scorpio, Pisces
Honeysuckle	1st or 2nd	Scorpio, Virgo
Hops	1st or 2nd	Scorpio, Libra
Horseradish	1st or 2nd	Cancer, Scorpio, Pisces
Houseplants	1st	Cancer, Scorpio, Pisces, Libra
Hyacinth	3rd	Cancer, Scorpio, Pisces
Iris	1st or 2nd	Cancer, Virgo
Kohlrabi	1st or 2nd	Cancer, Scorpio, Pisces, Libra
Leek	2nd or 3rd	Sagittarius
Lettuce	1st	Cancer, Scorpio, Pisces, Libra, Taurus
Lily	1st or 2nd	Cancer, Scorpio, Pisces
Maple tree	2nd or 3rd	Taurus, Virgo, Cancer, Pisces
Melon	2nd	Cancer, Scorpio, Pisces
Moon vine	1st or 2nd	Virgo

Plant	Quarter	Sign
Morning glory	1st or 2nd	Cancer, Scorpio, Pisces, Virgo
Oak tree	2nd or 3rd	Taurus, Virgo, Cancer, Pisces
Oats	1st or 2nd	Cancer, Scorpio, Pisces, Libra
Okra	1st or 2nd	Cancer, Scorpio, Pisces, Libra
Onion seed	2nd	Cancer, Scorpio, Sagittarius
Onion set	3rd or 4th	Cancer, Pisces, Taurus, Libra
Pansies	1st or 2nd	Cancer, Scorpio, Pisces
Parsley	1st	Cancer, Scorpio, Pisces, Libra
Parsnip	3rd	Cancer, Scorpio, Taurus, Capricorn
Peach tree	2nd or 3rd	Cancer, Taurus, Virgo, Libra
Peanuts	3rd	Cancer, Scorpio, Pisces
Pear tree	2nd or 3rd	Cancer, Scorpio, Pisces, Libra
Peas	2nd	Cancer, Scorpio, Pisces, Libra
Peony	1st or 2nd	Virgo
Peppers	2nd	Cancer, Scorpio, Pisces
Perennials	3rd	
Petunia	1st or 2nd	Libra, Virgo
Plum tree	2nd or 3rd	Cancer, Pisces, Taurus, Virgo
Poppies	1st or 2nd	Virgo
Portulaca	1st or 2nd	Virgo
Potatoes	3rd	Cancer, Scorpio, Libra, Taurus, Capricorn
Privet	1st or 2nd	Taurus, Libra
Pumpkin	2nd	Cancer, Scorpio, Pisces, Libra
Quince	1st or 2nd	Capricorn
Radishes	3rd	Cancer, Scorpio, Pisces, Libra, Capricorn
Rhubarb	3rd	Cancer, Pisces
Rice	1st or 2nd	Scorpio
Roses	1st or 2nd	Cancer, Virgo
Rutabaga	3rd	Cancer, Scorpio, Pisces, Taurus
Saffron	1st or 2nd	Cancer, Scorpio, Pisces
Sage	3rd	Cancer, Scorpio, Pisces

Plant	Quarter	Sign
Salsify	1st	Cancer, Scorpio, Pisces
Shallot	2nd	Scorpio
Spinach	1st	Cancer, Scorpio, Pisces
Squash	2nd	Cancer, Scorpio, Pisces, Libra
Strawberries	3rd	Cancer, Scorpio, Pisces
String beans	1st or 2nd	Taurus
Sunflowers	1st or 2nd	Libra, Cancer
Sweet peas	1st or 2nd	Any
Tomatoes	2nd	Cancer, Scorpio, Pisces, Capricorn
Trees, shade	3rd	Taurus, Capricorn
Trees, ornamental	2nd	Libra, Taurus
Trumpet vine	1st or 2nd	Cancer, Scorpio, Pisces
Tubers for seed	3rd	Cancer, Scorpio, Pisces, Libra
Tulips	1st or 2nd	Libra, Virgo
Turnips	3rd	Cancer, Scorpio, Pisces, Taurus, Capricorn, Libra
Valerian	1st or 2nd	Virgo, Gemini
Watermelon	1st or 2nd	Cancer, Scorpio, Pisces, Libra
Wheat	1st or 2nd	Cancer, Scorpio, Pisces, Libra

Companion Planting Guide

Plant	Companions	Hindered by
Asparagus	Tomatoes, parsley, basil	None known
Beans	Tomatoes, carrots, cucumbers, garlic, cabbage, beets, corn	Onions, gladiolas
Beets	Onions, cabbage, lettuce, mint, catnip	Pole beans
Broccoli	Beans, celery, potatoes, onions	Tomatoes
Cabbage	Peppermint, sage, thyme, tomatoes	Strawberries, grapes
Carrots	Peas, lettuce, chives, radishes, leeks, onions, sage	Dill, anise
Citrus trees	Guava, live oak, rubber trees, peppers	None known
Corn	Potatoes, beans, peas, melon, squash, pumpkin, sunflowers, soybeans	Quack grass, wheat, straw, mulch
Cucumbers	Beans, cabbage, radishes, sunflowers, lettuce, broccoli, squash	Aromatic herbs
Eggplant	Green beans, lettuce, kale	None known
Grapes	Peas, beans, blackberries	Cabbage, radishes
Melons	Corn, peas	Potatoes, gourds
Onions, leeks	Beets, chamomile, carrots, lettuce	Peas, beans, sage
Parsnip	Peas	None known
Peas	Radishes, carrots, corn, cucumbers, beans, tomatoes, spinach, turnips	Onion, garlic
Potatoes	Beans, corn, peas, cabbage, hemp, cucumbers, eggplant, catnip	Raspberries, pumpkins, tomatoes, sunflowers
Radishes	Peas, lettuce, nasturtiums, cucumbers	Hyssop
Spinach	Strawberries	None known
Squash/ Pumpkin	Nasturtiums, corn, mint, catnip	Potatoes
Tomatoes	Asparagus, parsley, chives, onions, carrots, marigolds, nasturtiums, dill	Black walnut roots, fennel, potatoes
Turnips	Peas, beans, brussels sprouts	Potatoes

Plant	Companions	Uses
Anise	Coriander	Flavor candy, pastry, cheeses, cookies
Basil	Tomatoes	Dislikes rue; repels flies and mosquitoes
Borage	Tomatoes, squash	Use in teas
Buttercup	Clover	Hinders delphinium, peonies, monkshood, columbine
Catnip		Repels flea beetles
Chamomile	Peppermint, wheat, onions, cabbage	Roman chamomile may control damping-off disease; use in herbal sprays
Chervil	Radishes	Good in soups and other dishes
Chives	Carrots	Use in spray to deter black spot on roses
Coriander	Plant anywhere	Hinders seed formation in fennel
Cosmos		Repels corn earworms
Dill	Cabbage	Hinders carrots and tomatoes
Fennel	Plant in borders	Disliked by all garden plants
Horseradish		Repels potato bugs
Horsetail		Makes fungicide spray
Hyssop		Attracts cabbage flies; harmful to radishes
Lavender	Plant anywhere	Use in spray to control insects on cotton, repels clothes moths
Lovage		Lures horn worms away from tomatoes
Marigolds		Pest repellent; use against Mexican bean beetles and nematodes
Mint	Cabbage, tomatoes	Repels ants, flea beetles, cabbage worm butterflies
Morning glory	Corn	Helps melon germination
Nasturtium	Cabbage, cucumbers	Deters aphids, squash bugs, pumpkin beetles
Okra	Eggplant	Attracts leafhopper (lure insects from other plants)
Parsley	Tomatoes, asparagus	Freeze chopped-up leaves to flavor foods
Purslane		Good ground cover
Rosemary		Repels cabbage moths, bean beetles, carrot flies
Savory		Plant with onions for added sweetness
Tansy		Deters Japanese beetles, striped cucumber beetles, squash bugs
Thyme		Repels cabbage worms
Yarrow		Increases essential oils of neighbors

Moon Void-of-Course

Kim Rogers-Gallagher

The Moon circles the Earth in about twenty-eight days, moving through each zodiac sign in two and a half days. As she passes through the thirty degrees of each sign, she "visits" with the planets in numerical order, forming aspects with them. Because she moves one degree in just two to two and a half hours, her influence on each planet lasts only a few hours. She eventually reaches the planet that's in the highest degree of any sign and forms what will be her final aspect before leaving the sign. From this point until she enters the next sign, she is referred to as void-of-course.

Think of it this way: the Moon is the emotional "tone" of the day, carrying feelings with her particular to the sign she's "wearing" at the moment. After she has contacted each of the planets, she symbolically "rests" before changing her costume, so her instinct is temporarily on hold. It's during this time that many people feel "fuzzy" or "vague." Plans or decisions made now often do not pan out. Without the instinctual "knowing" the Moon provides as she touches each planet, we tend to be unrealistic or exercise poor judgment. The traditional definition of the void Moon is that "nothing will come of this." Actions initiated under a void Moon are often wasted, irrelevant, or incorrect—usually because information is hidden, missing, or has been overlooked.

Although it's not a good time to initiate plans, routine tasks seem to go along just fine. This period is ideal for reflection. On the lighter side, remember there are good uses for the void Moon. It is the period when the universe seems to be most open to loopholes. It's a great time to make plans you don't want to fulfill or schedule things you don't want to do. See the tables on pages 76–81 for a schedule of the Moon's void-of-course times.

Last Aspect   **Moon Enters New Sign**

		January		
2	5:16 pm	2	Gemini	9:44 pm
4	7:08 pm	5	Cancer	9:15 am
7	5:23 pm	7	Leo	9:40 pm
9	8:52 pm	10	Virgo	10:15 am
12	6:06 pm	12	Libra	9:56 pm
15	3:40 am	15	Scorpio	7:08 am
17	9:27 am	17	Sagittarius	12:33 pm
19	5:09 am	19	Capricorn	2:11 pm
21	10:52 am	21	Aquarius	1:29 pm
23	5:19 am	23	Pisces	12:36 pm
25	11:12 am	25	Aries	1:48 pm
27	4:01 pm	27	Taurus	6:42 pm
30	12:52 am	30	Gemini	3:35 am
		February		
1	6:58 am	1	Cancer	3:11 pm
4	1:19 am	4	Leo	3:48 am
6	9:15 am	6	Virgo	4:14 pm
9	1:40 am	9	Libra	3:47 am
11	11:41 am	11	Scorpio	1:34 pm
13	6:52 pm	13	Sagittarius	8:31 pm
15	8:06 pm	16	Capricorn	12:00 am
17	11:18 pm	18	Aquarius	12:35 am
19	9:00 pm	19	Pisces	11:56 pm
21	11:06 pm	22	Aries	12:14 am
24	2:22 am	24	Taurus	3:29 am
26	9:42 am	26	Gemini	10:48 am
28	8:07 pm	28	Cancer	9:40 pm

Last Aspect   Moon Enters New Sign

March				
3	9:22 am	3	Leo	10:16 am
5	10:18 pm	5	Virgo	10:38 pm
8	9:07 am	8	Libra	9:44 am
10	6:37 pm	10	Scorpio	7:06 pm
13	2:58 am	13	Sagittarius	3:21 am
15	4:50 am	15	Capricorn	8:06 am
17	10:14 am	17	Aquarius	10:25 am
19	6:33 am	19	Pisces	11:12 am
21	11:58 am	21	Aries	12:01 pm
23	1:13 pm	23	Taurus	2:42 pm
25	12:19 pm	25	Gemini	8:42 pm
27	9:39 pm	28	Cancer	6:22 am
30	9:45 am	30	Leo	6:31 pm
April				
2	2:03 am	2	Virgo	6:57 am
4	9:50 am	4	Libra	5:51 pm
6	8:43 am	7	Scorpio	2:29 am
9	5:09 am	9	Sagittarius	8:57 am
11	6:48 am	11	Capricorn	1:33 pm
13	10:14 am	13	Aquarius	4:42 pm
15	11:16 am	15	Pisces	6:57 pm
17	2:57 pm	17	Aries	9:09 pm
20	12:13 am	20	Taurus	12:30 am
21	11:41 pm	22	Gemini	6:11 am
24	8:15 am	24	Cancer	2:58 pm
26	7:41 pm	27	Leo	2:30 am
29	6:53 am	29	Virgo	2:59 pm

Last Aspect   Moon Enters New Sign

		May			
1	7:53 pm	2		Libra	2:09 am
4	5:17 am	4		Scorpio	10:32 am
6	10:38 am	6		Sagittarius	4:04 pm
8	4:28 pm	8		Capricorn	7:33 pm
10	7:52 pm	10		Aquarius	10:05 pm
12	11:15 pm	13		Pisces	12:39 am
14	10:56 pm	15		Aries	3:56 am
17	5:10 am	17		Taurus	8:28 am
19	1:51 pm	19		Gemini	2:48 pm
21	6:12 pm	21		Cancer	11:28 pm
24	5:12 am	24		Leo	10:35 am
26	2:38 am	26		Virgo	11:05 pm
29	5:46 am	29		Libra	10:51 am
31	10:53 am	31		Scorpio	7:45 pm
		June			
2	8:51 pm	3		Sagittarius	1:03 am
4	11:24 pm	5		Capricorn	3:31 am
7	12:40 am	7		Aquarius	4:42 am
9	12:24 am	9		Pisces	6:14 am
11	9:20 am	11		Aries	9:20 am
13	2:27 pm	13		Taurus	2:31 pm
15	9:36 pm	15		Gemini	9:46 pm
18	2:24 am	18		Cancer	6:58 am
20	5:43 pm	20		Leo	6:04 pm
22	1:01 pm	23		Virgo	6:35 am
25	6:24 pm	25		Libra	6:57 pm
28	4:19 am	28		Scorpio	4:55 am
30	10:20 am	30		Sagittarius	10:59 am

Last Aspect **Moon Enters New Sign**

		July		
2	9:33 am	2	Capricorn	1:20 pm
4	12:45 pm	4	Aquarius	1:30 pm
6	9:42 am	6	Pisces	1:33 pm
8	2:22 pm	8	Aries	3:19 pm
10	7:11 pm	10	Taurus	7:55 pm
13	2:11 am	13	Gemini	3:26 am
15	8:35 am	15	Cancer	1:13 pm
17	11:06 pm	18	Leo	12:39 am
20	10:08 am	20	Virgo	1:13 pm
23	12:06 am	23	Libra	1:54 am
25	11:05 am	25	Scorpio	12:55 pm
27	6:36 pm	27	Sagittarius	8:24 pm
29	7:51 pm	29	Capricorn	11:44 pm
31	10:13 pm	31	Aquarius	11:58 pm
		August		
2	5:15 pm	2	Pisces	11:05 pm
4	9:21 pm	4	Aries	11:19 pm
7	12:13 am	7	Taurus	2:25 am
9	6:39 am	9	Gemini	9:05 am
11	1:27 pm	11	Cancer	6:52 pm
14	3:46 am	14	Leo	6:36 am
16	5:38 am	16	Virgo	7:14 pm
19	4:51 am	19	Libra	7:53 am
21	4:31 pm	21	Scorpio	7:22 pm
24	1:10 am	24	Sagittarius	4:07 am
26	7:56 am	26	Capricorn	9:05 am
28	7:49 am	28	Aquarius	10:32 am
29	11:04 pm	30	Pisces	9:56 am

Last Aspect   Moon Enters New Sign

		September		
1	6:36 am	1	Aries	9:25 am
3	7:57 am	3	Taurus	11:00 am
5	12:46 pm	5	Gemini	4:07 pm
7	6:22 pm	8	Cancer	1:00 am
10	8:47 am	10	Leo	12:36 pm
12	11:06 am	13	Virgo	1:18 am
15	9:49 am	15	Libra	1:44 pm
17	9:06 pm	18	Scorpio	12:58 am
20	6:21 am	20	Sagittarius	10:06 am
22	3:32 pm	22	Capricorn	4:20 pm
24	4:05 pm	24	Aquarius	7:29 pm
26	8:38 am	26	Pisces	8:18 pm
28	4:58 pm	28	Aries	8:17 pm
30	5:50 pm	30	Taurus	9:18 pm
		October		
2	9:20 pm	3	Gemini	1:03 am
5	2:34 am	5	Cancer	8:32 am
7	3:12 pm	7	Leo	7:24 pm
10	5:37 am	10	Virgo	8:02 am
12	4:10 pm	12	Libra	8:22 pm
15	3:01 am	15	Scorpio	7:04 am
17	11:44 am	17	Sagittarius	3:36 pm
19	3:02 pm	19	Capricorn	9:55 pm
22	2:00 am	22	Aquarius	2:06 am
23	3:04 pm	24	Pisces	4:33 am
26	2:39 am	26	Aries	6:02 am
28	4:20 am	28	Taurus	7:44 am
30	7:36 am	30	Gemini	11:08 am

Last Aspect		**Moon Enters New Sign**		
		November		
1	8:36 am	1	Cancer	5:30 pm
3	11:28 pm	4	Leo	3:21 am
6	2:25 am	6	Virgo	2:39 pm
8	11:55 pm	9	Libra	3:08 am
11	10:05 am	11	Scorpio	1:39 pm
13	6:03 pm	13	Sagittarius	9:23 pm
15	5:57 pm	16	Capricorn	2:41 am
18	3:27 am	18	Aquarius	6:28 am
20	5:50 am	20	Pisces	9:29 am
22	10:10 am	22	Aries	12:19 pm
24	12:40 pm	24	Taurus	3:29 pm
26	4:52 pm	26	Gemini	7:40 pm
28	8:03 pm	29	Cancer	1:54 am
		December		
1	8:07 am	1	Leo	11:00 am
3	9:11 pm	3	Virgo	10:50 pm
6	8:50 am	6	Libra	11:35 am
8	8:05 pm	8	Scorpio	10:35 pm
11	3:57 am	11	Sagittarius	6:11 am
13	1:48 am	13	Capricorn	10:31 am
15	11:04 am	15	Aquarius	12:56 pm
17	7:04 am	17	Pisces	2:58 pm
19	4:03 pm	19	Aries	5:47 pm
21	9:47 pm	21	Taurus	9:50 pm
24	1:40 am	24	Gemini	3:15 am
26	2:55 am	26	Cancer	10:15 am
28	5:57 pm	28	Leo	7:23 pm
31	12:18 am	31	Virgo	6:53 am

The Moon's Rhythm

The Moon journeys around Earth in an elliptical orbit that takes about 27.33 days, which is known as a sidereal month (period of revolution of one body about another). She can move up to 15 degrees or as few as 11 degrees in a day, with the fastest motion occurring when the Moon is at perigee (closest approach to Earth). The Moon is never retrograde, but when her motion is slow, the effect is similar to a retrograde period.

Astrologers have observed that people born on a day when the Moon is fast will process information differently from those who are born when the Moon is slow in motion. People born when the Moon is fast process information quickly and tend to react quickly, while those born during a slow Moon will be more deliberate.

The time from New Moon to New Moon is called the synodic month (involving a conjunction), and the average time span between this Sun-Moon alignment is 29.53 days. Since 29.53 won't divide into 365 evenly, we can have a month with two Full Moons or two New Moons.

Moon Aspects

The aspects the Moon will make during the times you are considering are also important. A trine or sextile, and sometimes a conjunction, are considered favorable aspects. A trine or sextile between the Sun and Moon is an excellent foundation for success. Whether or not a conjunction is considered favorable depends upon the planet the Moon is making a conjunction to. If it's joining the Sun, Venus, Mercury, Jupiter, or even Saturn, the aspect is favorable. If the Moon joins Pluto or Mars, however, that would not be considered favorable. There may be exceptions, but it would depend on what you are electing to do. For example, a trine to Pluto might hasten the end of a relationship you want to be free of.

It is important to avoid times when the Moon makes an aspect to or is conjoining any retrograde planet, unless, of course, you want the thing started to end in failure.

After the Moon has completed an aspect to a planet, that planetary energy has passed. For example, if the Moon squares Saturn at 10:00 am, you can disregard Saturn's influence on your activity if it will occur after that time. You should always look ahead at aspects the Moon will make on the day in question, though, because if the Moon opposes Mars at 11:30 pm on that day, you can expect events that stretch into the evening to be affected by the Moon-Mars aspect. A testy conversation might lead to an argument, or more.

Moon Signs

Much agricultural work is ruled by earth signs—Virgo, Capricorn, and Taurus. The air signs—Gemini, Aquarius, and Libra—rule flying and intellectual pursuits.

Each planet has one or two signs in which its characteristics are enhanced or "dignified," and the planet is said to "rule" that sign. The Sun rules Leo and the Moon rules Cancer, for example. The ruling planet for each sign is listed below. These should not be considered complete lists. We recommend that you purchase a book of planetary rulerships for more complete information.

Aries Moon

The energy of an Aries Moon is masculine, dry, barren, and fiery. Aries provides great start-up energy, but things started at this time may be the result of impulsive action that lacks research or necessary support. Aries lacks staying power.

Use this assertive, outgoing Moon sign to initiate change, but have a plan in place for someone to pick up the reins when you're impatient to move on to the next thing. Work that requires skillful but not necessarily patient use of tools—cutting down trees, hammering, etc.—is appropriate in Aries. Expect things to occur rapidly but to also quickly pass. If you are prone to injury or accidents, exercise caution and good judgment in Aries-related activities.

RULER: Mars

IMPULSE: Action

RULES: Head and face

Taurus Moon

A Taurus Moon's energy is feminine, semi-fruitful, and earthy. The Moon is exalted—very strong—in Taurus. Taurus is known as the farmer's sign because of its associations with farmland and precipitation that is the typical day-long "soaker" variety. Taurus energy is good to incorporate into your plans when patience, practicality, and perseverance are needed. Be aware, though, that you may also experience stubbornness in this sign.

Things started in Taurus tend to be long lasting and to increase in value. This can be very supportive energy in a marriage election. On the downside, the fixed energy of this sign resists change or the letting go of even the most difficult situations. A divorce following a marriage that occurred during a Taurus Moon may be difficult and costly to end. Things begun now tend to become habitual and hard to alter. If you want to make changes in something you started, it would be better to wait for Gemini. This is a good time to get a loan, but expect the people in charge of money to be cautious and slow to make decisions.

RULER: Venus

IMPULSE: Stability

RULES: Neck, throat, and voice

Gemini Moon

A Gemini Moon's energy is masculine, dry, barren, and airy. People are more changeable than usual and may prefer to follow intellectual pursuits and play mental games rather than apply themselves to practical concerns.

This sign is not favored for agricultural matters, but it is an excellent time to prepare for activities, to run errands, and write letters. Plan to use a Gemini Moon to exchange ideas, meet people, go on vacations that include walking or biking, or be in situations that require versatility and quick thinking on your feet.

RULER: Mercury

IMPULSE: Versatility

RULES: Shoulders, hands, arms, lungs, and nervous system

Cancer Moon

A Cancer Moon's energy is feminine, fruitful, moist, and very strong. Use this sign when you want to grow things—flowers, fruits, vegetables, commodities, stocks, or collections—for example. This sensitive sign stimulates rapport between people. Considered the most fertile of the signs, it is often associated with mothering. You can use this moontime to build personal friendships that support mutual growth.

Cancer is associated with emotions and feelings. Prominent Cancer energy promotes growth, but it can also turn people pouty and prone to withdrawing into their shells.

RULER: The Moon

IMPULSE: Tenacity

RULES: Chest area, breasts, and stomach

Leo Moon

A Leo Moon's energy is masculine, hot, dry, fiery, and barren. Use it whenever you need to put on a show, make a presentation, or entertain colleagues or guests. This is a proud yet playful energy that exudes self-confidence and is often associated with romance.

This is an excellent time for fundraisers and ceremonies or to be straightforward, frank, and honest about something. It is advisable not to put yourself in a position of needing public approval or where you might have to cope with underhandedness, as trouble in these areas can bring out the worst Leo traits. There is a tendency in this sign to become arrogant or self-centered.

RULER: The Sun

IMPULSE: I am

RULES: Heart and upper back

Virgo Moon

A Virgo Moon is feminine, dry, barren, earthy energy. It is favorable for anything that needs painstaking attention—especially those things where exactness rather than innovation is preferred.

Use this sign for activities when you must analyze information or when you must determine the value of something. Virgo is the sign of bargain hunting. It's friendly toward agricultural matters with an emphasis on animals and harvesting vegetables. It is an excellent time to care for animals, especially training them and veterinary work.

This sign is most beneficial when decisions have already been made and now need to be carried out. The inclination here is to see details rather than the bigger picture.

There is a tendency in this sign to overdo. Precautions should be taken to avoid becoming too dull from all work and no play. Build relaxation and pleasure into your routine from the beginning.

RULER: Mercury

IMPULSE: Discriminating

RULES: Abdomen and intestines

Libra Moon

A Libra Moon's energy is masculine, semi-fruitful, and airy. This energy will benefit any attempt to bring beauty to a place or thing. Libra is considered good energy for starting things of an intellectual nature. Libra is the sign of partnership and unions, which makes it an excellent time to form partnerships of any kind, to make agreements, and to negotiate. Even though this sign is good for initiating things, it is crucial to work with a partner who will provide incentive and encouragement. A Libra Moon accentuates teamwork (particularly teams of two) and artistic work (especially work that involves color). Make use of this sign when you are decorating your home or shopping for better-quality clothing.

RULER: Venus

IMPULSE: Balance

RULES: Lower back, kidneys, and buttocks

Scorpio Moon

The Scorpio Moon is feminine, fruitful, cold, and moist. It is useful when intensity (that sometimes borders on obsession) is needed. Scorpio is considered a very psychic sign. Use this Moon sign when you must back up something you strongly believe in, such as union or employer relations. There is strong group loyalty here, but a Scorpio Moon is also a good time to end connections thoroughly. This is also a good time to conduct research.

The desire nature is so strong here that there is a tendency to manipulate situations to get what one wants or to not see one's responsibility in an act.

RULER: Pluto, Mars (traditional)

IMPULSE: Transformation

RULES: Reproductive organs, genitals, groin, and pelvis

Sagittarius Moon

The Moon's energy is masculine, dry, barren, and fiery in Sagittarius, encouraging flights of imagination and confidence in the flow of life. Sagittarius is the most philosophical sign. Candor and honesty are enhanced when the Moon is here. This is an excellent time to "get things off your chest" and to deal with institutions of higher learning, publishing companies, and the law. It's also a good time for sport and adventure.

Sagittarians are the crusaders of this world. This is a good time to tackle things that need improvement, but don't try to be the diplomat while influenced by this energy. Opinions can run strong, and the tendency to proselytize is increased.

RULER: Jupiter

IMPULSE: Expansion

RULES: Thighs and hips

Capricorn Moon

In Capricorn the Moon's energy is feminine, semi-fruitful, and earthy. Because Cancer and Capricorn are polar opposites, the Moon's energy is thought to be weakened here. This energy encourages the need for structure, discipline, and organization. This is a good time to set goals and plan for the future, tend to family business, and to take care of details requiring patience or a businesslike manner. Institutional activities are favored. This sign should be avoided if you're seeking favors, as those in authority can be insensitive under this influence.

RULER: Saturn

IMPULSE: Ambitious

RULES: Bones, skin, and knees

Aquarius Moon

An Aquarius Moon's energy is masculine, barren, dry, and airy. Activities that are unique, individualistic, concerned with human- itarian issues, society as a whole, and making improvements are favored under this Moon. It is this quality of making improve- ments that has caused this sign to be associated with inventors and new inventions.

An Aquarius Moon promotes the gathering of social groups for friendly exchanges. People tend to react and speak from an intel- lectual rather than emotional viewpoint when the Moon is in this sign.

RULER: Uranus and Saturn

IMPULSE: Reformer

RULES: Calves and ankles

Pisces Moon

A Pisces Moon is feminine, fruitful, cool, and moist. This is an excel- lent time to retreat, meditate, sleep, pray, or make that dreamed-of escape into a fantasy vacation. However, things are not always what they seem to be with the Moon in Pisces. Personal boundaries tend to be fuzzy, and you may not be seeing things clearly. People tend to be idealistic under this sign, which can prevent them from seeing reality.

There is a live-and-let-live philosophy attached to this sign, which in the idealistic world may work well enough, but chaos is frequently the result. That's why this sign is also associated with alcohol and drug abuse, drug trafficking, and counterfeiting. On the lighter side, many musicians and artists are ruled by Pisces. It's only when they move too far away from reality that the dark side of substance abuse, suicide, or crime takes away life.

RULER: Jupiter and Neptune

IMPULSE: Empathetic

RULES: Feet

More about Zodiac Signs

Element (Triplicity)

Each of the zodiac signs is classified as belonging to an element; these are the four basic elements:

Fire Signs

Aries, Sagittarius, and Leo are action-oriented, outgoing, energetic, and spontaneous.

Earth Signs

Taurus, Capricorn, and Virgo are stable, conservative, practical, and oriented to the physical and material realm.

Air Signs

Gemini, Aquarius, and Libra are sociable and critical, and they tend to represent intellectual responses rather than feelings.

Water Signs

Cancer, Scorpio, and Pisces are emotional, receptive, intuitive, and can be very sensitive.

Quality (Quadruplicity)

Each zodiac sign is further classified as being cardinal, mutable, or fixed. There are four signs in each quadruplicity, one sign from each element.

Cardinal Signs

Aries, Cancer, Libra, and Capricorn represent beginnings and newly initiated action. They initiate each new season in the cycle of the year.

Fixed Signs

Taurus, Leo, Scorpio, and Aquarius want to maintain the status quo through stubbornness and persistence; they represent that "between" time. For example, Leo is the month when summer really feels like summer.

Mutable Signs

Pisces, Gemini, Virgo, and Sagittarius adapt to change and tolerate situations. They represent the last month of each season, when things are changing in preparation for the coming season.

Nature and Fertility

In addition to a sign's element and quality, each sign is further classified as either fruitful, semi-fruitful, or barren. This classification is the most important for readers who use the gardening information in the *Moon Sign Book* because the timing of most events depends on the fertility of the sign occupied by the Moon. The water signs of Cancer, Scorpio, and Pisces are the most fruitful. The semi-fruitful signs are the earth signs Taurus and Capricorn, and the air sign Libra. The barren signs correspond to fire signs Aries, Leo, and Sagittarius; air signs Gemini and Aquarius; and earth sign Virgo.

Good Timing

Sharon Leah

Electional astrology is the art of electing times to begin any undertaking. Say, for example, you want to start a business. That business will experience ups and downs, as well as reach its potential, according to the promise held in the universe at the time the business was started—its birth time. The horoscope (birth chart) set for the date, time, and place that a business starts would indicate the outcome—its potential to succeed.

So, you might ask yourself the question: If the horoscope for a business start can show success or failure, why not begin at a time that is more favorable to the venture? Well, you can.

While no time is perfect, there are better times and better days to undertake specific activities. There are thousands of examples that prove electional astrology is not only practical, but that it can make a difference in our lives. There are rules for electing times to begin various activities—even shopping. You'll find detailed instructions about how to make elections beginning on page 107.

Personalizing Elections

The election rules in this almanac are based upon the planetary positions at the time for which the election is made. They do not depend on any type of birth chart. However, a birth chart based upon the time, date, and birthplace of an event has advantages. No election is effective for every person. For example, you may leave home to begin a trip at the same time as a friend, but each of you will have a different experience according to whether or not your birth chart favors the trip.

Not all elections require a birth chart, but the timing of very important events—business starts, marriages, etc.—would benefit from the additional accuracy a birth chart provides. To order a birth chart for yourself or a planned event, visit our website at www.llewellyn.com.

Some Things to Consider

You've probably experienced good timing in your life. Maybe you were at the right place at the right time to meet a friend whom you hadn't seen in years. Frequently, when something like that happens, it is the result of following an intuitive impulse—that "gut instinct." Consider for a moment that you were actually responding to planetary energies. Electional astrology is a tool that can help you to align with energies, present and future, that are available to us through planetary placements.

Significators

Decide upon the important significators (planet, sign, and house ruling the matter) for which the election is being made. The Moon is the most important significator in any election, so the Moon should always be fortified (strong by sign and making favorable aspects to other planets). The Moon's aspects to other planets are more important than the sign the Moon is in.

Other important considerations are the significators of the Ascendant and Midheaven—the house ruling the election matter and the ruler of the sign on that house cusp. Finally, any planet or sign that has a general rulership over the matter in question should be taken into consideration.

Nature and Fertility

Determine the general nature of the sign that is appropriate for your election. For example, much agricultural work is ruled by the earth signs of Virgo, Capricorn, and Taurus; while the air signs—Gemini, Aquarius, and Libra—rule intellectual pursuits.

One Final Comment

Use common sense. If you must do something, like plant your garden or take an airplane trip on a day that doesn't have the best aspects, proceed anyway, but try to minimize problems. For example, leave early for the airport to avoid being left behind due to delays in the security lanes. When you have no other choice, do the best that you can under the circumstances at the time.

If you want to personalize your elections, please turn to page 107 for more information. If you want a quick and easy answer, you can refer to Llewellyn's Astro Almanac on the following pages.

Llewellyn's Astro Almanac

The Astro Almanac tables, beginning on the next page, can help you find the dates best suited to particular activities. The dates provided are determined from the Moon's sign, phase, and aspects to other planets. Please note that the Astro Almanac does not take personal factors, such as your Sun and Moon sign, into account. The dates are general, and they will apply for everyone. Some activities will not have ideal dates during a particular month.

Activity	January
Animals (Neuter or spay)	19–21
Animals (Sell or buy)	2, 27
Automobile (Buy)	4, 11, 20
Brewing	7, 16, 17
Build (Start foundation)	no ideal dates
Business (Conducting for self and others)	1, 12, 17, 25, 31
Business (Start new)	no ideal dates
Can Fruits and Vegetables	7, 16
Can Preserves	7, 16
Concrete (Pour)	8, 9
Construction (Begin new)	1, 3, 8, 12, 17, 21, 25, 30, 31
Consultants (Begin work with)	2, 3, 8, 11, 15, 17, 20, 21, 24, 25, 28, 30
Contracts (Bid on)	2, 3, 24, 25, 28, 30
Cultivate	no ideal dates
Decorating	2–5, 21–23, 30, 31
Demolition	8, 9, 17, 18
Electronics (Buy)	no ideal dates
Entertain Guests	2, 14
Floor Covering (Laying new)	8, 9, 10–15
Habits (Break)	20
Hair (Cut to increase growth)	1–4, 24, 27–31
Hair (Cut to decrease growth)	7, 17–20
Harvest (Grain for storage)	7–9, 10
Harvest (Root crops)	8, 9, 17–19
Investments (New)	1, 12, 31
Loan (Ask for)	1, 2, 27–30
Massage (Relaxing)	14, 23, 27
Mow Lawn (Decrease growth)	7–20
Mow Lawn (Increase growth)	1–5, 22–31
Mushrooms (Pick)	5–7
Negotiate (Business for the elderly)	4, 14, 27
Prune for Better Fruit	15–19
Prune to Promote Healing	20, 21
Wean Children	18–23
Wood Floors (Installing)	19–21
Write Letters or Contracts	6, 11, 20, 24

Activity	February
Animals (Neuter or spay)	15–17
Animals (Sell or buy)	2, 4
Automobile (Buy)	1, 7, 8, 17, 28
Brewing	12, 13
Build (Start foundation)	24
Business (Conducting for self and others)	10, 15, 24
Business (Start new)	no ideal dates
Can Fruits and Vegetables	12, 13
Can Preserves	12, 13
Concrete (Pour)	6, 18
Construction (Begin new)	4, 10, 14, 15, 18, 24, 27
Consultants (Begin work with)	4, 8, 14, 18, 22, 23, 27, 28
Contracts (Bid on)	4, 22, 23, 27, 28
Cultivate	18, 19
Decorating	1, 26–28
Demolition	5, 14, 15
Electronics (Buy)	18, 28
Entertain Guests	2, 27
Floor Covering (Laying new)	6–11, 18, 19
Habits (Break)	17, 18
Hair (Cut to increase growth)	4, 20, 21, 24–27
Hair (Cut to decrease growth)	14–17
Harvest (Grain for storage)	6
Harvest (Root crops)	5, 6, 14, 15, 18
Investments (New)	10
Loan (Ask for)	4, 24–26
Massage (Relaxing)	2
Mow Lawn (Decrease growth)	6–18
Mow Lawn (Increase growth)	1–4, 21–28
Mushrooms (Pick)	4–6
Negotiate (Business for the elderly)	11, 15, 28
Prune for Better Fruit	11–15
Prune to Promote Healing	16, 17
Wean Children	14–19
Wood Floors (Installing)	16, 17
Write Letters or Contracts	2, 7, 17, 18

Activity	March
Animals (Neuter or spay)	13, 15, 16, 19, 20
Animals (Sell or buy)	4, 27, 29
Automobile (Buy)	7, 15–17, 27
Brewing	11, 12, 20
Build (Start foundation)	no ideal dates
Business (Conducting for self and others)	1, 12, 17, 26, 31
Business (Start new)	23
Can Fruits and Vegetables	11, 12, 20
Can Preserves	11, 12
Concrete (Pour)	18
Construction (Begin new)	1, 4, 14, 17, 18, 26, 27, 31
Consultants (Begin work with)	4, 12, 14, 17, 18, 21, 22, 27
Contracts (Bid on)	4, 22, 27, 28
Cultivate	13, 14, 18
Decorating	25–28
Demolition	13, 14, 21
Electronics (Buy)	27
Entertain Guests	4, 24, 29
Floor Covering (Laying new)	8–10, 17, 18
Habits (Break)	15, 17–19
Hair (Cut to increase growth)	3, 23–27, 30
Hair (Cut to decrease growth)	13–16, 20
Harvest (Grain for storage)	13, 14
Harvest (Root crops)	13, 14, 17, 18
Investments (New)	1, 12, 31
Loan (Ask for)	3–5, 23–25, 30, 31
Massage (Relaxing)	4, 24, 29
Mow Lawn (Decrease growth)	8–20
Mow Lawn (Increase growth)	1–6, 22–31
Mushrooms (Pick)	6–8
Negotiate (Business for the elderly)	10, 15, 23, 28
Prune for Better Fruit	10–14
Prune to Promote Healing	15–17
Wean Children	13–19
Wood Floors (Installing)	15–17
Write Letters or Contracts	2, 7, 16, 20, 21, 29

Activity	April
Animals (Neuter or spay)	1, 3, 4, 24, 28, 29
Animals (Sell or buy)	1, 4, 24, 28, 29
Automobile (Buy)	3, 11, 12, 30
Brewing	7, 8, 16, 17
Build (Start foundation)	20
Business (Conducting for self and others)	10, 15, 25, 30
Business (Start new)	20
Can Fruits and Vegetables	7, 8, 16, 17
Can Preserves	7, 8
Concrete (Pour)	14, 15
Construction (Begin new)	1, 10, 15, 24, 25, 29, 30
Consultants (Begin work with)	1, 2, 10, 12, 15, 16, 19, 21, 24, 25, 29, 30
Contracts (Bid on)	1, 2, 21, 24, 25, 29, 30
Cultivate	10, 11, 14, 15, 18, 19
Decorating	4–6, 22–24
Demolition	9, 10, 17–19
Electronics (Buy)	no ideal dates
Entertain Guests	23, 28
Floor Covering (Laying new)	6, 13–15
Habits (Break)	14, 15, 17
Hair (Cut to increase growth)	20–23
Hair (Cut to decrease growth)	9–12, 16
Harvest (Grain for storage)	9–11
Harvest (Root crops)	9–11, 13–15, 17, 18
Investments (New)	10, 30
Loan (Ask for)	1, 2, 20, 21, 27–29
Massage (Relaxing)	13, 28
Mow Lawn (Decrease growth)	7–18
Mow Lawn (Increase growth)	1–4, 21–30
Mushrooms (Pick)	5–7
Negotiate (Business for the elderly)	7, 11, 20
Prune for Better Fruit	7–10
Prune to Promote Healing	12, 13
Wean Children	10–15
Wood Floors (Installing)	11–13
Write Letters or Contracts	3, 12, 17, 21, 26

Activity	May
Animals (Neuter or spay)	9, 13, 14
Animals (Sell or buy)	4, 22, 27, 28
Automobile (Buy)	1, 9, 10, 27, 28
Brewing	6, 13, 14
Build (Start foundation)	no ideal dates
Business (Conducting for self and others)	10, 14, 24, 30
Business (Start new)	27
Can Fruits and Vegetables	6, 13, 14
Can Preserves	6, 18
Concrete (Pour)	11, 18
Construction (Begin new)	8, 10, 12, 22, 24, 27, 30
Consultants (Begin work with)	8, 9, 12, 13, 17, 22, 27
Contracts (Bid on)	22, 27
Cultivate	7, 8, 12, 15, 16
Decorating	2–4, 19–21, 29–31
Demolition	6, 7, 15, 16
Electronics (Buy)	no ideal dates
Entertain Guests	18, 23
Floor Covering (Laying new)	10–12, 17–19
Habits (Break)	15, 16
Hair (Cut to increase growth)	19, 20, 24
Hair (Cut to decrease growth)	6–9, 13, 14, 17, 18
Harvest (Grain for storage)	6–8, 10, 11
Harvest (Root crops)	6–8, 10–12, 15, 16
Investments (New)	10, 30
Loan (Ask for)	19, 24–26
Massage (Relaxing)	4, 18, 23
Mow Lawn (Decrease growth)	6–18
Mow Lawn (Increase growth)	1–4, 20–31
Mushrooms (Pick)	4–6
Negotiate (Business for the elderly)	4, 17, 22
Prune for Better Fruit	5–8
Prune to Promote Healing	9, 10
Wean Children	7–12
Wood Floors (Installing)	8–10
Write Letters or Contracts	1, 10, 14, 17, 23, 28

Activity	June
Animals (Neuter or spay)	4–6, 9, 10
Animals (Sell or buy)	2, 18, 23, 27
Automobile (Buy)	5, 6, 16, 25
Brewing	10
Build (Start foundation)	no ideal dates
Business (Conducting for self and others)	8, 12, 23, 28
Business (Start new)	23
Can Fruits and Vegetables	10
Can Preserves	14, 15
Concrete (Pour)	8, 14, 15
Construction (Begin new)	5, 8, 12, 18, 23
Consultants (Begin work with)	5, 6, 9, 11, 14, 16, 18, 22, 23, 28
Contracts (Bid on)	22, 23, 28
Cultivate	no ideal dates
Decorating	18, 25–28
Demolition	3–5, 11, 12
Electronics (Buy)	16
Entertain Guests	16, 21, 27
Floor Covering (Laying new)	7, 8, 14–17
Habits (Break)	11–13, 16
Hair (Cut to increase growth)	3, 20, 30
Hair (Cut to decrease growth)	4–6, 10, 13–17
Harvest (Grain for storage)	4, 5, 7, 8
Harvest (Root crops)	4, 7, 8, 11–13, 16
Investments (New)	8, 28
Loan (Ask for)	20–23
Massage (Relaxing)	21, 27
Mow Lawn (Decrease growth)	4–16
Mow Lawn (Increase growth)	1, 2, 19–30
Mushrooms (Pick)	2–4
Negotiate (Business for the elderly)	1, 5, 18, 28
Prune for Better Fruit	3, 4
Prune to Promote Healing	5–7
Wean Children	3–9, 30
Wood Floors (Installing)	5–7
Write Letters or Contracts	6, 10, 16, 20

Activity	July
Animals (Neuter or spay)	4, 7, 8,
Animals (Sell or buy)	1, 29, 30
Automobile (Buy)	3, 4, 13, 22, 30, 31
Brewing	7, 8, 16
Build (Start foundation)	no ideal dates
Business (Conducting for self and others)	7, 12, 23, 28
Business (Start new)	3, 21, 30
Can Fruits and Vegetables	7, 8, 16
Can Preserves	11, 12, 16
Concrete (Pour)	5, 11, 12
Construction (Begin new)	3, 12, 16, 21, 23, 28, 30
Consultants (Begin work with)	3, 7, 8, 11, 13, 16, 19, 21, 25, 30
Contracts (Bid on)	1, 19, 21, 25, 30
Cultivate	10, 13–15
Decorating	23–25
Demolition	8, 9
Electronics (Buy)	13, 25
Entertain Guests	15, 20, 25
Floor Covering (Laying new)	4–6, 11–15
Habits (Break)	10, 14, 15
Hair (Cut to increase growth)	1, 2, 28–30
Hair (Cut to decrease growth)	7, 10–14
Harvest (Grain for storage)	4, 5, 8, 9
Harvest (Root crops)	4–6, 8–10, 13–15
Investments (New)	7, 28
Loan (Ask for)	18–20
Massage (Relaxing)	20, 25
Mow Lawn (Decrease growth)	4–16
Mow Lawn (Increase growth)	1, 2, 18–31
Mushrooms (Pick)	2–4, 31
Negotiate (Business for the elderly)	11, 30
Prune for Better Fruit	no ideal dates
Prune to Promote Healing	3, 4
Wean Children	1–6, 28–31
Wood Floors (Installing)	3, 4
Write Letters or Contracts	4, 8, 17, 22, 31

Activity	August
Animals (Neuter or spay)	4, 31
Animals (Sell or buy)	20, 25, 27
Automobile (Buy)	18, 26, 27
Brewing	3, 4, 12, 13, 31
Build (Start foundation)	no ideal dates
Business (Conducting for self and others)	5, 10, 21, 26
Business (Start new)	18, 26, 27
Can Fruits and Vegetables	3, 4, 12, 13, 31
Can Preserves	7, 8, 12, 13
Concrete (Pour)	2, 7, 8, 15
Construction (Begin new)	5, 10, 13, 18, 21, 26, 27
Consultants (Begin work with)	3, 8, 13, 18, 23, 27, 31
Contracts (Bid on)	18, 23, 27
Cultivate	10, 11, 14, 15
Decorating	1, 19–21, 28, 29
Demolition	5–7, 14, 15
Electronics (Buy)	no ideal dates
Entertain Guests	11, 15, 20
Floor Covering (Laying new)	2, 7–11, 14–16
Habits (Break)	9, 11, 14
Hair (Cut to increase growth)	24–27
Hair (Cut to decrease growth)	3, 7–10, 14, 31
Harvest (Grain for storage)	2, 4, 5
Harvest (Root crops)	1, 2, 5, 6, 9–11, 14, 15
Investments (New)	5, 26
Loan (Ask for)	16
Massage (Relaxing)	15, 20
Mow Lawn (Decrease growth)	2–15, 31
Mow Lawn (Increase growth)	17–29
Mushrooms (Pick)	1, 2, 29–31
Negotiate (Business for the elderly)	7, 26
Prune for Better Fruit	no ideal dates
Prune to Promote Healing	no ideal dates
Wean Children	1, 2, 24–29
Wood Floors (Installing)	no ideal dates
Write Letters or Contracts	4, 13, 18, 27, 31

Activity	September
Animals (Neuter or spay)	no ideal dates
Animals (Sell or buy)	21, 27
Automobile (Buy)	13, 14, 22–24
Brewing	8–10
Build (Start foundation)	18
Business (Conducting for self and others)	4, 9, 20, 24
Business (Start new)	22, 23
Can Fruits and Vegetables	8, 9
Can Preserves	4, 5, 8, 9
Concrete (Pour)	4, 5, 11
Construction (Begin new)	4, 9, 14, 23, 24
Consultants (Begin work with)	4, 8, 9, 13, 14, 18, 23, 27
Contracts (Bid on)	18, 23, 25, 27
Cultivate	7, 11–14
Decorating	15–17, 24–26
Demolition	1, 2, 10–12, 29
Electronics (Buy)	no ideal dates
Entertain Guests	6, 11, 16
Floor Covering (Laying new)	3–7, 11–14
Habits (Break)	7, 10, 12
Hair (Cut to increase growth)	20–23, 27
Hair (Cut to decrease growth)	3–7, 10, 30
Harvest (Grain for storage)	1, 2, 5, 6, 30
Harvest (Root crops)	1, 2, 5–7, 10–12, 29, 30
Investments (New)	4, 24
Loan (Ask for)	no ideal dates
Massage (Relaxing)	11, 16
Mow Lawn (Decrease growth)	1–13, 30
Mow Lawn (Increase growth)	15–28
Mushrooms (Pick)	28–30
Negotiate (Business for the elderly)	3, 22, 30
Prune for Better Fruit	no ideal dates
Prune to Promote Healing	no ideal dates
Wean Children	21–26
Wood Floors (Installing)	no ideal dates
Write Letters or Contracts	9, 13, 14, 24, 28

Activity	October
Animals (Neuter or spay)	no ideal dates
Animals (Sell or buy)	20, 24
Automobile (Buy)	12, 19, 21
Brewing	6, 7
Build (Start foundation)	15
Business (Conducting for self and others)	3, 9, 19, 24
Business (Start new)	19, 20, 28
Can Fruits and Vegetables	6, 7
Can Preserves	1, 6, 7, 29
Concrete (Pour)	1, 8, 9, 29
Construction (Begin new)	3, 6, 9, 11, 19, 20
Consultants (Begin work with)	1, 2, 6, 8, 11, 14, 19, 20, 24, 29
Contracts (Bid on)	19, 20, 24
Cultivate	8–12
Decorating	14, 15, 22, 23
Demolition	7–9
Electronics (Buy)	14
Entertain Guests	5
Floor Covering (Laying new)	1, 2, 3, 4, 8, 9, 10, 11, 12, 13, 14, 29, 30, 31
Habits (Break)	9, 10
Hair (Cut to increase growth)	17–22, 25, 28
Hair (Cut to decrease growth)	1–4, 7, 29–31
Harvest (Grain for storage)	3, 4, 30, 31
Harvest (Root crops)	3, 4, 7–9, 30, 31
Investments (New)	3, 24
Loan (Ask for)	no ideal dates
Massage (Relaxing)	29
Mow Lawn (Decrease growth)	1–13, 29–31
Mow Lawn (Increase growth)	15–27
Mushrooms (Pick)	27–29
Negotiate (Business for the elderly)	5, 15, 19, 28
Prune for Better Fruit	no ideal dates
Prune to Promote Healing	no ideal dates
Wean Children	18–23
Wood Floors (Installing)	no ideal dates
Write Letters or Contracts	7, 12, 14, 21, 25

Activity	November
Animals (Neuter or spay)	no ideal dates
Animals (Sell or buy)	14, 16, 19
Automobile (Buy)	8, 16, 17
Brewing	2, 3, 12, 29, 30
Build (Start foundation)	no ideal dates
Business (Conducting for self and others)	2, 7, 17, 22
Business (Start new)	16, 24
Can Fruits and Vegetables	2, 3, 12, 29, 30
Can Preserves	2, 3, 12, 29, 30
Concrete (Pour)	4
Construction (Begin new)	2, 7, 16, 17, 22, 29
Consultants (Begin work with)	2, 3, 7, 8, 14, 16, 19, 20, 23, 25, 29
Contracts (Bid on)	14, 16, 19, 20, 23, 25
Cultivate	6–8
Decorating	18–20, 26
Demolition	4
Electronics (Buy)	19
Entertain Guests	3, 9, 28
Floor Covering (Laying new)	1, 4, 6–11, 28
Habits (Break)	6
Hair (Cut to increase growth)	13–17, 20, 21, 24–26
Hair (Cut to decrease growth)	4, 28
Harvest (Grain for storage)	1, 4
Harvest (Root crops)	1, 4, 6, 27, 28
Investments (New)	2, 22
Loan (Ask for)	24–26
Massage (Relaxing)	3, 9, 19
Mow Lawn (Decrease growth)	1–4, 6–12, 28–30
Mow Lawn (Increase growth)	14–26
Mushrooms (Pick)	26–28
Negotiate (Business for the elderly)	1, 11, 24
Prune for Better Fruit	11, 12
Prune to Promote Healing	no ideal dates
Wean Children	14–20
Wood Floors (Installing)	no ideal dates
Write Letters or Contracts	3, 8, 14, 17, 30

Activity	December
Animals (Neuter or spay)	11, 12
Animals (Sell or buy)	13, 14
Automobile (Buy)	4, 5, 13, 14
Brewing	9, 10, 27, 28
Build (Start foundation)	no ideal dates
Business (Conducting for self and others)	2, 7, 17, 21
Business (Start new)	13, 22
Can Fruits and Vegetables	9, 10, 27, 28
Can Preserves	9, 10, 27, 28
Concrete (Pour)	2, 3, 29, 30
Construction (Begin new)	2, 4, 7, 13, 17, 21, 26, 31
Consultants (Begin work with)	4, 9, 13, 14, 18, 22, 26, 30, 31
Contracts (Bid on)	13, 14, 18, 22, 26
Cultivate	5
Decorating	15–17, 24, 25
Demolition	1, 2, 11, 12, 29, 30
Electronics (Buy)	no ideal dates
Entertain Guests	3, 28
Floor Covering (Laying new)	1–8, 29–31
Habits (Break)	no ideal dates
Hair (Cut to increase growth)	13, 14, 18, 21–25
Hair (Cut to decrease growth)	1, 11, 12, 28
Harvest (Grain for storage)	1, 2, 3, 28–31
Harvest (Root crops)	1, 2, 3, 11, 29, 30
Investments (New)	2, 21
Loan (Ask for)	21–24
Massage (Relaxing)	3, 28
Mow Lawn (Decrease growth)	1–11
Mow Lawn (Increase growth)	13–25
Mushrooms (Pick)	25–27
Negotiate (Business for the elderly)	13, 26
Prune for Better Fruit	9–12
Prune to Promote Healing	no ideal dates
Wean Children	11–17
Wood Floors (Installing)	no ideal dates
Write Letters or Contracts	5, 14, 19, 27

Choose the Best Time for Your Activities

When rules for elections refer to "favorable" and "unfavorable" aspects to your Sun or other planets, please refer to the Favorable and Unfavorable Days Tables and Lunar Aspectarian for more information. You'll find instructions beginning on page 129 and the tables beginning on page 136.

The material in this section came from several sources including: *The New A to Z Horoscope Maker and Delineator* by Llewellyn George (Llewellyn, 1999), *Moon Sign Book* (Llewellyn, 1945), and *Electional Astrology* by Vivian Robson (Slingshot Publishing, 2000). Robson's book was originally published in 1937.

Advertise (Internet)

The Moon should be conjunct, sextile, or trine Mercury or Uranus and in the sign of Gemini, Capricorn, or Aquarius.

Advertise (Print)

Write ads on a day favorable to your Sun. The Moon should be conjunct, sextile, or trine Mercury or Venus. Avoid hard aspects to Mars and Saturn. Ad campaigns produce the best results when the Moon is well aspected in Gemini (to enhance communication) or Capricorn (to build business).

Animals

Take home new pets when the day is favorable to your Sun, or when the Moon is trine, sextile, or conjunct Mercury, Jupiter or Venus, or in the sign of Virgo or Pisces. However, avoid days when the Moon is either square or opposing the Sun, Mars, Saturn, Uranus, Neptune, or Pluto. When selecting a pet, have the Moon well aspected by the planet that rules the animal. Cats are ruled by the Sun, dogs by Mercury, birds by Venus, horses by Jupiter, and fish by Neptune. Buy large animals when the Moon is in Sagittarius or Pisces and making favorable aspects to Jupiter or Mercury. Buy animals smaller than sheep when the Moon is in Virgo with favorable aspects to Mercury or Venus.

Animals (Breed)

Animals are easiest to handle when the Moon is in Taurus, Cancer, Libra, or Pisces, but try to avoid the Full Moon. To encourage healthy births, animals should be mated so births occur when the Moon is increasing in Taurus, Cancer, Pisces, or Libra. Those born during a semi-fruitful sign (Taurus and Capricorn) will produce leaner meat. Libra yields beautiful animals for showing and racing.

Animals (Neuter or Spay)

Have livestock and pets neutered or spayed when the Moon is in Sagittarius, Capricorn, or Pisces, after it has passed through Scorpio, the sign that rules reproductive organs. Avoid the week before and after the Full Moon.

Animals (Sell or Buy)

In either buying or selling, it is important to keep the Moon and Mercury free from any aspect to Mars. Aspects to Mars will create discord and increase the likelihood of wrangling over price and quality. The Moon should be passing from the first quarter to full and sextile or trine Venus or Jupiter. When buying racehorses, let the Moon be in an air sign. The Moon should be in air signs when you buy birds. If the birds are to be pets, let the Moon be in good aspect to Venus.

Animals (Train)

Train pets when the Moon is in Virgo or trine to Mercury.

Animals (Train Dogs to Hunt)

Let the Moon be in Aries in conjunction with Mars, which makes them courageous and quick to learn. But let Jupiter also be in aspect to preserve them from danger in hunting.

Automobiles

When buying an automobile, select a time when the Moon is conjunct, sextile, or trine to Mercury, Saturn, or Uranus and in the sign of Gemini or Capricorn. Avoid times when Mercury is in retrograde motion.

Baking Cakes

Your cakes will have a lighter texture if you see that the Moon is in Gemini, Libra, or Aquarius and in good aspect to Venus or Mercury. If you are decorating a cake or confections are being made, have the Moon placed in Libra.

Beauty Treatments (Massage, etc.)

See that the Moon is in Taurus, Cancer, Leo, Libra, or Aquarius and in favorable aspect to Venus. In the case of plastic surgery, aspects to Mars should be avoided, and the Moon should not be in the sign ruling the part to be operated on.

Borrow (Money or Goods)

See that the Moon is not placed between 15 degrees Libra and 15 degrees Scorpio. Let the Moon be waning and in Leo, Scorpio (16 to 30 degrees), Sagittarius, or Pisces. Venus should be in good aspect to the Moon, and the Moon should not be square, opposing, or conjunct either Saturn or Mars.

Brewing

Start brewing during the third or fourth quarter, when the Moon is in Cancer, Scorpio, or Pisces.

Build (Start Foundation)

Turning the first sod for the foundation marks the beginning of the building. For best results, excavate the site when the Moon is in the first quarter of a fixed sign and making favorable aspects to Saturn.

Business (Start New)

When starting a business, have the Moon be in Taurus, Virgo, or Capricorn and increasing. The Moon should be sextile or trine Jupiter or Saturn, but avoid oppositions or squares. The planet ruling the business should be well aspected too.

Buy Goods

Buy during the third quarter, when the Moon is in Taurus for quality or in a mutable sign (Gemini, Sagittarius, Virgo, or Pisces) for savings. Good aspects to Venus or the Sun are desirable. If you are buying for yourself, it is good if the day is favorable for your Sun sign. You may also apply rules for buying specific items.

Canning

Can fruits and vegetables when the Moon is in either the third or fourth quarter and in the water sign Cancer or Pisces. Preserves and jellies use the same quarters and the signs Cancer, Pisces, or Taurus.

Clothing

Buy clothing on a day that is favorable for your Sun sign and when Venus or Mercury is well aspected. Avoid aspects to Mars and Saturn. Buy your clothing when the Moon is in Taurus if you want to remain satisfied. Do not buy clothing or jewelry when the Moon is in Scorpio or Aries. See that the Moon is sextile or trine the Sun during the first or second quarters.

Collections

Try to make collections on days when your natal Sun is well aspected. Avoid days when the Moon is opposing or square Mars or Saturn. If possible, the Moon should be in a cardinal sign (Aries, Cancer, Libra, or Capricorn). It is more difficult to collect when the Moon is in Taurus or Scorpio.

Concrete

Pour concrete when the Moon is in the third quarter of the fixed sign Taurus, Leo, or Aquarius.

Construction (Begin New)

The Moon should be sextile or trine Jupiter. According to Hermes, no building should be begun when the Moon is in Scorpio or Pisces. The best time to begin building is when the Moon is in Aquarius.

Consultants (Work with)

The Moon should be conjunct, sextile, or trine Mercury or Jupiter.

Contracts (Bid On)

The Moon should be in Gemini or Capricorn and either the Moon or Mercury should be conjunct, sextile, or trine Jupiter.

Copyrights/Patents

The Moon should be conjunct, trine, or sextile either Mercury or Jupiter.

Coronations and Installations

Let the Moon be in Leo and in favorable aspect to Venus, Jupiter, or Mercury. The Moon should be applying to these planets.

Cultivate

Cultivate when the Moon is in a barren sign and waning, ideally the fourth quarter in Aries, Gemini, Leo, Virgo, or Aquarius. The third quarter in the sign of Sagittarius will also work.

Cut Timber

Timber cut during the waning Moon does not become worm-eaten; it will season well and not warp, decay, or snap during burning. Cut when the Moon is in Taurus, Gemini, Virgo, or Capricorn—especially in August. Avoid the water signs. Look for favorable aspects to Mars.

Decorating or Home Repairs

Have the Moon waxing and in the sign of Libra, Gemini, or Aquarius. Avoid squares or oppositions to either Mars or Saturn. Venus in good aspect to Mars or Saturn is beneficial.

Demolition

Let the waning Moon be in Leo, Sagittarius, or Aries.

Dental and Dentists

Visit the dentist when the Moon is in Virgo, or pick a day marked favorable for your Sun sign. Mars should be marked sextile, conjunct, or trine; avoid squares or oppositions to Saturn, Uranus, or Jupiter.

Teeth are best removed when the Moon is in Gemini, Virgo, Sagittarius, or Pisces and during the first or second quarter. Avoid the Full Moon! The day should be favorable for your lunar cycle, and Mars and Saturn should be marked conjunct, trine, or sextile. Fillings should be done in the third or fourth quarters in the sign of Taurus, Leo, Scorpio, or Pisces. The same applies for dentures.

Dressmaking

William Lilly wrote in 1676: "Make no new clothes, or first put them on when the Moon is in Scorpio or afflicted by Mars, for they will be apt to be torn and quickly worn out." Design, repair, and sew clothes in the first and second quarters of Taurus, Leo, or Libra on a day marked favorable for your Sun sign. Venus, Jupiter, and Mercury should be favorably aspected, but avoid hard aspects to Mars or Saturn.

Egg-Setting (see p. 161)

Eggs should be set so chicks will hatch during fruitful signs. To set eggs, subtract the number of days given for incubation or gestation from the fruitful dates. Chickens incubate in twenty-one days, turkeys and geese in twenty-eight days.

A freshly laid egg loses quality rapidly if it is not handled properly. Use plenty of clean litter in the nests to reduce the number of dirty or cracked eggs. Gather eggs daily in mild weather and at least two times daily in hot or cold weather. The eggs should be placed in a cooler immediately after gathering and stored at 50 to 55°F. Do not store eggs with foods or products that give off pungent odors since eggs may absorb the odors.

Eggs saved for hatching purposes should not be washed. Only clean and slightly soiled eggs should be saved for hatching. Dirty eggs should not be incubated. Eggs should be stored in a cool place with the large ends up. It is not advisable to store the eggs longer than one week before setting them in an incubator.

Electricity and Gas (Install)

The Moon should be in a fire sign, and there should be no squares, oppositions, or conjunctions with Uranus (ruler of electricity), Neptune (ruler of gas), Saturn, or Mars. Hard aspects to Mars can cause fires.

Electronics (Buying)

Choose a day when the Moon is in an air sign (Gemini, Libra, Aquarius) and well aspected by Mercury and/or Uranus when buying electronics.

Electronics (Repair)

The Moon should be sextile or trine Mars or Uranus and in a fixed sign (Taurus, Leo, Scorpio, Aquarius).

Entertain Friends

Let the Moon be in Leo or Libra and making good aspects to Venus. Avoid squares or oppositions to either Mars or Saturn by the Moon or Venus.

Eyes and Eyeglasses

Have your eyes tested and glasses fitted on a day marked favorable for your Sun sign, and on a day that falls during your favorable lunar cycle. Mars should not be in aspect with the Moon. The same applies for any treatment of the eyes, which should also be started during the Moon's first or second quarter.

Fence Posts

Set posts when the Moon is in the third or fourth quarter of the fixed sign Taurus or Leo.

Fertilize and Compost

Fertilize when the Moon is in a fruitful sign (Cancer, Scorpio, Pisces). Organic fertilizers are best when the Moon is waning. Use chemical fertilizers when the Moon is waxing. Start compost when the Moon is in the fourth quarter in a water sign.

Find Hidden Treasure

Let the Moon be in good aspect to Jupiter or Venus. If you erect a horoscope for this election, place the Moon in the Fourth House.

Find Lost Articles

Search for lost articles during the first quarter and when your Sun sign is marked favorable. Also check to see that the planet ruling the lost item is trine, sextile, or conjunct the Moon. The Moon rules household utensils; Mercury rules letters and books; and Venus rules clothing, jewelry, and money.

Fishing

During the summer months, the best time of the day to fish is from sunrise to three hours after and from two hours before sunset until one hour after. Fish do not bite in cooler months until the air is warm, from noon to three pm. Warm, cloudy days are good. The most favorable winds are from the south and southwest.

Easterly winds are unfavorable. The best days of the month for fishing are when the Moon changes quarters, especially if the change occurs on a day when the Moon is in a water sign (Cancer, Scorpio, Pisces). The best period in any month is the day after the Full Moon.

Friendship

The need for friendship is greater when the Moon is in Aquarius or when Uranus aspects the Moon. Friendship prospers when Venus or Uranus is trine, sextile, or conjunct the Moon. The Moon in Gemini facilitates the chance meeting of acquaintances and friends.

Grafting or Budding

Grafting is the process of introducing new varieties of fruit on less desirable trees. For this process you should use the increasing phase of the Moon in fruitful signs such as Cancer, Scorpio, or Pisces. Capricorn may be used, too. Cut your grafts while trees are dormant, from December to March. Keep them in a cool, dark place, not too dry or too damp. Do the grafting before the sap starts to flow and while the Moon is waxing, preferably while it is in Cancer, Scorpio, or Pisces. The type of plant should determine both cutting and planting times.

Habit (Breaking)

To end an undesirable habit, and this applies to ending everything from a bad relationship to smoking, start on a day when the Moon is in the fourth quarter and in the barren sign of Gemini, Leo, or Aquarius. Aries, Virgo, and Capricorn may be suitable as well, depending on the habit you want to be rid of. Make sure that your lunar cycle is favorable. Avoid lunar aspects to Mars or Jupiter. However, favorable aspects to Pluto are helpful.

Haircuts

Cut hair when the Moon is in Gemini, Sagittarius, Pisces, Taurus, or Capricorn, but not in Virgo. Look for favorable aspects to Venus.

For faster growth, cut hair when the Moon is increasing in Cancer or Pisces. To make hair grow thicker, cut when the Moon is full in the signs of Taurus, Cancer, or Leo. If you want your hair to grow more slowly, have the Moon be decreasing in Aries, Gemini, or Virgo, and have the Moon square or opposing Saturn.

Permanents, straightening, and hair coloring will take well if the Moon is in Taurus or Leo and trine or sextile Venus. Avoid hair treatments if Mars is marked as square or in opposition, especially if heat is to be used. For permanents, a trine to Jupiter is helpful. The Moon also should be in the first quarter. Check the lunar cycle for a favorable day in relation to your Sun sign.

Harvest Crops

Harvest root crops when the Moon is in a dry sign (Aries, Leo, Sagittarius, Gemini, Aquarius) and waning. Harvest grain for storage just after the Full Moon, avoiding Cancer, Scorpio, or Pisces. Harvest in the third and fourth quarters in dry signs. Dry crops in the third quarter in fire signs.

Health

A diagnosis is more likely to be successful when the Moon is in Aries, Cancer, Libra, or Capricorn and less so when in Gemini, Sagittarius, Pisces, or Virgo. Begin a recuperation program or enter a hospital when the Moon is in a cardinal or fixed sign and the day is favorable to your Sun sign. For surgery, see "Surgical Procedures." Buy medicines when the Moon is in Virgo or Scorpio.

Home (Buy New)

If you desire a permanent home, buy when the New Moon is in a fixed sign—Taurus or Leo, for example. Each sign will affect your decision in a different way. A house bought when the Moon is in Taurus is likely to be more practical and have a country look— right down to the split-rail fence. A house purchased when the Moon is in Leo will more likely be a real showplace.

If you're buying for speculation and a quick turnover, be certain that the Moon is in a cardinal sign (Aries, Cancer, Libra, Capricorn). Avoid buying when the Moon is in a fixed sign (Leo, Scorpio, Aquarius, Taurus).

Home (Make Repairs)

In all repairs, avoid squares, oppositions, or conjunctions to the planet ruling the place or thing to be repaired. For example, bathrooms are ruled by Scorpio and Cancer. You would not want to start a project in those rooms when the Moon or Pluto is receiving hard aspects. The front entrance, hall, dining room, and porch are ruled by the Sun So you would want to avoid times when Saturn or Mars are square, opposing, or conjunct the Sun. Also, let the Moon be waxing.

Home (Sell)

Make a strong effort to list your property for sale when the Sun is marked favorable in your sign and in good aspect to Jupiter. Avoid adverse aspects to as many planets as possible.

Home Furnishings (Buy New)

Saturn days (Saturday) are good for buying, and Jupiter days (Thursday) are good for selling. Items bought on days when Saturn is well aspected tend to wear longer and purchases tend to be more conservative.

Job (Start New)

Jupiter and Venus should be sextile, trine, or conjunct the Moon. A day when your Sun is receiving favorable aspects is preferred.

Legal Matters

Good Moon-Jupiter aspects improve the outcome in legal decisions. To gain damages through a lawsuit, begin the process during the increasing Moon. To avoid paying damages, a court date during the decreasing Moon is desirable. Good Moon-Sun aspects strengthen your chance of success. A well-aspected Moon in Cancer or Leo, making good aspects to the Sun, brings the best results in custody cases. In divorce cases, a favorable Moon-Venus aspect is best.

Loan (Ask For)

A first and second quarter phase favors the lender, the third and fourth quarters favor the borrower. Good aspects of Jupiter and Venus to the Moon are favorable to both, as is having the Moon in Leo or Taurus.

Machinery, Appliances, or Tools (Buy)

Tools, machinery, and other implements should be bought on days when your lunar cycle is favorable and when Mars and Uranus are trine, sextile, or conjunct the Moon. Any quarter of the Moon is suitable. When buying gas or electrical appliances, the Moon should be in Aquarius.

Make a Will

Let the Moon be in a fixed sign (Taurus, Leo, Scorpio, or Aquarius) to ensure permanence. If the Moon is in a cardinal sign (Aries, Cancer, Libra, or Capricorn), the will could be altered. Let the Moon be waxing—increasing in light—and in good aspect to Saturn, Venus, or Mercury. In case the will is made in an emergency during illness and the Moon is slow in motion, void-of-course, combust, or under the Sun's beams, the testator will die and the will remain unaltered. There is some danger that it will be lost or stolen, however.

Marriage

The best time for marriage to take place is when the Moon is increasing, but not yet full. Good signs for the Moon to be in are Taurus, Cancer, Leo, or Libra.

The Moon in Taurus produces the most steadfast marriages, but if the partners later want to separate, they may have a difficult time. Make sure that the Moon is well aspected, especially to Venus or Jupiter. Avoid aspects to Mars, Uranus, or Pluto and the signs Aries, Gemini, Virgo, Scorpio, or Aquarius.

The values of the signs are as follows:

- Aries is not favored for marriage
- Taurus from 0 to 19 degrees is good, the remaining degrees are less favorable
- Cancer is unfavorable unless you are marrying a widow
- Leo is favored, but it may cause one party to deceive the other as to his or her money or possessions
- Virgo is not favored except when marrying a widow
- Libra is good for engagements but not for marriage
- Scorpio from 0 to 15 degrees is good, but the last 15 degrees are entirely unfortunate. The woman may be fickle, envious, and quarrelsome
- Sagittarius is neutral

- Capricorn, from 0 to 10 degrees, is difficult for marriage; however, the remaining degrees are favorable, especially when marrying a widow
- Aquarius is not favored
- Pisces is favored, although marriage under this sign can incline a woman to chatter a lot

These effects are strongest when the Moon is in the sign. If the Moon and Venus are in a cardinal sign, happiness between the couple may not continue long.

On no account should the Moon apply to Saturn or Mars, even by good aspect.

Medical Treatment for the Eyes

Let the Moon be increasing in light and motion and making favorable aspects to Venus or Jupiter and be unaspected by Mars. Keep the Moon out of Taurus, Capricorn, or Virgo. If an aspect between the Moon and Mars is unavoidable, let it be separating.

Medical Treatment for the Head

If possible, have Mars and Saturn free of hard aspects. Let the Moon be in Aries or Taurus, decreasing in light, in conjunction or aspect with Venus or Jupiter and free of hard aspects. The Sun should not be in any aspect to the Moon.

Medical Treatment for the Nose

Let the Moon be in Cancer, Leo, or Virgo and not aspecting Mars or Saturn and also not in conjunction with a retrograde or weak planet.

Mining

Saturn rules mining. Begin work when Saturn is marked conjunct, trine, or sextile. Mine for gold when the Sun is marked conjunct, trine, or sextile. Mercury rules quicksilver, Venus rules copper, Jupiter rules tin, Saturn rules lead and coal, Uranus rules radioactive elements, Neptune rules oil, the Moon rules water. Mine for these items when the ruling planet is marked conjunct, trine, or sextile.

Move to New Home

If you have a choice, and sometimes you don't, make sure that Mars is not aspecting the Moon. Move on a day favorable to your Sun sign or when the Moon is conjunct, sextile, or trine the Sun.

Mow Lawn

Mow in the first and second quarters (waxing phase) to increase growth and lushness, and in the third and fourth quarters (waning phase) to decrease growth.

Negotiate

When you are choosing a time to negotiate, consider what the meeting is about and what you want to have happen. If it is agreement or compromise between two parties that you desire, have the Moon be in the sign of Libra. When you are making contracts, it is best to have the Moon in the same element. For example, if your concern is communication, then elect a time when the Moon is in an air sign. If, on the other hand, your concern is about possessions, an earth sign would be more appropriate. Fixed signs are unfavorable, with the exception of Leo; so are cardinal signs, except for Capricorn. If you are negotiating the end of something, use the rules that apply to ending habits.

Occupational Training

When you begin training, see that your lunar cycle is favorable that day and that the planet ruling your occupation is marked conjunct or trine.

Paint

Paint buildings during the waning Libra or Aquarius Moon. If the weather is hot, paint when the Moon is in Taurus. If the weather is cold, paint when the Moon is in Leo. Schedule the painting to start in the fourth quarter as the wood is drier and paint will penetrate wood better. Avoid painting around the New Moon, though, as the wood is likely to be damp, making the paint subject to scalding when hot weather hits it. If the temperature is below 70°F, it is not advisable to paint while the Moon is in Cancer, Scorpio, or Pisces as the paint is apt to creep, check, or run.

Party (Host or Attend)

A party timed so the Moon is in Gemini, Leo, Libra, or Sagittarius, with good aspects to Venus and Jupiter, will be fun and well attended. There should be no aspects between the Moon and Mars or Saturn.

Pawn

Do not pawn any article when Jupiter is receiving a square or opposition from Saturn or Mars or when Jupiter is within 17 degrees of the Sun, for you will have little chance to redeem the items.

Pick Mushrooms

Mushrooms, one of the most promising traditional medicines in the world, should be gathered at the Full Moon.

Plant

Root crops, like carrots and potatoes, are best if planted in the sign Taurus or Capricorn. Beans, peas, tomatoes, peppers, and other fruit-bearing plants are best if planted in a sign that supports seed growth. Leaf plants, like lettuce, broccoli, or cauliflower, are best planted when the Moon is in a water sign.

It is recommended that you transplant during a decreasing Moon, when forces are streaming into the lower part of the plant. This helps root growth.

Promotion (Ask For)

Choose a day favorable to your Sun sign. Mercury should be marked conjunct, trine, or sextile. Avoid days when Mars or Saturn is aspected.

Prune

Prune during the third and fourth quarter of a Scorpio Moon to retard growth and to promote better fruit. Prune when the Moon is in cardinal Capricorn to promote healing.

Reconcile with People

If the reconciliation is with a woman, let Venus be strong and well aspected. If elders or superiors are involved, see that Saturn is receiving good aspects; if the reconciliation is between young people or between an older and younger person, see that Mercury is well aspected.

Romance

There is less control of when a romance starts, but romances begun under an increasing Moon are more likely to be permanent or satisfying, while those begun during the decreasing Moon tend to transform the participants. The tone of the relationship can be guessed from the sign the Moon is in. Romances begun with the Moon in Aries may be impulsive. Those begun in Capricorn will take greater effort to bring to a desirable conclusion, but they may be very rewarding. Good aspects between the Moon and Venus will have a positive influence on the relationship. Avoid unfavorable aspects to Mars, Uranus, and Pluto. A decreasing Moon, particularly the fourth quarter, facilitates ending a relationship and causes the least pain.

Roof a Building

Begin roofing a building during the third or fourth quarter, when the Moon is in Aries or Aquarius. Shingles laid during the New Moon have a tendency to curl at the edges.

Sauerkraut

The best-tasting sauerkraut is made just after the Full Moon in the fruitful signs of Cancer, Scorpio, or Pisces.

Select a Child's Sex

Count from the last day of menstruation to the first day of the next cycle and divide the interval between the two dates in half. Pregnancy in the first half produces females, but copulation should take place with the Moon in a feminine sign. Pregnancy in the latter half, up to three days before the beginning of menstruation, produces males, but copulation should take place with the Moon in a masculine sign. The three-day period before the next period again produces females.

Sell or Canvass

Begin these activities during a day favorable to your Sun sign. Otherwise, sell on days when Jupiter, Mercury, or Mars is trine, sextile, or conjunct the Moon. Avoid days when Saturn is square or opposing the Moon, for that always hinders business and causes discord. If the Moon is passing from the first quarter to full, it is best to have the Moon swift in motion and in good aspect with Venus and/or Jupiter.

Sign Papers

Sign contracts or agreements when the Moon is increasing in a fruitful sign and on a day when the Moon is making favorable aspects to Mercury. Avoid days when Mars, Saturn, or Neptune are square or opposite the Moon.

Spray and Weed

Spray pests and weeds during the fourth quarter when the Moon is in the barren sign Leo or Aquarius and making favorable aspects to Pluto. Weed during a waning Moon in a barren sign.

Staff (Fire)

Have the Moon in the third or fourth quarter, but not full. The Moon should not be square any planets.

Staff (Hire)

The Moon should be in the first or second quarter, and preferably in the sign of Gemini or Virgo. The Moon should be conjunct, trine, or sextile Mercury or Jupiter.

Stocks (Buy)

The Moon should be in Taurus or Capricorn, and there should be a sextile or trine to Jupiter or Saturn.

Surgical Procedures

Blood flow, like ocean tides, appears to be related to Moon phases. To reduce hemorrhage after a surgery, schedule it within one week before or after a New Moon. Schedule surgery to occur during the increase of the Moon if possible, as wounds heal better and vitality is greater than during the decrease of the Moon. Avoid surgery within one week before or after the Full Moon. Select a date when the Moon is past the sign governing the part of the body involved in the operation. For example, abdominal operations should be done when the Moon is in Sagittarius, Capricorn, or Aquarius. The further removed the Moon sign is from the sign ruling the afflicted part of the body, the better.

For successful operations, avoid times when the Moon is applying to any aspect of Mars. (This tends to promote inflammation and complications.) See the Lunar Aspectarian on odd pages 137–159 to find days with negative Mars aspects and positive Venus and Jupiter aspects. Never operate with the Moon in the same sign as a person's Sun sign or Ascendant. Let the Moon be in a fixed sign and avoid square or opposing aspects. The Moon should not be void-of-course. Cosmetic surgery should be done in the increase of the Moon, when the Moon is not square or in opposition to Mars. Avoid days when the Moon is square or opposing Saturn or the Sun.

Travel (Air)

Start long trips when the Moon is making favorable aspects to the Sun For enjoyment, aspects to Jupiter are preferable; for visiting, look for favorable aspects to Mercury. To prevent accidents, avoid squares or oppositions to Mars, Saturn, Uranus, or Pluto. Choose a day when the Moon is in Sagittarius or Gemini and well aspected to Mercury, Jupiter, or Uranus. Avoid adverse aspects of Mars, Saturn, or Uranus.

Visit

On setting out to visit a person, let the Moon be in aspect with any retrograde planet, for this ensures that the person you're visiting will be at home. If you desire to stay a long time in a place, let the Moon be in good aspect to Saturn. If you desire to leave the place quickly, let the Moon be in a cardinal sign.

Wean Children

To wean a child successfully, do so when the Moon is in Sagittarius, Capricorn, Aquarius, or Pisces—signs that do not rule vital human organs. By observing this astrological rule, much trouble for parents and child may be avoided.

Weight (Reduce)

If you want to lose weight, the best time to get started is when the Moon is in the third or fourth quarter and in the barren sign of Virgo. Review the section on How to Use the Moon Tables and Lunar Aspectarian beginning on page 136 to help you select a date that is favorable to begin your weight-loss program.

Wine and Drink Other Than Beer

Start brewing when the Moon is in Pisces or Taurus. Sextiles or trines to Venus are favorable, but avoid aspects to Mars or Saturn.

Write

Write for pleasure or publication when the Moon is in Gemini. Mercury should be making favorable aspects to Uranus and Neptune.

How to Use the Moon Tables and Lunar Aspectarian

Timing activities is one of the most important things you can do to ensure success. In many Eastern countries, timing by the planets is so important that practically no event takes place without first setting up a chart for it. Weddings have occurred in the middle of the night because the influences were at the best then. You may not want to take it that far, but you can still make use of the influences of the Moon whenever possible. It's easy and it works!

Llewellyn's Moon Sign Book has information to help you plan just about any activity: weddings, fishing, making purchases, cutting your hair, traveling, and more. We provide the guidelines you need to pick the best day out of the several from which you have to choose. The Moon Tables are the *Moon Sign Book's* primary method for choosing dates. Following are instructions, examples, and directions on how to read the Moon Tables. More advanced information on using the tables containing the Lunar Aspectarian and favorable and unfavorable days (found on odd-numbered pages opposite the Moon Tables), Moon void-of-course and retrograde information to choose the dates best for you is also included.

The Five Basic Steps

Step 1: Directions for Choosing Dates

Look up the directions for choosing dates for the activity that you wish to begin, then go to step 2.

Step 2: Check the Moon Tables

You'll find two tables for each month of the year beginning on page 136. The Moon Tables (on the left-hand pages) include the day, date, and sign the Moon is in; the element and nature of the sign; the Moon's phase; and when it changes sign or phase. If there is a time listed after a date, that time is the time when the Moon moves into that zodiac sign. Until then, the Moon is considered to be in the sign for the previous day.

The abbreviation Full signifies Full Moon and New signifies New Moon. The times listed with dates indicate when the Moon changes sign. The times listed after the phase indicate when the Moon changes phase.

Turn to the month you would like to begin your activity. You will be using the Moon's sign and phase information most often when you begin choosing your own dates. Use the Time Zone Map on page 164 and the Time Zone Conversions table on page 165 to convert time to your own time zone.

When you find dates that meet the criteria for the correct Moon phase and sign for your activity, you may have completed the process. For certain simple activities, such as getting a haircut, the phase and sign information is all that is needed. If the directions for your activity include information on certain lunar aspects, however, you should consult the Lunar Aspectarian. An example of this would be if the directions told you not to perform a certain activity when the Moon is square (Q) Jupiter.

Step 3: Check the Lunar Aspectarian

On the pages opposite the Moon Tables you will find tables containing the Lunar Aspectarian and Favorable and Unfavorable Days. The Lunar Aspectarian gives the aspects (or angles) of the Moon to other planets. Some aspects are favorable, while others are not. To use the Lunar Aspectarian, find the planet that the directions list as favorable for your activity, and run down the column to the date desired. For example, you should avoid aspects to Mars if you are planning surgery. So you would look for Mars across the top and then run down that column looking for days where there are no aspects to Mars (as signified by empty boxes). If you want to find a **favorable** aspect (sextile (X) or trine (T)) to Mercury, run your finger down the column under Mercury until you find an X or T. **Adverse** aspects to planets are squares (Q) or oppositions (O). A conjunction (C) is sometimes beneficial, sometimes not, depending on the activity or planets involved.

Step 4: Favorable and Unfavorable Days

The tables listing favorable and unfavorable days are helpful when you want to choose your personal best dates because your Sun sign is taken into consideration. The twelve Sun signs are listed on the right side of the tables. Once you have determined which days meet your criteria for phase, sign, and aspects, you can determine whether or not those days are positive for you by checking the favorable and unfavorable days for your Sun sign.

To find out if a day is positive for you, find your Sun sign and then look down the column. If it is marked F, it is very favorable. The Moon is in the same sign as your Sun on a favorable day. If it is marked f, it is slightly favorable; U is very unfavorable; and u means slightly unfavorable. A day marked very unfavorable (U) indicates that the Moon is in the sign opposing your Sun

Once you have selected good dates for the activity you are about to begin, you can go straight to "Using What You've Learned," beginning on the next page. To learn how to fine-tune your selections even further, read on.

Step 5: Void-of-Course Moon and Retrogrades

This last step is perhaps the most advanced portion of the procedure. It is generally considered poor timing to make decisions, sign important papers, or start special activities during a Moon void-of-course period or during a Mercury retrograde. Once you have chosen the best date for your activity based on steps one through four, you can check the Void-of-Course tables, beginning on page 76, to find out if any of the dates you have chosen have void periods.

The Moon is said to be void-of-course after it has made its last aspect to a planet within a particular sign, but before it has moved into the next sign. Put simply, the Moon is "resting" during the void-of-course period, so activities initiated at this time generally don't come to fruition. You will notice that there are many void periods during the year, and it is nearly impossible to avoid all of them. Some people choose to ignore these altogether and do not take them into consideration when planning activities.

Next, you can check the Retrograde Planets tables on page 160 to see what planets are retrograde during your chosen date(s).

A planet is said to be retrograde when it appears to move backward in the sky as viewed from Earth. Generally, the farther a planet is away from the Sun, the longer it can stay retrograde. Some planets will retrograde for several months at a time. Avoiding retrogrades is not as important in lunar planning as avoiding the Moon void-of-course, with the exception of the planet Mercury.

Mercury rules thought and communication, so it is advisable not to sign important papers, initiate important business or legal work, or make crucial decisions during these times. As with the Moon void-of-course, it is difficult to avoid all planetary retrogrades when beginning events, and you may choose to ignore this step of the process. Following are some examples using some or all of the steps outlined above.

Using What You've Learned

Let's say it's a new year and you want to have your hair cut. It's thin and you would like it to look fuller, so you find the directions for hair care and you see that for thicker hair you should cut hair while the Moon is Full and in the sign of Taurus, Cancer, or Leo. You should avoid the Moon in Aries, Gemini, or Virgo. Look at the January Moon Table on page 136. You see that the Full Moon is on January 6 at 6:08 pm. The Moon is in Leo on January 7 and moves into Virgo on January 10 at 10:15 am, so January 7–9 meet both the phase and sign criteria.

Let's move on to a more difficult example using the sign and phase of the Moon. You want to buy a permanent home. After checking the instructions for purchasing a house: "Home (Buy New)" on page 117, you see that you should buy a home when the Moon is in Taurus, Cancer, or Leo. You need to get a loan, so you should also look under "Loan (Ask For)" on page 119. Here it says that the third and fourth quarters favor the borrower (you). You are going to buy the house in October, so go to page 154. The Moon is in the third quarter Oct 1–5 and Oct 29–31 and fourth quarter Oct 6–13. The Moon is in Leo at 7:24 pm on Oct 7 until Oct 10 at 8:02 am; in Taurus from Oct 1 until Oct 3 at 1:03 am and at 7:44 am on Oct 28 until Oct 30 at 11:08 am; in Cancer from 8:32 am on Oct 5 to Oct 7 at 7:24 pm. The best days for obtaining a loan would be October 1, 2, 5–9.

Just match up the best sign and phase (quarter) to come up with the best date. With all activities, be sure to check the favorable and unfavorable days for your Sun sign in the table adjoining the Lunar Aspectarian. If there is a choice between several dates, pick the one most favorable for you. Because buying a home is an important business decision, you may also wish to see if the Moon is void or if Mercury is retrograde during these dates.

Now let's look at an example that uses signs, phases, and aspects. Our example is starting new home construction. We will use the month of February. Look under "Build (Start Foundation)" on page 110 and you'll see that the Moon should be in the first quarter of a fixed sign—Leo, Taurus, Aquarius, or Scorpio. You should select a time when the Moon is not making unfavorable aspects to Saturn. (Conjunctions are usually considered unfavorable if they are to Mars, Saturn, or Neptune.) Look in the February Moon Table on page 138. You will see that the Moon is in the first quarter Feb 20–26 and in Taurus from 3:29 am on Feb 24 until 10:48 am on Feb 26. Now, look to the February Lunar Aspectarian. We see that there is an unfavorable square to Saturn the 26; therefore, Feb 24–25 would be the best dates to start a foundation.

A Note about Time and Time Zones

All tables in the Moon Sign Book use Eastern Time. You must calculate the difference between your time zone and the Eastern Time Zone. Please refer to the Time Zone Conversions chart on page 165 for help with time conversions. The sign the Moon is in at midnight is the sign shown in the Aspectarian and Favorable and Unfavorable Days tables.

How Does the Time Matter?

Due to the three-hour time difference between the East and West Coasts of the United States, those of you living on the East Coast may be, for example, under the influence of a Virgo

Moon, while those of you living on the West Coast will still have a Leo Moon influence.

We follow a commonly held belief among astrologers: whatever sign the Moon is in at the start of a day—12:00 am Eastern Time—is considered the dominant influence of the day. That sign is indicated in the Moon Tables. If the date you select for an activity shows the Moon changing signs, you can decide how important the sign change may be for your specific election and adjust your election date and time accordingly.

Use Common Sense

Some activities depend on outside factors. Obviously, you can't go out and plant when there is a foot of snow on the ground. You should adjust to the conditions at hand. If the weather was bad during the first quarter, when it was best to plant crops, do it during the second quarter while the Moon is in a fruitful sign. If the Moon is not in a fruitful sign during the first or second quarter, choose a day when it is in a semi-fruitful sign. The best advice is to choose either the sign or phase that is most favorable, when the two don't coincide.

To Summarize

First, look up the activity under the proper heading, then look for the information given in the tables. Choose the best date considering the number of positive factors in effect. If most of the dates are favorable, there is no problem choosing the one that will fit your schedule. However, if there aren't any really good dates, pick the ones with the least number of negative influences. Please keep in mind that the information found here applies in the broadest sense to the events you want to plan or are considering. To be the most effective, when you use electional astrology, you should also consider your own birth chart in relation to a chart drawn for the time or times you have under consideration. The best advice we can offer you is: read the entire introduction to each section.

January Moon Table

Date	Sign	Element	Nature	Phase
1 Sun	Taurus	Earth	Semi-fruitful	2nd
2 Mon 9:44 pm	Gemini	Air	Barren	2nd
3 Tue	Gemini	Air	Barren	2nd
4 Wed	Gemini	Air	Barren	2nd
5 Thu 9:15 am	Cancer	Water	Fruitful	2nd
6 Fri	Cancer	Water	Fruitful	Full 6:08 pm
7 Sat 9:40 pm	Leo	Fire	Barren	3rd
8 Sun	Leo	Fire	Barren	3rd
9 Mon	Leo	Fire	Barren	3rd
10 Tue 10:15 am	Virgo	Earth	Barren	3rd
11 Wed	Virgo	Earth	Barren	3rd
12 Thu 9:56 pm	Libra	Air	Semi-fruitful	3rd
13 Fri	Libra	Air	Semi-fruitful	3rd
14 Sat	Libra	Air	Semi-fruitful	4th 9:10 pm
15 Sun 7:08 am	Scorpio	Water	Fruitful	4th
16 Mon	Scorpio	Water	Fruitful	4th
17 Tue 12:33 pm	Sagittarius	Fire	Barren	4th
18 Wed	Sagittarius	Fire	Barren	4th
19 Thu 2:11 pm	Capricorn	Earth	Semi-fruitful	4th
20 Fri	Capricorn	Earth	Semi-fruitful	4th
21 Sat 1:29 pm	Aquarius	Air	Barren	New 3:53 pm
22 Sun	Aquarius	Air	Barren	1st
23 Mon 12:36 pm	Pisces	Water	Fruitful	1st
24 Tue	Pisces	Water	Fruitful	1st
25 Wed 1:48 pm	Aries	Fire	Barren	1st
26 Thu	Aries	Fire	Barren	1st
27 Fri 6:42 pm	Taurus	Earth	Semi-fruitful	1st
28 Sat	Taurus	Earth	Semi-fruitful	2nd 10:19 am
29 Sun	Taurus	Earth	Semi-fruitful	2nd
30 Mon 3:35 am	Gemini	Air	Barren	2nd
31 Tue	Gemini	Air	Barren	2nd

January Aspectarian/Favorable & Unfavorable Days

Date	Sun	Mercury	Venus	Mars	Jupiter	Saturn	Uranus	Neptune	Pluto
1	T						C		
2		T	T				Q	X	T
3				C	X				
4						T		Q	
5					Q				
6	O	O					X		
7								T	O
8			O	X	T				
9						O	Q		
10									
11		T		Q			T		
12	T							O	T
13		Q		T	O				
14	Q		T			T			
15		X							Q
16			Q				O		
17	X					T	Q	T	X
18			X	O					
19					Q	X		Q	
20		C					T		
21	C				X			X	C
22			T				Q		
23		C				C			
24		X		Q			X		
25	X				C			C	X
26		Q		X					
27			X			X			Q
28	Q	T					C		
29						Q		X	
30			Q	C	X				T
31	T								

Date	Aries	Taurus	Gemini	Cancer	Leo	Virgo	Libra	Scorpio	Sagittarius	Capricorn	Aquarius	Pisces
1		F		f	u	f		U		f	u	f
2		F		f	u	f		U		f	u	f
3	f		F		f	u	f		U		f	u
4	f		F		f	u	f		U		f	u
5	f		F		f	u	f		U		f	u
6	u	f		F		f	u	f		U		f
7	u	f		F		f	u	f		U		f
8	f	u	f		F		f	u	f		U	
9	f	u	f		F		f	u	f		U	
10	f	u	f		F		f	u	f		U	
11		f	u	f		F		f	u	f		U
12		f	u	f		F		f	u	f		U
13	U		f	u	f		F		f	u	f	
14	U		f	u	f		F		f	u	f	
15	U		f	u	f		F		f	u	f	
16		U		f	u	f		F		f	u	f
17		U		f	u	f		F		f	u	f
18	f		U		f	u	f		F		f	u
19	f		U		f	u	f		F		f	u
20	u	f		U		f	u	f		F		f
21	u	f		U		f	u	f		F		f
22	f	u	f		U		f	u	f		F	
23	f	u	f		U		f	u	f		F	
24		f	u	f		U		f	u	f		F
25		f	u	f		U		f	u	f		F
26	F		f	u	f		U		f	u	f	
27	F		f	u	f		U		f	u	f	u
28		F		f	u	f		U		f	u	f
29		F		f	u	f		U		f	u	f
30		F		f	u	f		U		f	u	f
31	f		F		f	u	f		U		f	u

February Moon Table

Date	Sign	Element	Nature	Phase
1 Wed 3:11 pm	Cancer	Water	Fruitful	2nd
2 Thu	Cancer	Water	Fruitful	2nd
3 Fri	Cancer	Water	Fruitful	2nd
4 Sat 3:48 am	Leo	Fire	Barren	2nd
5 Sun	Leo	Fire	Barren	Full 1:29 pm
6 Mon 4:14 pm	Virgo	Earth	Barren	3rd
7 Tue	Virgo	Earth	Barren	3rd
8 Wed	Virgo	Earth	Barren	3rd
9 Thu 3:47 am	Libra	Air	Semi-fruitful	3rd
10 Fri	Libra	Air	Semi-fruitful	3rd
11 Sat 1:34 pm	Scorpio	Water	Fruitful	3rd
12 Sun	Scorpio	Water	Fruitful	3rd
13 Mon 8:31 pm	Sagittarius	Fire	Barren	4th 11:01 am
14 Tue	Sagittarius	Fire	Barren	4th
15 Wed	Sagittarius	Fire	Barren	4th
16 Thu 12:00 am	Capricorn	Earth	Semi-fruitful	4th
17 Fri	Capricorn	Earth	Semi-fruitful	4th
18 Sat 12:35 am	Aquarius	Air	Barren	4th
19 Sun 11:56 pm	Pisces	Water	Fruitful	4th
20 Mon	Pisces	Water	Fruitful	New 2:06 am
21 Tue	Pisces	Water	Fruitful	1st
22 Wed 12:14 am	Aries	Fire	Barren	1st
23 Thu	Aries	Fire	Barren	1st
24 Fri 3:29 am	Taurus	Earth	Semi-fruitful	1st
25 Sat	Taurus	Earth	Semi-fruitful	1st
26 Sun 10:48 am	Gemini	Air	Barren	1st
27 Mon	Gemini	Air	Barren	2nd 3:06 am
28 Tue 9:40 pm	Cancer	Water	Fruitful	2nd

February Aspectarian/Favorable & Unfavorable Days

Date	Sun	Mercury	Venus	Mars	Jupiter	Saturn	Uranus	Neptune	Pluto
1						T		Q	
2		T			Q		X		
3		O						T	
4					T				O
5	O			X		Q			
6							O		
7			O	Q		T			
8		T						O	
9					O				T
10	T			T					
11		Q				T			Q
12								O	
13	Q		T			Q		T	X
14		X		O	T				
15	X		Q			X		Q	
16					Q				
17			X				T	X	C
18		C			X				
19			T				C	Q	
20	C								
21			Q				X	C	X
22		C			C				
23		X		X					
24	X						X		Q
25		Q						C	
26							Q	X	T
27	Q		X	C	X				
28		T				T		Q	

Date	Aries	Taurus	Gemini	Cancer	Leo	Virgo	Libra	Scorpio	Sagittarius	Capricorn	Aquarius	Pisces
1	f		F		f	u	f		U		f	u
2	u	f		F		f	u	f		U		f
3	u	f		F		f	u	f		U		f
4	u	f		F		f	u	f		U		f
5	f	u	f		F		f	u	f		U	
6	f	u	f		F		f	u	f		U	
7		f	u	f		F		f	u	f		U
8		f	u	f		F		f	u	f		U
9		f	u	f		F		f	u	f		U
10	U		f	u	f		F		f	u	f	
11	U		f	u	f		F		f	u	f	
12		U		f	u	f		F		f	u	f
13		U		f	u	f		F		f	u	f
14	f		U		f	u	f		F		f	u
15	f		U		f	u	f		F		f	u
16	u	f		U		f	u	f		F		f
17	u	f		U		f	u	f		F		f
18	f	u	f		U		f	u	f		F	
19	f	u	f		U		f	u	f		F	
20		f	u	f		U		f	u	f		F
21		f	u	f		U		f	u	f		F
22	F		f	u	f		U		f	u	f	
23	F		f	u	f		U		f	u	f	
24	F		f	u	f		U		f	u	f	
25		F		f	u	f		U		f	u	f
26		F		f	u	f		U		f	u	f
27	f		F		f	u	f		U		f	u
28	f		F		f	u	f		U		f	u

March Moon Table

Date	Sign	Element	Nature	Phase
1 Wed	Cancer	Water	Fruitful	2nd
2 Thu	Cancer	Water	Fruitful	2nd
3 Fri 10:16 am	Leo	Fire	Barren	2nd
4 Sat	Leo	Fire	Barren	2nd
5 Sun 10:38 pm	Virgo	Earth	Barren	2nd
6 Mon	Virgo	Earth	Barren	2nd
7 Tue	Virgo	Earth	Barren	Full 7:40 am
8 Wed 9:44 am	Libra	Air	Semi-fruitful	3rd
9 Thu	Libra	Air	Semi-fruitful	3rd
10 Fri 7:06 pm	Scorpio	Water	Fruitful	3rd
11 Sat	Scorpio	Water	Fruitful	3rd
12 Sun	Scorpio	Water	Fruitful	3rd
13 Mon 3:21 am	Sagittarius	Fire	Barren	3rd
14 Tue	Sagittarius	Fire	Barren	4th 10:08 pm
15 Wed 8:06 am	Capricorn	Earth	Semi-fruitful	4th
16 Thu	Capricorn	Earth	Semi-fruitful	4th
17 Fri 10:25 am	Aquarius	Air	Barren	4th
18 Sat	Aquarius	Air	Barren	4th
19 Sun 11:12 am	Pisces	Water	Fruitful	4th
20 Mon	Pisces	Water	Fruitful	4th
21 Tue 12:01 pm	Aries	Fire	Barren	New 1:23 pm
22 Wed	Aries	Fire	Barren	1st
23 Thu 2:42 pm	Taurus	Earth	Semi-fruitful	1st
24 Fri	Taurus	Earth	Semi-fruitful	1st
25 Sat 8:42 pm	Gemini	Air	Barren	1st
26 Sun	Gemini	Air	Barren	1st
27 Mon	Gemini	Air	Barren	1st
28 Tue 6:22 am	Cancer	Water	Fruitful	2nd 10:32 pm
29 Wed	Cancer	Water	Fruitful	2nd
30 Thu 6:31 pm	Leo	Fire	Barren	2nd
31 Fri	Leo	Fire	Barren	2nd

March Aspectarian/Favorable & Unfavorable Days

Date	Sun	Mercury	Venus	Mars	Jupiter	Saturn	Uranus	Neptune	Pluto
1	T		Q		Q				
2							X	T	
3									O
4			T		T		Q		
5					X	O			
6		O							
7	O				Q		T	O	
8									T
9						O			
10			O	T	T				Q
11									
12	T	T					O	T	
13						Q			X
14	Q	Q		O	T			Q	
15		T				X			
16					Q		T		
17	X	X	Q					X	C
18				X			Q		
19			X	T			C		
20								X	
21	C	C	Q					C	X
22				C					
23				X		X			Q
24			C			C			
25								X	T
26	X					Q			
27		X		X				Q	
28	Q				C	T			
29			X		Q		X		
30		Q						T	O
31	T								

Date	Aries	Taurus	Gemini	Cancer	Leo	Virgo	Libra	Scorpio	Sagittarius	Capricorn	Aquarius	Pisces
1	u	f		F		f	u	f		U		f
2	u	f		F		f	u	f		U		f
3	u	f		F		f	u	f		U		f
4	f	u	f		F		f	u	f		U	
5	f	u	f		F		f	u	f		U	
6		f	u	f		F		f	u	f		U
7		f	u	f		F		f	u	f		U
8		f	u	f		F		f	u	f		U
9	U		f	u	f		F		f	u	f	
10	U		f	u	f		F		f	u	f	
11		U		f	u	f		F		f	u	f
12		U		f	u	f		F		f	u	f
13		U		f	u	f		F		f	u	f
14			U		f	u	f		F		f	u
15			U		f	u	f		F		f	u
16	f			U		f	u	f		F		f
17	f			U		f	u	f		F		f
18	u	f			U		f	u	f		F	f
19	u	f			U		f	u	f		F	f
20	f	u	f			U		f	u	f		F
21	f	u	f			U		f	u	f		F
22	F	f	u	f			U	f	u	f		
23	F	f	u	f			U	f	u	f		
24	f	F	f	u	f			U	f	u	f	
25	f	F	f	u	f			U	f	u	f	
26	f		F	f	u	f			U		f	u
27	f		F	f	u	f			U		f	u
28	f		F	f	u	f			U		f	u
29	u	f		F		f	u	f		U		f
30	u	f		F		f	u	f		U		f
31	f	u	f		F		f	u	f		U	

April Moon Table

Date	Sign	Element	Nature	Phase
1 Sat	Leo	Fire	Barren	2nd
2 Sun 6:57 am	Virgo	Earth	Barren	2nd
3 Mon	Virgo	Earth	Barren	2nd
4 Tue 5:51 pm	Libra	Air	Semi-fruitful	2nd
5 Wed	Libra	Air	Semi-fruitful	2nd
6 Thu	Libra	Air	Semi-fruitful	Full 12:34 am
7 Fri 2:29 am	Scorpio	Water	Fruitful	3rd
8 Sat	Scorpio	Water	Fruitful	3rd
9 Sun 8:57 am	Sagittarius	Fire	Barren	3rd
10 Mon	Sagittarius	Fire	Barren	3rd
11 Tue 1:33 pm	Capricorn	Earth	Semi-fruitful	3rd
12 Wed	Capricorn	Earth	Semi-fruitful	3rd
13 Thu 4:42 pm	Aquarius	Air	Barren	4th 5:11 am
14 Fri	Aquarius	Air	Barren	4th
15 Sat 6:57 pm	Pisces	Water	Fruitful	4th
16 Sun	Pisces	Water	Fruitful	4th
17 Mon 9:09 pm	Aries	Fire	Barren	4th
18 Tue	Aries	Fire	Barren	4th
19 Wed	Aries	Fire	Barren	4th
20 Thu 12:30 am	Taurus	Earth	Semi-fruitful	New 12:13 am
21 Fri	Taurus	Earth	Semi-fruitful	1st
22 Sat 6:11 am	Gemini	Air	Barren	1st
23 Sun	Gemini	Air	Barren	1st
24 Mon 2:58 pm	Cancer	Water	Fruitful	1st
25 Tue	Cancer	Water	Fruitful	1st
26 Wed	Cancer	Water	Fruitful	1st
27 Thu 2:30 am	Leo	Fire	Barren	2nd 5:20 pm
28 Fri	Leo	Fire	Barren	2nd
29 Sat 2:59 pm	Virgo	Earth	Barren	2nd
30 Sun	Virgo	Earth	Barren	2nd

April Aspectarian/Favorable & Unfavorable Days

Date	Sun	Mercury	Venus	Mars	Jupiter	Saturn	Uranus	Neptune	Pluto
1			Q		T			Q	
2		T		X		O			
3							T		
4			T					O	T
5				Q					
6	O				O				
7		O		T	T				Q
8						O			
9			O			Q		T	X
10	T				T				
11						X		Q	
12		T		O		T			
13	Q		T	Q				X	C
14		Q						Q	
15	X				X				
16		X	Q	T		C			
17							X	C	X
18			X	Q					
19						C			
20	C					X			Q
21		C		X		C	X		
22						Q			T
23			C						
24						X		Q	
25	X	X			C		T		
26						Q	X	T	
27	Q								O
28		Q	X					Q	
29				T					
30	T	T						O	

Date	Aries	Taurus	Gemini	Cancer	Leo	Virgo	Libra	Scorpio	Sagittarius	Capricorn	Aquarius	Pisces
1	f	u	f		F			f	u	f	U	
2	f	u	f		F			f	u	f	U	
3		f	u	f		F			f	u	f	U
4		f	u	f		F			f	u	f	U
5	U		f	u	f		F			f	u	f
6	U		f	u	f		F			f	u	f
7	f	U		f	u	f		F			f	u
8	f	U		f	u	f		F			f	u
9	f	U		f	u	f		F			f	u
10	u	f	U		f	u	f		F			f
11	u	f	U		f	u	f		F			f
12	f	u	f	U		f	u	f		F		
13	f	u	f	U		f	u	f		F		
14		f	u	f	U		f	u	f		F	
15		f	u	f	U		f	u	f		F	
16			f	u	f	U		f	u	f		F
17			f	u	f	U		f	u	f		F
18	F			f	u	f	U		f	u	f	
19	F			f	u	f	U		f	u	f	
20		F			f	u	f	U		f	u	f
21		F			f	u	f	U		f	u	f
22		F			f	u	f	U		f	u	f
23	f		F			f	u	f	U		f	u
24	f		F			f	u	f	U		f	u
25	u	f		F			f	u	f	U		f
26	u	f		F			f	u	f	U		f
27	f	u	f		F			f	u	f	U	
28	f	u	f		F			f	u	f	U	
29	f	u	f		F			f	u	f	U	
30		f	u	f		F			f	u	f	U

May Moon Table

Date	Sign	Element	Nature	Phase
1 Mon	Virgo	Earth	Barren	2nd
2 Tue 2:09 am	Libra	Air	Semi-fruitful	2nd
3 Wed	Libra	Air	Semi-fruitful	2nd
4 Thu 10:32 am	Scorpio	Water	Fruitful	2nd
5 Fri	Scorpio	Water	Fruitful	Full 1:34 pm
6 Sat 4:04 pm	Sagittarius	Fire	Barren	3rd
7 Sun	Sagittarius	Fire	Barren	3rd
8 Mon 7:33 pm	Capricorn	Earth	Semi-fruitful	3rd
9 Tue	Capricorn	Earth	Semi-fruitful	3rd
10 Wed 10:05 pm	Aquarius	Air	Barren	3rd
11 Thu	Aquarius	Air	Barren	3rd
12 Fri	Aquarius	Air	Barren	4th 10:28 am
13 Sat 12:39 am	Pisces	Water	Fruitful	4th
14 Sun	Pisces	Water	Fruitful	4th
15 Mon 3:56 am	Aries	Fire	Barren	4th
16 Tue	Aries	Fire	Barren	4th
17 Wed 8:28 am	Taurus	Earth	Semi-fruitful	4th
18 Thu	Taurus	Earth	Semi-fruitful	4th
19 Fri 2:48 pm	Gemini	Air	Barren	New 11:53 am
20 Sat	Gemini	Air	Barren	1st
21 Sun 11:28 pm	Cancer	Water	Fruitful	1st
22 Mon	Cancer	Water	Fruitful	1st
23 Tue	Cancer	Water	Fruitful	1st
24 Wed 10:35 am	Leo	Fire	Barren	1st
25 Thu	Leo	Fire	Barren	1st
26 Fri 11:05 pm	Virgo	Earth	Barren	1st
27 Sat	Virgo	Earth	Barren	2nd 11:22 am
28 Sun	Virgo	Earth	Barren	2nd
29 Mon 10:51 am	Libra	Air	Semi-fruitful	2nd
30 Tue	Libra	Air	Semi-fruitful	2nd
31 Wed 7:45 pm	Scorpio	Water	Fruitful	2nd

May Aspectarian/Favorable & Unfavorable Days

Date	Sun	Mercury	Venus	Mars	Jupiter	Saturn	Uranus	Neptune	Pluto
1			Q	X			T	O	
2									T
3				Q					
4			T		O	T			Q
5	O	O						O	
6				T				T	X
7						Q			
8			O		T			Q	
9		T					X		
10	T				O	Q	T	X	C
11		Q							
12	Q			X		Q			
13		X	T				C		
14	X			T			X	C	
15			Q						X
16									
17		C		Q	C	X			Q
18			X				C		
19	C			X				X	T
20						Q			
21								Q	
22		X			X	T			
23		C					X		
24	X			C	Q			T	O
25		Q							
26								Q	
27	Q	T			T	O			
28			X				T		
29				X				O	T
30	T								
31			Q						Q

Date	Aries	Taurus	Gemini	Cancer	Leo	Virgo	Libra	Scorpio	Sagittarius	Capricorn	Aquarius	Pisces
1		f	u	f	F		f	u	f			U
2	U		f	u	f	F		f	u	f		
3	U		f	u	f	F		f	u	f		
4	U		f	u	f	F		f	u	f		
5		U		f	u	f	F		f	u	f	
6		U		f	u	f	F		f	u	f	
7			U		f	u	f	F		f	u	f
8			U		f	u	f	F		f	u	f
9	f			U		f	u	f	F		f	u
10	f			U		f	u	f	F		f	u
11	u	f			U		f	u	f	F		f
12	u	f			U		f	u	f	F		f
13	f	u	f			U		f	u	f	F	
14	f	u	f			U		f	u	f	F	
15	f	u	f			U		f	u	f	F	
16		f	u	f			U		f	u	f	F
17		f	u	f			U		f	u	f	F
18	F		f	u	f			U		f	u	f
19	F		f	u	f			U		f	u	f
20	f	F		f	u	f			U		f	u
21	f	F		f	u	f			U		f	u
22	u	f	F		f	u	f			U		f
23	u	f	F		f	u	f			U		f
24	u	f	F		f	u	f			U		f
25	f	u	f	F		f	u	f			U	
26	f	u	f	F		f	u	f			U	
27		f	u	f	F		f	u	f			U
28		f	u	f	F		f	u	f			U
29		f	u	f	F		f	u	f			U
30	U		f	u	f	F		f	u	f		
31	U		f	u	f	F		f	u	f		

June Moon Table

Date	Sign	Element	Nature	Phase
1 Thu	Scorpio	Water	Fruitful	2nd
2 Fri	Scorpio	Water	Fruitful	2nd
3 Sat 1:03 am	Sagittarius	Fire	Barren	Full 11:42 pm
4 Sun	Sagittarius	Fire	Barren	3rd
5 Mon 3:31 am	Capricorn	Earth	Semi-fruitful	3rd
6 Tue	Capricorn	Earth	Semi-fruitful	3rd
7 Wed 4:42 am	Aquarius	Air	Barren	3rd
8 Thu	Aquarius	Air	Barren	3rd
9 Fri 6:14 am	Pisces	Water	Fruitful	3rd
10 Sat	Pisces	Water	Fruitful	4th 3:31 pm
11 Sun 9:20 am	Aries	Fire	Barren	4th
12 Mon	Aries	Fire	Barren	4th
13 Tue 2:31 pm	Taurus	Earth	Semi-fruitful	4th
14 Wed	Taurus	Earth	Semi-fruitful	4th
15 Thu 9:46 pm	Gemini	Air	Barren	4th
16 Fri	Gemini	Air	Barren	4th
17 Sat	Gemini	Air	Barren	4th
18 Sun 6:58 am	Cancer	Water	Fruitful	New 12:37 am
19 Mon	Cancer	Water	Fruitful	1st
20 Tue 6:04 pm	Leo	Fire	Barren	1st
21 Wed	Leo	Fire	Barren	1st
22 Thu	Leo	Fire	Barren	1st
23 Fri 6:35 am	Virgo	Earth	Barren	1st
24 Sat	Virgo	Earth	Barren	1st
25 Sun 6:57 pm	Libra	Air	Semi-fruitful	1st
26 Mon	Libra	Air	Semi-fruitful	2nd 3:50 am
27 Tue	Libra	Air	Semi-fruitful	2nd
28 Wed 4:55 am	Scorpio	Water	Fruitful	2nd
29 Thu	Scorpio	Water	Fruitful	2nd
30 Fri 10:59 am	Sagittarius	Fire	Barren	2nd

June Aspectarian/Favorable & Unfavorable Days

Date	Sun	Mercury	Venus	Mars	Jupiter	Saturn	Uranus	Neptune	Pluto
1				Q	O	T			
2		O	T				O	T	
3	O			T		Q			X
4								Q	
5					T	X			
6		T					T		
7			O	O	Q			X	C
8	T					Q			
9		Q			X	C			
10	Q						X		
11		X	T					C	X
12	X			T					
13									Q
14			Q	Q	C	X			
15							C	X	T
16		C	X			Q			
17				X					
18	C				X	T		Q	
19									
20							X	T	O
21			C	Q					
22		X	C			Q			
23	X				T	O			
24									
25		Q				T	O	T	
26	Q								
27			X	X					
28	T	T			O	T			Q
29			Q				O		
30				Q		Q		T	X

Date	Aries	Taurus	Gemini	Cancer	Leo	Virgo	Libra	Scorpio	Sagittarius	Capricorn	Aquarius	Pisces
1		U		f	u	f		F		f	u	f
2		U		f	u	f		F		f	u	f
3	f		U		f	u	f		F		f	u
4	f		U		f	u	f		F		f	u
5	f		U		f	u	f		F		f	u
6	u	f		U		f	u	f		F		f
7	u	f		U		f	u	f		F		f
8	f	u	f		U		f	u	f		F	
9	f	u	f		U		f	u	f		F	
10		f	u	f		U		f	u	f		F
11		f	u	f		U		f	u	f		F
12	F		f	u	f		U		f	u	f	
13	F		f	u	f		U		f	u	f	
14		F		f	u	f		U		f	u	f
15		F		f	u	f		U		f	u	f
16	f		F		f	u	f		U		f	u
17	f		F		f	u	f		U		f	u
18	f		F		f	u	f		U		f	u
19	u	f		F		f	u	f		U		f
20	u	f		F		f	u	f		U		f
21	f	u	f		F		f	u	f		U	
22	f	u	f		F		f	u	f		U	
23	f	u	f		F		f	u	f		U	
24		f	u	f		F		f	u	f		U
25		f	u	f		F		f	u	f		U
26	U		f	u	f		F		f	u	f	
27	U		f	u	f		F		f	u	f	
28	U		f	u	f		F		f	u	f	
29		U		f	u	f		F		f	u	f
30		U		f	u	f		F		f	u	f

July Moon Table

Date	Sign	Element	Nature	Phase
1 Sat	Sagittarius	Fire	Barren	2nd
2 Sun 1:20 pm	Capricorn	Earth	Semi-fruitful	2nd
3 Mon	Capricorn	Earth	Semi-fruitful	Full 7:39 am
4 Tue 1:30 pm	Aquarius	Air	Barren	3rd
5 Wed	Aquarius	Air	Barren	3rd
6 Thu 1:33 pm	Pisces	Water	Fruitful	3rd
7 Fri	Pisces	Water	Fruitful	3rd
8 Sat 3:19 pm	Aries	Fire	Barren	3rd
9 Sun	Aries	Fire	Barren	4th 9:48 pm
10 Mon 7:55 pm	Taurus	Earth	Semi-fruitful	4th
11 Tue	Taurus	Earth	Semi-fruitful	4th
12 Wed	Taurus	Earth	Semi-fruitful	4th
13 Thu 3:26 am	Gemini	Air	Barren	4th
14 Fri	Gemini	Air	Barren	4th
15 Sat 1:13 pm	Cancer	Water	Fruitful	4th
16 Sun	Cancer	Water	Fruitful	4th
17 Mon	Cancer	Water	Fruitful	New 2:32 pm
18 Tue 12:39 am	Leo	Fire	Barren	1st
19 Wed	Leo	Fire	Barren	1st
20 Thu 1:13 pm	Virgo	Earth	Barren	1st
21 Fri	Virgo	Earth	Barren	1st
22 Sat	Virgo	Earth	Barren	1st
23 Sun 1:54 am	Libra	Air	Semi-fruitful	1st
24 Mon	Libra	Air	Semi-fruitful	1st
25 Tue 12:55 pm	Scorpio	Water	Fruitful	2nd 6:07 pm
26 Wed	Scorpio	Water	Fruitful	2nd
27 Thu 8:24 pm	Sagittarius	Fire	Barren	2nd
28 Fri	Sagittarius	Fire	Barren	2nd
29 Sat 11:44 pm	Capricorn	Earth	Semi-fruitful	2nd
30 Sun	Capricorn	Earth	Semi-fruitful	2nd
31 Mon 11:58 pm	Aquarius	Air	Barren	2nd

July Aspectarian/Favorable & Unfavorable Days

Date	Sun	Mercury	Venus	Mars	Jupiter	Saturn	Uranus	Neptune	Pluto
1			T						
2				T				Q	
3	O	O			T	X			
4						T	X	C	
5					Q				
6			O	O			Q		
7	T				X	C			
8		T					X	C	X
9	Q								
10		Q	T	T					Q
11					C	X			
12	X		Q				C	X	
13		X		Q		Q			T
14									
15			X	X				Q	
16					X	T			
17	C						X	T	O
18									
19		C			Q		Q		
20			C						
21					C	T	O		
22								T	O
23	X								T
24									
25	Q	X	X						Q
26					X	O	T		
27		Q	Q				O	T	X
28	T			Q		Q			
29			T					Q	
30		T		T	T	X			
31							T	X	C

Date	Aries	Taurus	Gemini	Cancer	Leo	Virgo	Libra	Scorpio	Sagittarius	Capricorn	Aquarius	Pisces
1	f		U		f	u	f		F		f	u
2	f		U		f	u	f		F		f	u
3	u	f		U		f	u	f		F		f
4	u	f		U		f	u	f		F		f
5	f	u	f		U		f	u	f		F	
6	f	u	f		U		f	u	f		F	
7		f	u	f		U		f	u	f		F
8		f	u	f		U		f	u	f		F
9	F		f	u	f		U		f	u	f	
10	F		f	u	f		U		f	u	f	
11		F		f	u	f		U		f	u	f
12		F		f	u	f		U		f	u	f
13		F		f	u	f		U		f	u	f
14	f		F		f	u	f		U		f	u
15	f		F		f	u	f		U		f	u
16	u	f		F		f	u	f		U		f
17	u	f		F		f	u	f		U		f
18	f	u	f		F		f	u	f		U	
19	f	u	f		F		f	u	f		U	
20	f	u	f		F		f	u	f		U	
21		f	u	f		F		f	u	f		U
22		f	u	f		F		f	u	f		U
23	U		f	u	f		F		f	u	f	
24	U		f	u	f		F		f	u	f	
25	U		f	u	f		F		f	u	f	
26		U		f	u	f		F		f	u	f
27		U		f	u	f		F		f	u	f
28	f		U		f	u	f		F		f	u
29	f		U		f	u	f		F		f	u
30	u	f		U		f	u	f		F		f
31	u	f		U		f	u	f		F		f

August Moon Table

Date	Sign	Element	Nature	Phase
1 Tue	Aquarius	Air	Barren	Full 2:32 pm
2 Wed 11:05 pm	Pisces	Water	Fruitful	3rd
3 Thu	Pisces	Water	Fruitful	3rd
4 Fri 11:19 pm	Aries	Fire	Barren	3rd
5 Sat	Aries	Fire	Barren	3rd
6 Sun	Aries	Fire	Barren	3rd
7 Mon 2:25 am	Taurus	Earth	Semi-fruitful	3rd
8 Tue	Taurus	Earth	Semi-fruitful	4th 6:28 am
9 Wed 9:05 am	Gemini	Air	Barren	4th
10 Thu	Gemini	Air	Barren	4th
11 Fri 6:52 pm	Cancer	Water	Fruitful	4th
12 Sat	Cancer	Water	Fruitful	4th
13 Sun	Cancer	Water	Fruitful	4th
14 Mon 6:36 am	Leo	Fire	Barren	4th
15 Tue	Leo	Fire	Barren	4th
16 Wed 7:14 pm	Virgo	Earth	Barren	New 5:38 am
17 Thu	Virgo	Earth	Barren	1st
18 Fri	Virgo	Earth	Barren	1st
19 Sat 7:53 am	Libra	Air	Semi-fruitful	1st
20 Sun	Libra	Air	Semi-fruitful	1st
21 Mon 7:22 pm	Scorpio	Water	Fruitful	1st
22 Tue	Scorpio	Water	Fruitful	1st
23 Wed	Scorpio	Water	Fruitful	1st
24 Thu 4:07 am	Sagittarius	Fire	Barren	2nd 5:57 am
25 Fri	Sagittarius	Fire	Barren	2nd
26 Sat 9:05 am	Capricorn	Earth	Semi-fruitful	2nd
27 Sun	Capricorn	Earth	Semi-fruitful	2nd
28 Mon 10:32 am	Aquarius	Air	Barren	2nd
29 Tue	Aquarius	Air	Barren	2nd
30 Wed 9:56 am	Pisces	Water	Fruitful	Full 9:36 pm
31 Thu	Pisces	Water	Fruitful	3rd

August Aspectarian/Favorable & Unfavorable Days

Date	Sun	Mercury	Venus	Mars	Jupiter	Saturn	Uranus	Neptune	Pluto
1	O				Q				
2			O				Q		
3		O		O	X	C			
4						X	C	X	
5	T								
6			T						
7							X		Q
8	Q	T	Q	T	C		C		
9							Q	X	T
10	X	Q		Q					
11			X					Q	
12						T			
13		X		X	X		X		
14								T	O
15			C		Q				
16	C						Q		
17							O		
18		C		C	T		T		
19								O	T
20			X						
21	X								Q
22						T			
23		X	Q		O		O	T	
24	Q			X		Q			X
25		Q	T						
26	T			Q		X		Q	
27		T			T		T		
28				T				X	C
29			O		Q		Q		
30	O					C			
31		O			X		X		

Date	Aries	Taurus	Gemini	Cancer	Leo	Virgo	Libra	Scorpio	Sagittarius	Capricorn	Aquarius	Pisces
1	f	u	f		U		f	u	f		F	
2	f	u	f		U		f	u	f		F	
3		f	u	f		U		f	u	f		F
4		f	u	f		U		f	u	f		F
5	F		f	u	f		U		f	u	f	
6	F		f	u	f		U		f	u	f	
7		F		f	u	f		U		f	u	f
8		F		f	u	f		U		f	u	f
9		F		f	u	f		U		f	u	f
10	f		F		f	u	f		U		f	u
11	f		F		f	u	f		U		f	u
12	u	f		F		f	u	f		U		f
13	u	f		F		f	u	f		U		f
14	u	f		F		f	u	f		U		f
15	f	u	f		F		f	u	f		U	
16	f	u	f		F		f	u	f		U	
17		f	u	f		F		f	u	f		U
18		f	u	f		F		f	u	f		U
19		f	u	f		F		f	u	f		U
20	U		f	u	f		F		f	u	f	
21	U		f	u	f		F		f	u	f	
22		U		f	u	f		F		f	u	f
23		U		f	u	f		F		f	u	f
24		U		f	u	f		F		f	u	f
25	f		U		f	u	f		F		f	u
26	f		U		f	u	f		F		f	u
27	u	f		U		f	u	f		F		f
28	u	f		U		f	u	f		F		f
29	f	u	f		U		f	u	f		F	
30	f	u	f		U		f	u	f		F	
31		f	u	f		U		f	u	f		F

September Moon Table

Date	Sign	Element	Nature	Phase
1 Fri 9:25 am	Aries	Fire	Barren	3rd
2 Sat	Aries	Fire	Barren	3rd
3 Sun 11:00 am	Taurus	Earth	Semi-fruitful	3rd
4 Mon	Taurus	Earth	Semi-fruitful	3rd
5 Tue 4:07 pm	Gemini	Air	Barren	3rd
6 Wed	Gemini	Air	Barren	4th 6:21 pm
7 Thu	Gemini	Air	Barren	4th
8 Fri 1:00 am	Cancer	Water	Fruitful	4th
9 Sat	Cancer	Water	Fruitful	4th
10 Sun 12:36 pm	Leo	Fire	Barren	4th
11 Mon	Leo	Fire	Barren	4th
12 Tue	Leo	Fire	Barren	4th
13 Wed 1:18 am	Virgo	Earth	Barren	4th
14 Thu	Virgo	Earth	Barren	New 9:40 pm
15 Fri 1:44 pm	Libra	Air	Semi-fruitful	1st
16 Sat	Libra	Air	Semi-fruitful	1st
17 Sun	Libra	Air	Semi-fruitful	1st
18 Mon 12:58 am	Scorpio	Water	Fruitful	1st
19 Tue	Scorpio	Water	Fruitful	1st
20 Wed 10:06 am	Sagittarius	Fire	Barren	1st
21 Thu	Sagittarius	Fire	Barren	1st
22 Fri 4:20 pm	Capricorn	Earth	Semi-fruitful	2nd 3:32 pm
23 Sat	Capricorn	Earth	Semi-fruitful	2nd
24 Sun 7:29 pm	Aquarius	Air	Barren	2nd
25 Mon	Aquarius	Air	Barren	2nd
26 Tue 8:18 pm	Pisces	Water	Fruitful	2nd
27 Wed	Pisces	Water	Fruitful	2nd
28 Thu 8:17 pm	Aries	Fire	Barren	2nd
29 Fri	Aries	Fire	Barren	Full 5:58 am
30 Sat 9:18 pm	Taurus	Earth	Semi-fruitful	3rd

September Aspectarian/Favorable & Unfavorable Days

Date	Sun	Mercury	Venus	Mars	Jupiter	Saturn	Uranus	Neptune	Pluto
1				O				C	X
2			T						
3							X		Q
4	T	T	Q		C				
5						Q	C	X	T
6	Q	Q	X	T					
7							Q		
8		X		Q	T				
9	X				X		X		
10								T	O
11			C	X	Q				
12							Q		
13		C			O				
14	C				T		T		
15								O	T
16			X	C					
17									Q
18		X			T				
19		Q		O		O			
20	X					Q		T	X
21		Q	T	X					
22	Q					X	Q		
23		T		Q	T				
24	T						T	X	C
25						Q			
26			O	T		C	Q		
27					X				
28		O					X	C	X
29	O								
30			T	O		X			Q

Date	Aries	Taurus	Gemini	Cancer	Leo	Virgo	Libra	Scorpio	Sagittarius	Capricorn	Aquarius	Pisces
1		f	u	f	U			f	u	f		F
2	F		f	u	f		U		f	u	f	
3	F		f	u	f		U		f	u	f	
4		F		f	u	f		U		f	u	f
5		F		f	u	f		U		f	u	f
6	f		F		f	u	f		U		f	u
7	f		F		f	u	f		U		f	u
8	u	f		F		f	u	f		U		f
9	u	f		F		f	u	f		U		f
10	u	f		F		f	u	f		U		f
11	f	u	f		F		f	u	f		U	
12	f	u	f		F		f	u	f		U	
13		f	u	f		F		f	u	f		U
14		f	u	f		F		f	u	f		U
15		f	u	f		F		f	u	f		U
16	U		f	u	f		F		f	u	f	
17	U		f	u	f		F		f	u	f	
18		U		f	u	f		F		f	u	f
19		U		f	u	f		F		f	u	f
20		U		f	u	f		F		f	u	f
21	f		U		f	u	f		F		f	u
22	f		U		f	u	f		F		f	u
23	u	f		U		f	u	f		F		f
24	u	f		U		f	u	f		F		f
25	f	u	f		U		f	u	f		F	
26	f	u	f		U		f	u	f		F	
27		f	u	f		U		f	u	f		F
28		f	u	f		U		f	u	f		F
29	F		f	u	f		U		f	u	f	
30	F		f	u	f		U		f	u	f	

October Moon Table

Date	Sign	Element	Nature	Phase
1 Sun	Taurus	Earth	Semi-fruitful	3rd
2 Mon	Taurus	Earth	Semi-fruitful	3rd
3 Tue 1:03 am	Gemini	Air	Barren	3rd
4 Wed	Gemini	Air	Barren	3rd
5 Thu 8:32 am	Cancer	Water	Fruitful	3rd
6 Fri	Cancer	Water	Fruitful	4th 9:48 am
7 Sat 7:24 pm	Leo	Fire	Barren	4th
8 Sun	Leo	Fire	Barren	4th
9 Mon	Leo	Fire	Barren	4th
10 Tue 8:02 am	Virgo	Earth	Barren	4th
11 Wed	Virgo	Earth	Barren	4th
12 Thu 8:22 pm	Libra	Air	Semi-fruitful	4th
13 Fri	Libra	Air	Semi-fruitful	4th
14 Sat	Libra	Air	Semi-fruitful	New 1:55 pm
15 Sun 7:04 am	Scorpio	Water	Fruitful	1st
16 Mon	Scorpio	Water	Fruitful	1st
17 Tue 3:36 pm	Sagittarius	Fire	Barren	1st
18 Wed	Sagittarius	Fire	Barren	1st
19 Thu 9:55 pm	Capricorn	Earth	Semi-fruitful	1st
20 Fri	Capricorn	Earth	Semi-fruitful	1st
21 Sat	Capricorn	Earth	Semi-fruitful	2nd 11:29 pm
22 Sun 2:06 am	Aquarius	Air	Barren	2nd
23 Mon	Aquarius	Air	Barren	2nd
24 Tue 4:33 am	Pisces	Water	Fruitful	2nd
25 Wed	Pisces	Water	Fruitful	2nd
26 Thu 6:02 am	Aries	Fire	Barren	2nd
27 Fri	Aries	Fire	Barren	2nd
28 Sat 7:44 am	Taurus	Earth	Semi-fruitful	Full 4:24 pm
29 Sun	Taurus	Earth	Semi-fruitful	3rd
30 Mon 11:08 am	Gemini	Air	Barren	3rd
31 Tue	Gemini	Air	Barren	3rd

October Aspectarian/Favorable & Unfavorable Days

Date	Sun	Mercury	Venus	Mars	Jupiter	Saturn	Uranus	Neptune	Pluto
1					C				
2		T	Q				C	X	T
3	T					Q			
4				T					
5		Q	X			T		Q	
6	Q				X				
7			Q				X	T	O
8		X				Q			
9	X					Q			
10			C	X		O			
11						T			
12							T	O	T
13									
14	C	C							
15			X	C		T			Q
16					O				
17						Q	O	T	X
18		Q							
19	X	X					X		Q
20			T	X	T				
21	Q						T	X	C
22		Q		Q	Q				
23						Q			
24	T	T			T	X	C		
25			O				X	C	
26									X
27									
28	O						X		Q
29		O	T	O	C		C		
30						Q		X	T
31									

Date	Aries	Taurus	Gemini	Cancer	Leo	Virgo	Libra	Scorpio	Sagittarius	Capricorn	Aquarius	Pisces
1	F		f	u	f			U		f	u	f
2	F		f	u	f			U		f	u	f
3	f	F		f	u	f			U		f	u
4	f	F		f	u	f			U		f	u
5	f	F		f	u	f			U		f	u
6	u	f	F		f	u	f			U		f
7	u	f	F		f	u	f			U		f
8	f	u	f	F		f	u	f			U	
9	f	u	f	F		f	u	f			U	
10	f	u	f	F		f	u	f			U	
11		f	u	f	F		f	u	f			U
12		f	u	f	F		f	u	f			U
13	U		f	u	f	F		f	u	f		
14	U		f	u	f	F		f	u	f		
15	U		f	u	f	F		f	u	f		
16		U		f	u	f	F		f	u	f	
17		U		f	u	f	F		f	u	f	
18			U		f	u	f	F		f	u	f
19			U		f	u	f	F		f	u	f
20	f			U		f	u	f	F		f	u
21	f			U		f	u	f	F		f	u
22	u	f			U		f	u	f	F		f
23	u	f			U		f	u	f	F		f
24	f	u	f			U		f	u	f	F	
25	f	u	f			U		f	u	f	F	
26		f	u	f			U		f	u	f	F
27	F		f	u	f			U		f	u	f
28	F		f	u	f			U		f	u	f
29	f	F		f	u	f			U		f	u
30	f	F		f	u	f			U		f	u
31	u	f	F		f	u	f			U		f

November Moon Table

Date	Sign	Element	Nature	Phase
1 Wed 5:30 pm	Cancer	Water	Fruitful	3rd
2 Thu	Cancer	Water	Fruitful	3rd
3 Fri	Cancer	Water	Fruitful	3rd
4 Sat 3:21 am	Leo	Fire	Barren	3rd
5 Sun	Leo	Fire	Barren	4th 3:37 am
6 Mon 2:39 pm	Virgo	Earth	Barren	4th
7 Tue	Virgo	Earth	Barren	4th
8 Wed	Virgo	Earth	Barren	4th
9 Thu 3:08 am	Libra	Air	Semi-fruitful	4th
10 Fri	Libra	Air	Semi-fruitful	4th
11 Sat 1:39 pm	Scorpio	Water	Fruitful	4th
12 Sun	Scorpio	Water	Fruitful	4th
13 Mon 9:23 pm	Sagittarius	Fire	Barren	New 4:27 am
14 Tue	Sagittarius	Fire	Barren	1st
15 Wed	Sagittarius	Fire	Barren	1st
16 Thu 2:41 am	Capricorn	Earth	Semi-fruitful	1st
17 Fri	Capricorn	Earth	Semi-fruitful	1st
18 Sat 6:28 am	Aquarius	Air	Barren	1st
19 Sun	Aquarius	Air	Barren	1st
20 Mon 9:29 am	Pisces	Water	Fruitful	2nd 5:50 am
21 Tue	Pisces	Water	Fruitful	2nd
22 Wed 12:19 pm	Aries	Fire	Barren	2nd
23 Thu	Aries	Fire	Barren	2nd
24 Fri 3:29 pm	Taurus	Earth	Semi-fruitful	2nd
25 Sat	Taurus	Earth	Semi-fruitful	2nd
26 Sun 7:40 pm	Gemini	Air	Barren	2nd
27 Mon	Gemini	Air	Barren	Full 4:16 am
28 Tue	Gemini	Air	Barren	3rd
29 Wed 1:54 am	Cancer	Water	Fruitful	3rd
30 Thu	Cancer	Water	Fruitful	3rd

November Aspectarian/Favorable & Unfavorable Days

Date	Sun	Mercury	Venus	Mars	Jupiter	Saturn	Uranus	Neptune	Pluto
1			Q		T			Q	
2	T			T	X				
3		T	X				X	T	O
4				Q					
5	Q			Q		Q			
6		Q					O		
7	X				T				
8		X		X			T	O	T
9			C						
10									
11						T			Q
12				O					
13	C			C		Q	O	T	X
14		C	X						
15								Q	
16			Q		T	X			
17	X			X			T	X	
18				Q					C
19		X	T					Q	
20	Q			Q	X	C			
21		Q					X		
22	T			T				C	X
23		T	O						
24						X			Q
25					C				
26			O			Q	C	X	T
27	O								
28		O	T					Q	
29					X	T			
30								X	

Date	Aries	Taurus	Gemini	Cancer	Leo	Virgo	Libra	Scorpio	Sagittarius	Capricorn	Aquarius	Pisces
1	f		F		f	u	f		U		f	u
2	u	f		F		f	u	f		U		f
3	u	f		F		f	u	f		U		f
4	u	f		F		f	u	f		U		f
5	f	u	f		F		f	u	f		U	
6	f	u	f		F		f	u	f		U	
7		f	u	f		F		f	u	f		U
8		f	u	f		F		f	u	f		U
9		f	u	f		F		f	u	f		U
10	U		f	u	f		F		f	u	f	
11	U		f	u	f		F		f	u	f	
12		U		f	u	f		F		f	u	f
13		U		f	u	f		F		f	u	f
14	f		U		f	u	f		F		f	u
15	f		U		f	u	f		F		f	u
16	u	f		U		f	u	f		F		f
17	u	f		U		f	u	f		F		f
18	u	f		U		f	u	f		F		f
19	f	u	f		U		f	u	f		F	
20	f	u	f		U		f	u	f		F	
21		f	u	f		U		f	u	f		F
22		f	u	f		U		f	u	f		F
23	F		f	u	f		U		f	u	f	
24	F		f	u	f		U		f	u	f	
25		F	U		f	u	f		F		f	u
26		F		f	u	f		U		f	u	f
27	f		F		f	u	f		U		f	u
28	f		F		f	u	f		U		f	u
29	u	f		F		f	u	f		U		f
30	u	f		F		f	u	f		U		f

December Moon Table

Date	Sign	Element	Nature	Phase
1 Fri 11:00 am	Leo	Fire	Barren	3rd
2 Sat	Leo	Fire	Barren	3rd
3 Sun 10:50 pm	Virgo	Earth	Barren	3rd
4 Mon	Virgo	Earth	Barren	3rd
5 Tue	Virgo	Earth	Barren	4th 12:49 am
6 Wed 11:35 am	Libra	Air	Semi-fruitful	4th
7 Thu	Libra	Air	Semi-fruitful	4th
8 Fri 10:35 pm	Scorpio	Water	Fruitful	4th
9 Sat	Scorpio	Water	Fruitful	4th
10 Sun	Scorpio	Water	Fruitful	4th
11 Mon 6:11 am	Sagittarius	Fire	Barren	4th
12 Tue	Sagittarius	Fire	Barren	New 6:32 pm
13 Wed 10:31 am	Capricorn	Earth	Semi-fruitful	1st
14 Thu	Capricorn	Earth	Semi-fruitful	1st
15 Fri 12:56 pm	Aquarius	Air	Barren	1st
16 Sat	Aquarius	Air	Barren	1st
17 Sun 2:58 pm	Pisces	Water	Fruitful	1st
18 Mon	Pisces	Water	Fruitful	1st
19 Tue 5:47 pm	Aries	Fire	Barren	2nd 1:39 pm
20 Wed	Aries	Fire	Barren	2nd
21 Thu 9:50 pm	Taurus	Earth	Semi-fruitful	2nd
22 Fri	Taurus	Earth	Semi-fruitful	2nd
23 Sat	Taurus	Earth	Semi-fruitful	2nd
24 Sun 3:15 am	Gemini	Air	Barren	2nd
25 Mon	Gemini	Air	Barren	2nd
26 Tue 10:15 am	Cancer	Water	Fruitful	Full 7:33 pm
27 Wed	Cancer	Water	Fruitful	3rd
28 Thu 7:23 pm	Leo	Fire	Barren	3rd
29 Fri	Leo	Fire	Barren	3rd
30 Sat	Leo	Fire	Barren	3rd
31 Sat 12:08 pm	Taurus	Earth	Semi-fruitful	2nd

December Aspectarian/Favorable & Unfavorable Days

Date	Sun	Mercury	Venus	Mars	Jupiter	Saturn	Uranus	Neptune	Pluto
1			Q	T				T	O
2	T				Q				
3			X				Q		
4		T		Q	T	O			
5	Q							T	
6		Q						O	T
7	X			X					
8									Q
9		X	C		O	T			
10						O	T		
11					Q				X
12	C			C					
13					T	X		Q	
14		C	X				T		
15					Q		X	C	
16			Q	X			Q		
17	X					C			
18		X	T	Q	X				
19	Q						X	C	X
20		Q							
21	T			T					Q
22		T			C	X			
23			O			C	X		
24					Q				T
25					O				
26	O	O			X	T		Q	
27							X		
28			T					T	O
29				Q					
30		T					Q		
31			Q	T	T	O			

Date	Aries	Taurus	Gemini	Cancer	Leo	Virgo	Libra	Scorpio	Sagittarius	Capricorn	Aquarius	Pisces
1	u	f		F		f	u	f		U		f
2	f	u	f		F		f	u	f		U	
3	f	u	f		F		f	u	f		U	
4		f	u	f		F		f	u	f		U
5		f	u	f		F		f	u	f		U
6		f	u	f		F		f	u	f		U
7	U		f	u	f		F		f	u	f	
8	U		f	u	f		F		f	u	f	
9		U		f	u	f		F		f	u	f
10		U		f	u	f		F		f	u	f
11		U		f	u	f		F		f	u	f
12	f		U		f	u	f		F		f	u
13	f		U		f	u	f		F		f	u
14	u	f		U		f	u	f		F		f
15	u	f		U		f	u	f		F		f
16	f	u	f		U		f	u	f		F	
17	f	u	f		U		f	u	f		F	
18		f	u	f		U		f	u	f		F
19		f	u	f		U		f	u	f		F
20	F		f	u	f		U		f	u	f	
21	F		f	u	f		U		f	u	f	
22		F		f	u	f		U		f	u	f
23		F		f	u	f		U		f	u	f
24		F		f	u	f		U		f	u	f
25	f		F		f	u	f		U		f	u
26	f		F		f	u	f		U		f	u
27	u	f	F			f	u	f		U		f
28	u	f	F			f	u	f		U		f
29	f	u	f		F		f	u	f		U	
30	f	u	f		F		f	u	f		U	
31	f	u	f		F		f	u	f		U	

2023 Retrograde Planets

Planet	Begin	Eastern	Pacific	End	Eastern	Pacific
Uranus	8/24/22	9:54 am	**6:54 am**	1/22	5:59 pm	**2:59 pm**
Mars	10/30/22	9:26 am	**6:26 am**	1/12	3:56 pm	**12:56 pm**
Mercury	12/29/22	4:32 am	**1:32 am**	1/18	8:12 am	**5:12 am**
Mercury	4/21	4:35 am	**1:35 am**	5/14	11:17 pm	**8:17 pm**
Pluto	5/1	1:09 pm	**10:09 am**	10/10	9:10 pm	**6:10 pm**
Saturn	6/17	1:27 pm	**10:27 am**	11/4	3:03 am	**12:03 am**
Neptune	6/30	5:07 pm	**2:07 pm**	12/6	8:20 am	**5:20 am**
Venus	7/22	9:33 pm	**6:33 pm**	9/3	9:20 pm	**6:20 pm**
Mercury	8/23	3:59 pm	**12:59 pm**	9/15	4:21 pm	**1:21 pm**
Uranus	8/28	10:39 pm	**7:39 pm**	1/26/24		**11:35 pm**
Uranus	8/28	10:39 pm	**7:39 pm**	1/27/24	2:35 am	
Jupiter	9/4	10:10 am	**7:10 am**	12/30	9:40 pm	**6:40 pm**
Mercury	12/12		**11:09 pm**	1/1/24	10:08 pm	**7:08 pm**
Mercury	12/13	2:09 am		1/1/24	10:08 pm	**7:08 pm**

Eastern Time in plain type, **Pacific Time in bold type**

	Dec 22	Jan 23	Feb	Mar	Apr	May	Jun	Jul	Aug	Sep	Oct	Nov	Dec	Jan 24
☿		▓			▓					▓				▓
♃										▓	▓	▓	▓	
♀								▓	▓					
♄							▓	▓	▓	▓				
♇					▓	▓	▓	▓	▓					
♆							▓	▓	▓	▓	▓			
♅	▓	▓							▓	▓	▓	▓	▓	
♂	▓	▓												

Egg-Setting Dates

To Have Eggs by this Date	Sign	Qtr.	Date to Set Eggs
Jan 23, 12:36 pm–Jan 25, 1:48 pm	Pisces	1st	Jan 02, 2023
Jan 27, 6:42 pm–Jan 30, 3:35 am	Taurus	1st	Jan 06
Feb 1, 3:11 pm–Feb 4, 3:48 am	Cancer	2nd	Jan 11
Feb 20, 2:06 am–Feb 22, 12:14 am	Pisces	1st	Jan 30
Feb 24, 3:29 am–Feb 26, 10:48 am	Taurus	1st	Feb 03
Feb 28, 9:40 pm–Mar 3, 10:16 am	Cancer	2nd	Feb 07
Mar 23, 2:42 pm–Mar 25, 8:42 pm	Taurus	1st	Mar 02
Mar 28, 6:22 am–Mar 30, 6:31 pm	Cancer	1st	Mar 07
Apr 4, 5:51 pm–Apr 6, 12:34 am	Libra	2nd	Mar 14
Apr 20, 12:30 am–Apr 22, 6:11 am	Taurus	1st	Mar 30
Apr 24, 2:58 pm–Apr 27, 2:30 am	Cancer	1st	Apr 03
May 2, 2:09 am–May 4, 10:32 am	Libra	2nd	Apr 11
May 19, 11:53 am–May 19, 2:48 pm	Taurus	1st	Apr 28
May 21, 11:28 pm–May 24, 10:35 am	Cancer	1st	Apr 30
May 29, 10:51 am–May 31, 7:45 pm	Libra	2nd	May 08
Jun 18, 6:58 am–Jun 20, 6:04 pm	Cancer	1st	May 28
Jun 25, 6:57 pm–Jun 28, 4:55 am	Libra	1st	Jun 04
Jul 17, 2:32 pm–Jul 18, 12:39 am	Cancer	1st	Jun 26
Jul 23, 1:54 am–Jul 25, 12:55 pm	Libra	1st	Jul 02
Aug 19, 7:53 am–Aug 21, 7:22 pm	Libra	1st	Jul 29
Aug 30, 9:56 am–Aug 30, 9:36 pm	Pisces	2nd	Aug 09
Sep 15, 1:44 pm–Sep 18, 12:58 am	Libra	1st	Aug 25
Sep 26, 8:18 pm–Sep 28, 8:17 pm	Pisces	2nd	Sep 05
Oct 14, 1:55 pm–Oct 15, 7:04 am	Libra	1st	Sep 23
Oct 24, 4:33 am–Oct 26, 6:02 am	Pisces	2nd	Oct 03
Oct 28, 7:44 am–Oct 28, 4:24 pm	Taurus	2nd	Oct 07
Nov 20, 9:29 am–Nov 22, 12:19 pm	Pisces	2nd	Oct 30
Nov 24, 3:29 pm–Nov 26, 7:40 pm	Taurus	2nd	Nov 03
Dec 17, 2:58 pm–Dec 19, 5:47 pm	Pisces	1st	Nov 26
Dec 21, 9:50 pm–Dec 24, 3:15 am	Taurus	2nd	Nov 30
Dec 26, 10:15 am–Dec 26, 7:33 pm	Cancer	2nd	Dec 05

Dates to Hunt and Fish

Date	Quarter	Sign
Jan. 5, 9:15 am–Jan. 7, 9:40 pm	2nd	Cancer
Jan. 15, 7:08 am–Jan. 17, 12:33 pm	4th	Scorpio
Jan. 23, 12:36 pm–Jan. 25, 1:48 pm	1st	Pisces
Feb. 1, 3:11 pm–Feb. 4, 3:48 am	2nd	Cancer
Feb. 11, 1:34 pm–Feb. 13, 8:31 pm	3rd	Scorpio
Feb. 19, 11:56 pm–Feb. 22, 12:14 am	4th	Pisces
Feb. 28, 9:40 pm–Mar. 3, 10:16 am	2nd	Cancer
Mar. 10, 7:06 pm–Mar. 13, 3:21 am	3rd	Scorpio
Mar. 13, 3:21 am–Mar. 15, 8:06 am	3rd	Sagittarius
Mar. 19, 11:12 am–Mar. 21, 12:01 pm	4th	Pisces
Mar. 28, 6:22 am–Mar. 30, 6:31 pm	1st	Cancer
Apr. 7, 2:29 am–Apr. 9, 8:57 am	3rd	Scorpio
Apr. 9, 8:57 am–Apr. 11, 1:33 pm	3rd	Sagittarius
Apr. 15, 6:57 pm–Apr. 17, 9:09 pm	4th	Pisces
Apr. 24, 2:58 pm–Apr. 27, 2:30 am	1st	Cancer
May 4, 10:32 am–May 6, 4:04 pm	2nd	Scorpio
May 6, 4:04 pm–May 8, 7:33 pm	3rd	Sagittarius
May 13, 12:39 am–May 15, 3:56 am	4th	Pisces
May 21, 11:28 pm–May 24, 10:35 am	1st	Cancer
May 31, 7:45 pm–Jun. 3, 1:03 am	2nd	Scorpio
Jun. 3, 1:03 am–Jun. 5, 3:31 am	2nd	Sagittarius
Jun. 9, 6:14 am–Jun. 11, 9:20 am	3rd	Pisces
Jun. 18, 6:58 am–Jun. 20, 6:04 pm	1st	Cancer
Jun. 28, 4:55 am–Jun. 30, 10:59 am	2nd	Scorpio
Jun. 30, 10:59 am–Jul. 2, 1:20 pm	2nd	Sagittarius
Jul. 6, 1:33 pm–Jul. 8, 3:19 pm	3rd	Pisces
Jul. 8, 3:19 pm–Jul. 10, 7:55 pm	3rd	Aries
Jul. 15, 1:13 pm–Jul. 18, 12:39 am	4th	Cancer
Jul. 25, 12:55 pm–Jul. 27, 8:24 pm	1st	Scorpio
Jul. 27, 8:24 pm–Jul. 29, 11:44 pm	2nd	Sagittarius
Aug. 2, 11:05 pm–Aug. 4, 11:19 pm	3rd	Pisces
Aug. 4, 11:19 pm–Aug. 7, 2:25 am	3rd	Aries
Aug. 11, 6:52 pm–Aug. 14, 6:36 am	4th	Cancer
Aug. 21, 7:22 pm–Aug. 24, 4:07 am	1st	Scorpio
Aug. 30, 9:56 am–Sep. 1, 9:25 am	2nd	Pisces
Sep. 1, 9:25 am–Sep. 3, 11:00 am	3rd	Aries
Sep. 8, 1:00 am–Sep. 10, 12:36 pm	4th	Cancer
Sep. 18, 12:58 am–Sep. 20, 10:06 am	1st	Scorpio
Sep. 26, 8:18 pm–Sep. 28, 8:17 pm	2nd	Pisces
Sep. 28, 8:17 pm–Sep. 30, 9:18 pm	2nd	Aries
Oct. 5, 8:32 am–Oct. 7, 7:24 pm	3rd	Cancer
Oct. 15, 7:04 am–Oct. 17, 3:36 pm	1st	Scorpio
Oct. 24, 4:33 am–Oct. 26, 6:02 am	2nd	Pisces
Oct. 26, 6:02 am–Oct. 28, 7:44 am	2nd	Aries
Nov. 1, 5:30 pm–Nov. 4, 3:21 am	3rd	Cancer
Nov. 11, 1:39 pm–Nov. 13, 9:23 pm	4th	Scorpio
Nov. 20, 9:29 am–Nov. 22, 12:19 pm	2nd	Pisces
Nov. 22, 12:19 pm–Nov. 24, 3:29 pm	2nd	Aries
Nov. 29, 1:54 am–Dec. 1, 11:00 am	3rd	Cancer
Dec. 8, 10:35 pm–Dec. 11, 6:11 am	4th	Scorpio
Dec. 17, 2:58 pm–Dec. 19, 5:47 pm	1st	Pisces
Dec. 19, 5:47 pm–Dec. 21, 9:50 pm	2nd	Aries
Dec. 26, 10:15 am–Dec. 28, 7:23 pm	2nd	Cancer

Dates to Destroy Weeds and Pests

Date	Sign	Qtr.
Jan 7, 9:40 pm–Jan 10, 10:15 am	Leo	3rd
Jan 10, 10:15 am–Jan 12, 9:56 pm	Virgo	3rd
Jan 17, 12:33 pm–Jan 19, 2:11 pm	Sagittarius	4th
Jan 21, 1:29 pm–Jan 21, 3:53 pm	Aquarius	4th
Feb 5, 1:29 pm–Feb 6, 4:14 pm	Leo	3rd
Feb 6, 4:14 pm–Feb 9, 3:47 am	Virgo	3rd
Feb 13, 8:31 pm–Feb 16, 12:00 am	Sagittarius	4th
Feb 18, 12:35 am–Feb 19, 11:56 pm	Aquarius	4th
Mar 7, 7:40 am–Mar 8, 9:44 am	Virgo	3rd
Mar 13, 3:21 am–Mar 14, 10:08 pm	Sagittarius	3rd
Mar 14, 10:08 pm–Mar 15, 8:06 am	Sagittarius	4th
Mar 17, 10:25 am–Mar 19, 11:12 am	Aquarius	4th
Mar 21, 12:01 pm–Mar 21, 1:23 pm	Aries	4th
Apr 9, 8:57 am–Apr 11, 1:33 pm	Sagittarius	3rd
Apr 13, 4:42 pm–Apr 15, 6:57 pm	Aquarius	4th
Apr 17, 9:09 pm–Apr 20, 12:13 am	Aries	4th
May 6, 4:04 pm–May 8, 7:33 pm	Sagittarius	3rd
May 10, 10:05 pm–May 12, 10:28 am	Aquarius	3rd
May 12, 10:28 am–May 13, 12:39 am	Aquarius	4th
May 15, 3:56 am–May 17, 8:28 am	Aries	4th
Jun 3, 11:42 pm–Jun 5, 3:31 am	Sagittarius	3rd
Jun 7, 4:42 am–Jun 9, 6:14 am	Aquarius	3rd
Jun 11, 9:20 am–Jun 13, 2:31 pm	Aries	4th
Jun 15, 9:46 pm–Jun 18, 12:37 am	Gemini	4th
Jul 4, 1:30 pm–Jul 6, 1:33 pm	Aquarius	3rd
Jul 8, 3:19 pm–Jul 9, 9:48 pm	Aries	3rd
Jul 9, 9:48 pm–Jul 10, 7:55 pm	Aries	4th
Jul 13, 3:26 am–Jul 15, 1:13 pm	Gemini	4th
Aug 1, 2:32 pm–Aug 2, 11:05 pm	Aquarius	3rd
Aug 4, 11:19 pm–Aug 7, 2:25 am	Aries	3rd
Aug 9, 9:05 am–Aug 11, 6:52 pm	Gemini	4th
Aug 14, 6:36 am–Aug 16, 5:38 am	Leo	4th
Sep 1, 9:25 am–Sep 3, 11:00 am	Aries	3rd
Sep 5, 4:07 pm–Sep 6, 6:21 pm	Gemini	3rd
Sep 6, 6:21 pm–Sep 8, 1:00 am	Gemini	4th
Sep 10, 12:36 pm–Sep 13, 1:18 pm	Leo	4th
Sep 13, 1:18 am–Sep 14, 9:40 pm	Virgo	4th
Sep 29, 5:58 am–Sep 30, 9:18 pm	Aries	3rd
Oct 3, 1:03 am–Oct 5, 8:32 am	Gemini	3rd
Oct 7, 7:24 pm–Oct 10, 8:02 am	Leo	4th
Oct 10, 8:02 am–Oct 12, 8:22 pm	Virgo	4th
Oct 30, 11:08 am–Nov 1, 5:30 pm	Gemini	3rd
Nov 4, 3:21 am–Nov 5, 3:37 am	Leo	3rd
Nov 5, 3:37 am–Nov 6, 2:39 pm	Leo	4th
Nov 6, 2:39 pm–Nov 9, 3:08 am	Virgo	4th
Nov 27, 4:16 am–Nov 29, 1:54 am	Gemini	3rd
Dec 1, 11:00 am–Dec 3, 10:50 pm	Leo	3rd
Dec 3, 10:50 pm–Dec 5, 12:49 am	Virgo	3rd
Dec 5, 12:49 am–Dec 6, 11:35 am	Virgo	4th
Dec 11, 6:11 am–Dec 12, 6:32 pm	Sagittarius	4th
Dec 28, 7:23 pm–Dec 31, 6:53 am	Leo	3rd

Time Zone Map

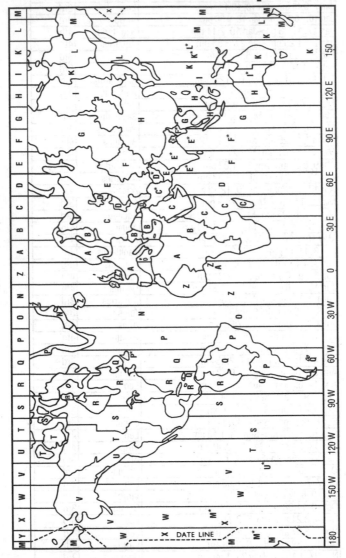

Time Zone Conversions

(R) EST—Used in book
(S) CST—Subtract 1 hour
(T) MST—Subtract 2 hours
(U) PST—Subtract 3 hours
(V) Subtract 4 hours
(V*) Subtract 4½ hours
(U*) Subtract 3½ hours
(W) Subtract 5 hours
(X) Subtract 6 hours
(Y) Subtract 7 hours
(Q) Add 1 hour
(P) Add 2 hours
(P*) Add 2½ hours
(O) Add 3 hours
(N) Add 4 hours
(Z) Add 5 hours
(A) Add 6 hours
(B) Add 7 hours
(C) Add 8 hours
(C*) Add 8½ hours

(D) Add 9 hours
(D*) Add 9½ hours
(E) Add 10 hours
(E*) Add 10½ hours
(F) Add 11 hours
(F*) Add 11½ hours
(G) Add 12 hours
(H) Add 13 hours
(I) Add 14 hours
(I*) Add 14½ hours
(K) Add 15 hours
(K*) Add 15½ hours
(L) Add 16 hours
(L*) Add 16½ hours
(M) Add 17 hours
(M*) Add 18 hours
(P*) Add 2½ hours

Important!

All times given in the *Moon Sign Book* are set in Eastern Time. The conversions shown here are for standard times only. Use the time zone conversions map and table to calculate the difference in your time zone. You must make the adjustment for your time zone and adjust for Daylight Saving Time where applicable.

Weather, Economic & Lunar Forecasts

An Introduction to Long-Range Weather Forecasting

Vincent Decker

Long-range weather forecasting based on planetary cycles, also known as astrometeorology, has been a field of study for centuries. The basic premise underlying the field is that the main heavenly bodies of our solar system exercise an influence over weather conditions on Earth.

Planets

The heat of summer and the chill of winter can be traced back to the Sun's apparent movement north and south of our terrestrial equator. The Moon, while mostly known for its effect on the oceans' tides, in astrometeorology also affects air tides in its circuit around the earth and serves as a triggering influence on solar and planetary configurations as they form. Under Mercury's domain, we find high pressure or fair weather as well as gentle breezes to hurricane-force winds. Venus is known for gentle showers, moderate temperatures, and snowfall or freezing rain in winter. Mars, the red planet, brings hot summers, mild winters, dry conditions, and fierce storms. Jupiter's trademark is a temperate and invigorating atmosphere under benign configurations. The traditional malefic Saturn engenders cold, damp conditions, and when aggravated by certain configurations, low-pressure systems. Like Mercury, the power of Uranus brings high-barometer and erratic wind velocities. Neptune is the pluvial planet *par excellence* capable of torrential downpours, flooding conditions, and warming trends. Pluto is held by some to be a warm influence while for others it is considered cold. In the forecasts included here, Pluto is considered a warm influence.

Aspects and Influences

The foregoing effects of the Sun, Moon, and planets are modified depending on the aspect that each one makes in relation to the other heavenly bodies. The traditional astrological aspects are employed: the conjunction, sextile, square, trine, opposition, and parallel of declination. Fair weather aspects are the sextile and trine. Disturbed weather is induced by the square and opposition. The kind of weather produced by the conjunction and parallel of declination vary depending on if the celestial bodies involved are of similar or contrary natures.

The signs of the zodiac in which the members of the solar system reside at any given moment also affect the manifestation of weather conditions. Heat and dryness are associated with the fire signs Aries, Leo, and Sagittarius. The water signs of Cancer, Scorpio, and Pisces enhance precipitation. Air signs such as Gemini,

Libra, and Aquarius relate to lower temperatures and wind, while the earth signs Taurus, Virgo, and Capricorn are generally wet and cold.

Forecasting

Although the aspects involved in the planetary configurations determine the time that weather processes will be at work (do keep in mind to allow a day or two leeway in all forecasting), it is by the use of key charts that the geographical locations of weather systems are ascertained. When a planet in a key chart is angular, that is to say it is on the cusp of the first, fourth, seventh, or tenth house, the influence associated with that planet will be strongest at that locale. The monthly alignments of the Sun and Moon such as New Moon, Full Moon, and Quarter Moons are examples of key charts. Other important charts include the cardinal solar ingresses and solar and lunar eclipses to name a few. Through setting up these key charts, noting the angular planets, the signs they tenant, and their aspects, as well as the kind of weather typical at the location in question, the long-range weather forecaster makes a judgment as to the type of weather to be expected. By faithfully comparing the forecasts with the actual ensuing weather, the forecaster has an opportunity to improve on method and results.

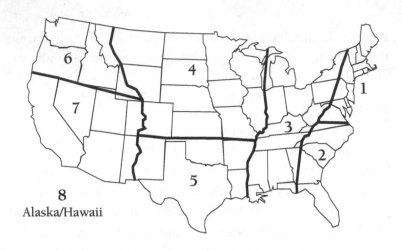

Weather Forecast for 2023

Vincent Decker

Winter

Generally, Zone 1 receives a warm and humid weather influence. Winter temperatures are mild with an increase in downfall. As is to be expected, other influences also contribute to the overall season. Colder and windier in January, then back to a milder influence as we move into February. March tends to stormier weather.

Zones 2 and 3 are affected by a cold, cloudy, and rainy influence. Toward the end of January, a mild and wet influence sweeps through the zones, exiting Zone 2 in early February. As the season progresses, a warmer and drier influence begins to take hold on western portions of Zone 3 in late February and by early March for Zone 2. Northern portions of these zones may not completely yield to the effect of the warmer and drier intruder.

Zones 4 and 5 show a variety of weather, ranging from energetic winter storms that traverse the plains to fair and breezy conditions. Generally, eastern portions of these zones see lower temperatures and more precipitation than central and western areas that are warmer and drier.

Northwestern sections of Zone 6 experience lower ranges of temperatures and some windy conditions. Further inland, temperatures are higher for Zones 6 and 7. As the season progresses, a mild and humid influence pushes eastward through both zones.

Western areas of Alaska experience higher-than-average temperatures for the season and dryness. Central sections also see higher-than-average temperatures but with higher-than-average moisture. The eastern portion of the zone is generally warmer than average with less humidity. Warmer temperatures and increased moisture are indicated for Hawaii.

2nd Quarter Moon December 29–January 6

Zone 1: Cold, windy, chance of precipitation over mid-Atlantic area. Generally colder temperatures, especially the fifth and sixth. New England fair around the second. Increasing chance of showers by the fourth. Western areas windy and stormy. **Zone 2:** Southern zone thunderstorms. Cold, windy, chance of precipitation over mid-Atlantic area. Generally lower temperatures. Windy and stormy weather likely. **Zone 3:** Strong front and thunderstorms sweep through zone. Generally colder weather. Southern portions may be warmer. Fronts bring showers and the potential for windy, stormy weather. **Zone 4:** West—colder with thunderstorms then chance of showers, becoming fair. Possible showers, breezy on the fifth. Central—possible showers, then fair. Cold, fair, breezy on the fourth. East—showers, then cold and fair on the fifth. **Zone 5:** West—colder with thunderstorms then chance of showers, becoming fair. Eastern sections subject to fronts, triggering storms and showers. **Zone 6:** The zone sees a mix of fronts producing showers, which transit eastward then clearing. **Zone 7:** Fronts push onshore bringing precipitation, which transit eastward. Inland, chance of showers and lower temperatures. **Zone**

8: Alaska: West—a cold front produces precipitation. Generally lower temperatures. Chance of showers over western and central portions. Eastern areas see a chance of thunderstorms then fair conditions before shower potential increases. Hawaii: Lower temperatures. Fronts bring shower potential.

Full Moon January 6–14

Zone 1: Period begins with a cold front and storm potential. Warmer, fair by the ninth. Around the twelfth, windy and stormy. Period ends with cold front, shower potential. **Zone 2:** Windy and stormy weather approaches from the west around the twelfth. Afterward fair, temperature increase. **Zone 3:** Winter storm conditions over all sections. The ninth through the eleventh, front with possible showers. By the twelfth, stronger storms northeast. Period ends with storms over southern regions. Northern sections are fair. **Zone 4:** West—winter storm assails the Rockies, then warmer, fair, westerly winds. Period ends with a low-pressure area likely over the Front Range area. Central and east—winter storm conditions in and around the Dakotas. More frontal activity around the ninth and fourteenth brings showers or thunderstorms. **Zone 5:** West—winter storm, then increasing warmth, fair conditions. East—winter storm. Possible showers or thunderstorms the ninth and fourteenth. **Zone 6:** West—Fronts, windy, stormy. Brief respite on the thirteenth. East—warmer, drier on the twelfth. **Zone 7:** West—lower-than-average temperatures. Some wind and rain. Brief warming on the thirteenth. East sees warming on the twelfth. **Zone 8:** Alaska: Windy and stormy throughout the zone, especially over west. Then increasing warmth and fair weather. Fair weather for the zone on the twelfth, ending with shower potential. Hawaii: Generally fair with average to above-average temperatures. Thunderstorms on the eleventh.

4th Quarter Moon January 14–21

Zone 1: West—Mostly higher ranges of temperatures. Low pressure and precipitation by the fifteenth. Cold and windy over New

England around the eighteenth through the twentieth. **Zone 2:** Zone sees some rising temperatures with dry weather. Around the seventeenth, a cold front may trigger strong storms. Period ends with increasing moisture, clouds, possible precipitation. **Zone 3:** The zone is cloudy with lower temperatures and precipitation. Eastern portions are warmer. The period begins with wind and rain or snow. Around the seventeenth, storminess possible over northern and eastern sections. **Zone 4:** West and central are colder, cloudy, wintery precipitation. West has low pressure over Wyoming-Colorado on the sixteenth. Strong winds, wintery precipitation over southwest on the eighteenth. More storminess for western portions on the twenty-first. Central has precipitation. East sees cloudy, lower temperatures, precipitation. **Zone 5:** West and central colder, cloudy, wintery precipitation. Strong wind, wintery precipitation in the western zone on the eighteenth. East is cloudy, lower temperatures, precipitation. **Zone 6:** Lower temperatures throughout the zone. Fronts bring wind and rain. Windy storms from west to east on the eighteenth and twenty-first. **Zone 7:** Lower temperatures throughout the zone. Fronts bring wind and rain. Low pressure off southern California coast brings rain and wind on the sixteenth. Windy storms from west to east the eighteenth and twenty-first. **Zone 8:** Alaska: Central area sees increasing temperatures and humidity. Southcentral portions heavy rain from fourteenth through the nineteenth. East is fine, warm, and dry. Cold, windy, and stormy conditions for the southwest on the eighteenth. Hawaii: Temperatures and humidity increase. Chance of rain on the nineteenth.

New Moon January 21–28
Zone 1: Storm system, wind, precipitation for Northeast and New England. Fair twenty-fourth through the twenty-sixth. New England possible windy and/or showery conditions the twenty-sixth. **Zone 2:** North sees wind, precipitation. Low-pressure, precipitation for southeast coast. Possible showers southward on

the twenty-fourth. Fair weather north on the twenty-sixth. **Zone 3:** Significant storm, wintery precipitation, colder, easterly winds throughout zone. Variable weather ensues. **Zone 4:** Winter storm conditions with severe thunderstorms, windy conditions, wintery precipitation, and colder temperatures. Around the twenty-fourth, western portions fair. **Zone 5:** Winter storm conditions with severe thunderstorms, windy conditions, wintery precipitation, and colder temperatures. Around the twenty-fourth, western portions fair. **Zone 6:** A cold wave affects zone the twenty-second through the twenty-sixth, northwest winds, possible storms from offshore. Storms push eastward. East is mild and breezy around the twenty-fourth. Possible showers around the twenty-seventh. **Zone 7:** A cold wave affects zone the twenty-second through the twenty-sixth, northwest winds, possible storms from offshore. Storms push eastward. East is mild and breezy around the twenty-fourth. Possible showers around the twenty-seventh. **Zone 8: Alaska:** South is cold, stormy especially. West sees increasing temperatures, moisture by the twenty-fifth, then windy. Central and east are milder, fair after the twenty-fourth. Eastern and western areas end with a slight chance of lower temperatures. **Hawaii:** Unseasonably colder air, wind. Possible thunderstorms as the period begins. Around the twenty-fifth, increasing moisture with a chance of showers.

2nd Quarter January 28–February 5

Zone 1: Initially, temperatures are below average then increase along with humidity, giving way to the likelihood of showers, some wind, and storm potential. **Zone 2:** Milder and perhaps breezy. A chance of precipitation. Period ends with windy storm potential north. **Zone 3:** Sharp winds and strong storms west. Afterward, warmer and breezy. Period ends with lower temperatures, increasing wind. Wintery precipitation pushes eastward. Low pressure over southwest zone. **Zone 4:** Western and central areas see clear conditions and higher temperatures. By the thirty-

first, strong winds and storms west. Around the second, central high plains see strong lows, generating wind and thunderstorms. Eastern sections see potential for sharp winds and strong storms. **Zone 5:** West and central areas see higher temperatures and fair conditions. Moving into February, thunderstorms, lower temperatures, windy, wintery precipitation. Eastern sections see sharp winds, strong storms, and low pressure over southeastern zone. **Zone 6:** A warming trend, then a stormy pattern sets in. Temperatures decline. Low-pressure areas bring precipitation and push eastward. **Zone 7:** A warming trend, then a stormy pattern sets in. Temperatures decline. Low-pressure areas bring precipitation and push eastward. Period ends with a strong low-pressure area over southern California. **Zone 8:** Alaska: Fair weather throughout the zone. Temperatures try to warm up. Around the second, storminess. Period ends warmer with storms along the southern coast. Hawaii: Beginning fair and cooler. Showers and/or thunderstorms from mid-period on.

Full Moon February 5–13
Zone 1: The period begins windy and perhaps stormy. Rising temperatures bring a chance of rain as the period progresses. New England ends on a windy and stormy note with declining temperatures. **Zone 2:** Initially windy and stormy. Rising temperatures with a chance of showers. Around the tenth, fair with lower temperatures over southern portions. **Zone 3:** Lower temperatures west with a chance of rain or snow, heavy at times, moving east. Windy and stormy northeast. Around the seventh, increasing temperatures generating storms. Period ends with low pressure over Great Lakes and possible lake effect snow. **Zone 4:** West has increasing warmth and dryness. By the tenth, a cold front and stormy conditions. Central is generally warmer with a chance of showers. Around the tenth, storm conditions develop. East starts warm then has lower ranges of temperatures with a chance of rain or snow, heavy at times. **Zone 5:** West sees increasing warmth and dryness. East begins warm then sees lower ranges of temperatures with a chance of rain or snow, heavy at times. **Zone 6:** Fair with rising temperatures. By the seventh, a strong front enters with rain and wind. Around the ninth, warming, windy and stormy. **Zone 7:** Fair with rising temperatures. By the seventh, a strong front enters with rain and wind. Around the ninth, warming, windy and stormy. **Zone 8:** Alaska: Southwestern and central portions see increasing winds and snow. Then fair periods interspersed with shower activity. Becoming progressively stormier. Western areas end cold with wintery precipitation. Hawaii: Increasing warmth and moisture with a chance of rain. Around the eighth, high pressure, lowering temperatures.

4th Quarter Moon February 13–20
Zone 1: Generally, lower temperatures. New England is windy with low pressure. Winter storm likely over the zone around the sixteenth and nineteenth, then central and southern areas fair.

Zone 2: Generally, lower temperatures. Chance of showers possibly heavy south, then turning fair on the fifteenth. **Zone 3:** Strong winter storm on the fifteenth over the Great Lakes and southward followed by a cold wave. Eastern portions fair toward the end. **Zone 4:** Generally, fair conditions over the zone. Potential winter storm east on the fifteenth, then fair. Central cold front on the seventeenth. **Zone 5:** Generally, fair conditions over the zone. East—strong storms the fifteenth. Central—cold front the seventeenth. **Zone 6:** Chance of showers. Increasing warmth, with cloudbursts central and east. Period ends fair. **Zone 7:** Chance of showers. Increasing warmth, with cloudbursts central and east. Period ends fair. **Zone 8:** Alaska: Generally lower temperatures. Low pressure west. Central and east see possible heavy rain the fifteenth, then becoming fair. Hawaii: Generally, lower temperatures, breezy to windy. Possible heavy rain, especially around the fifteenth, then becoming fair. Possible storms on the nineteenth.

New Moon February 20–27

Zone 1: Lower temperatures, wind, and wintery precipitation over the Northeast and New England. **Zone 2:** Northern areas have precipitation, cooler temperatures. Southern areas are stormy twenty-first and twenty-fifth. **Zone 3:** Great Lakes possible fog and/or precipitation with cooler temperatures following. South central increasing warmth and sharp winds. Wintery weather from the west brings falling temperatures, cloudiness, and wintery precipitation. **Zone 4:** Gusty winds and atmospheric disturbance for central areas. Fair conditions west with some warming the twenty-fifth. **Zone 5:** Gusty winds and atmospheric disturbance for central areas. Fair conditions west with some warming the twenty-fifth. **Zone 6:** Lower temperatures, windy conditions, and precipitation characterize the forecast period. **Zone 7:** Lower temperatures, windy conditions, and precipitation characterize the forecast period. Low pressure or wind event for Four Corners the twenty-second. **Zone 8:** Alaska: Far western Alaska and the Bering Strait see a winter storm pattern the twenty-second through the twenty-fourth. West and central see potential heavy rain the twenty-first. Central and east have increasing moisture, possible fog and/or heavy precipitation, cooler afterward. Mid-period colder, windy. Chance of precipitation, rising temperatures twenty-fourth through the twenty-sixth. Hawaii: Rising temperatures and some wind, then becoming rainy. Potential heavy rain the twenty-first.

2nd Quarter Moon February 27–March 7
Zone 1: Storm system centers over the Northeast. Expect clouds and precipitation. Period ends on a fair note with lower temperatures. **Zone 2:** A chance of precipitation, then falling temperatures and low pressure. The period ends cloudy and windy. **Zone 3:** A chance of precipitation from west to east. Then cold and cloudy with precipitation. A strong winter storm for southern Mississippi Valley second through the fourth. Period ends cloudy and windy. **Zone 4:** West sees potential heavy rain. Period ends cool and fair. Central is warmer, with sharp winds, then strong showers on the first. East sees winter storm for the southern Mississippi Valley the second through the fourth. Period ends cloudy and windy. **Zone 5:** West has potential heavy rain. Central is warmer, sharp winds, then cold front, strong showers on the first. East sees strong winter storm for southern Mississippi Valley the second through the fourth. **Zone 6:** Coastal fronts, wind, thunderstorms push eastward. Chance of rain east. Temperatures decline mid-period, generating precipitation. Period ends fair and cool. **Zone 7:** Northwest coastal fronts, wind, thunderstorms push eastward. Chance of rain east. Temperatures decline mid-period, generating precipitation. Special intensity over the southwest of zone. Period ends fair and cool. **Zone 8:** Alaska: West sees warming with sharp winds, then becoming cold, cloudy, and wet. Strong winter storm over the eastern Aleutian Islands and western Alaska the second through the fourth. Period ends cloudy and windy. Central and

east have warm, moist conditions with precipitation. Possibly heavy precipitation, then cool and fair. Hawaii: Warmth increases. Possibly strong precipitation. Period ends cool and fair.

Full Moon March 7–14

Zone 1: Temperatures rise. The zone is windy with possible precipitation. Storms over New England on the seventh. Potentially strong thunderstorms over eastern Maine on the twelfth. **Zone 2:** Temperatures rise. Chance of precipitation. Northern sections windy. South has dangerous thunderstorms or winds around the seventh. Possible heavy rain the twelfth through the fourteenth. **Zone 3:** Variable temperatures, chance of rain zone wide. Dangerous thunderstorms or winds the seventh. Southwest and east see severe thunderstorms, whipping winds twelfth through the fourteenth. Eastern sections potentially heavy rain and storms. **Zone 4:** Variable temperatures, showers, and possible windy conditions. Low pressure over northern plains. Intense central storms the tenth. Eastern areas warmer, breezy to windy with thunderstorm potential. **Zone 5:** Variable temperatures, showers, and possible windy conditions. West sees increasing warmth and low pressure. Intense western storms the tenth. Eastern areas are warmer, breezy to windy. Severe thunderstorms, whipping winds Ark-La-Tex region twelfth through the fourteenth. **Zone 6:** Seasonal temperatures, low pressure producing precipitation especially around the twelfth. Windy storm system in Pacific Northwest the tenth through the thirteenth. **Zone 7:** Seasonal temperatures and a chance of precipitation the twelfth. **Zone 8:** Alaska: West sees fluctuating temperatures, precipitation, strong around the twelfth. Bering Strait sees gale-force winds. Central sees rising temperatures, showers, strong around the twelfth. East sees rising temperatures, showers. Hawaii: Warmer temperatures, chance of showers. Possibly heavy around the twelfth.

Spring

Zone 1 will experience variable weather conditions, including partly cloudy skies and cooler temperatures, low-pressure areas, and southerly airflows bringing warmer temperatures as the season progresses.

The general weather conditions for Zones 2 and 3 range from partly cloudy conditions with lower-than-average temperatures for the season on the positive side to prevailing easterly winds, heavy low clouds, and low-pressure systems on the negative side.

Central and eastern portions of Zones 4 and 5, when affected in a positive manner by planetary alignments, experience fair conditions with temperatures that range below average and northwest winds that may be strong at times. Negative alignments result in a bleak atmosphere and stormy conditions with cold rain and erratic winds.

The western segment of Zones 4 and 5 shows general air movement from south to north, raising temperatures and bringing beneficial showers when receiving positive planetary alignments. Conversely, challenging alignments result in warm and humid conditions with heavier downfall.

Eastern portions of Zones 6 and 7 follow the same conditions as outlined for western segments of Zones 4 and 5. Western regions of the two zones are under a temperate influence regarding moisture and heat when alignments are positive. Negative configurations engender higher temperatures and thunderstorms.

Western segments of Alaska are slated for lower-than-average temperatures with partly cloudy skies under positive planetary alignments to increased downfall from a low-pressure system, heavy low clouds, and easterly winds. Central areas see variable conditions oscillating between high and low-pressure areas and fluctuating temperatures. The eastern zone experiences at times mild and pleasant conditions and southerly winds under positive configurations. When excited by negative configurations, higher humidity and squally storms or heavy precipitation sometimes accompanied by flooding. Hawaii sees warmer and drier conditions when under positive alignments, which can engender thunderstorm activity under negative configurations. As the season wears on, the islands are also under an opposite influence of a cooler and more moist nature, suppressing temperatures and bringing rain.

4th Quarter Moon March 14–21
Zone 1: Warm and fair. Increasing wind velocities. New England is stormy during the period, moderate to high risk of severe thunderstorms. **Zone 2:** North is warm and fair, slight risk of thunderstorms. South sees chance of low pressure, heavy rain. **Zone 3:** Great Lakes stormy and windy. North and east are stormy, possible heavy rain. West and central see potentially strong thunderstorms, wind. **Zone 4:** West has a slight risk of thunderstorms. Low over northern Rockies the nineteenth. Period ends stormy. Central and east have a chance of thunderstorms, wind. **Zone 5:** West has seasonal temperatures. Low risk of thunderstorms. Period ends stormy. Central and east see thunderstorm potential, wind. Possible low pressure over Arizona and New Mexico the seventeenth. **Zone 6:** West Coast has strong storms, high winds, rain. Period ends fair. East is stormy and windy the sixteenth. **Zone 7:** West Coast has strong storms, high winds, rain. Period ends fair. East is stormy and windy the sixteenth. Possible low pressure over Arizona and New Mexico the seventeenth. **Zone 8:** Alaska: West has potential for some heavy precipitation and windy storms. Period ends fair. Central and east warmer, chance of rain, some heavy, then stormy and windy. Hawaii: Temperatures increase, thunderstorms and rain, some heavy.

New Moon March 21–28
Zone 1: Some showers and thunderstorms. Otherwise, fair, rising temperatures. Period ends with declining temperatures. **Zone**

2: Fair, increasing warmth. Some scattered showers and thunderstorms. **Zone 3:** Rising temperatures with a chance of rain. Thunderstorms southwest the twenty-third through the twenty-eighth. North and east see scattered precipitation. Central sees some rain and storminess. Northeast warm and fair. **Zone 4:** West, generally, has rising temperatures, chance of thunderstorms. Central, generally, has rising temperatures, chance of thunderstorms, some severe on the twenty-fifth. Precipitation over northern plains around the twenty-fifth. East is warmer, thunderstorms. A low-pressure area develops over the Western Great Lakes area around the twenty-third. **Zone 5:** West and central have rising temperatures, scattered thunderstorms. East sees rising temperatures, scattered thunderstorms the twenty-sixth. Southeast sees possible severe thunderstorms the twenty-third and twenty-eighth. **Zone 6:** West is fair, breezy; coastal front or storms on the twenty-third and twenty-seventh. East sees rising temperatures, thunderstorm formation. **Zone 7:** West is fair, breezy; northwest coastal front or storms twenty-third and twenty-seventh. Rising temperatures along coastal areas the twenty-fifth. East sees rising temperatures, thunderstorm formation. **Zone 8:** Alaska: West and central see increasing warmth, scattered thunderstorms. Period ends warm. East is warmer, cloudy, with scattered precipitation. Hawaii: Generally warm and fair, chance of rain.

2nd Quarter Moon March 28–April 6

Zone 1: Cloudy and windy. Thunderstorms, heavy rain on the first. The period ends windy, thunderstorms. **Zone 2:** South and central are cloudy, windy, with rain. Low pressure, wind, rain over Tennessee the thirtieth. Period ends cloudy, cooler for south and central; warmer, fair in the north. **Zone 3:** North and east cloudy, windy then rainy, cloudy, and cooler. Central—low pressure, wind, and rain over Tennessee around the thirtieth then thunderstorms on the third. South—low pressure, wind, precipitation around Mississippi on the thirtieth. **Zone 4:** West is windy, cloudy, chance of showers and thunderstorms. North sees low pressure around the second. Period ends cloudy, cooler, low pressure over Wyoming. Central is windy and cloudy. Showers and thunderstorms the first through the third. East is colder, overcast, windy, with precipitation. **Zone 5:** West is warm, fair, windy. Chance of thunderstorms the third. Ending cloudy and cool. Central sees showers and thunderstorms the first through the third. East is cold, overcast, windy, with precipitation on the thirtieth. Low pressure over Louisiana. **Zone 6:** West is breezy, chance of showers, thunderstorms. East sees scattered showers, thunderstorms. **Zone 7:** West is breezy, chance of showers, thunderstorms. East sees scattered showers, thunderstorms. Period ends warmer, fair. **Zone 8:** Alaska: West is cloudy, windy, with scattered precipitation and thunderstorms. Low pressure over eastern Aleutian Islands the thirtieth and third. Period ends with high pressure, windy, warmer. Central is cloudy, windy, with scattered precipitation and thunderstorms. East has scattered precipitation and thunderstorms. Period ends warmer with chance of rain. Hawaii: Warm, fair. Cooler with a chance of rain on the third.

Full Moon April 6–13

Zone 1: New England sees high pressure, windy the seventh. Storm system the ninth, then warm and fair. Windy and rainy the twelfth. **Zone 2:** South is warmer, cloudy, fair. Rain over the zone on the ninth, then fair. Cooler, precipitation, windy the twelfth. **Zone 3:** Zone is warmer, cloudy, and fair. North sees some wind. West has thunderstorms the seventh. Western Great Lakes are cooler, with high pressure the seventh. East sees precipitation the twelfth. **Zone 4:** West is warm, fair, then cooler with gusty winds the ninth. Showers or storms the twelfth. Central and east are warm, fair, then cooler with gusty winds the seventh through the ninth. Warming by the eleventh. **Zone 5:** Low pressure over New Mexico the sixth and twelfth. Otherwise, warm, fair, then cooler with gusty winds the seventh through the ninth. Warming, fair by the eleventh. **Zone 6:** West has rising temperatures, fair conditions, windy. Precipitation the eighth. North central is windy, fair the twelfth. East is mostly fair, slight chance of rain. **Zone 7:** West has rising temperatures, fair. Precipitation the eighth. East is mostly fair, slight chance of rain. **Zone 8:** Alaska: West is warm, windy. High pressure south on the ninth. Cooler, chance of wind and rain the twelfth. Central has high pressure south the ninth, continuing fair. East is warmer, slight chance of showers. Hawaii: Generally fair conditions.

4th Quarter Moon April 13–20

Zone 1: Mid-Atlantic is warm, partly cloudy, then cooler temperatures, precipitation. Thunderstorms the fifteenth through the sixteenth. New England sees rising temperatures, some rain, especially around the seventeenth. **Zone 2:** Northern and central areas cooler, cloudy, chance of rain and thunderstorms, especially around the fifteenth through the sixteenth. South sees chance of rain. **Zone 3:** Northeast is cooler, cloudy, some showers. Southwest has possible heavy rain over the Mississippi area the fourteenth. Central sees showers the fourteenth through the sixteenth, then warming. **Zone 4:** Cold front crosses zone, some wind, showers the thirteenth through the sixteenth. Stormy east. **Zone 5:** Cold front crosses zone, some wind, and showers the thirteenth through the sixteenth. Possible heavy rain for Louisiana the fourteenth. Texas thunderstorms the nineteenth. **Zone 6:** West has chance of precipitation. Windy northwest. Low pressure and precipitation fourteenth through the sixteenth. East is warm, fair, ending with possible rain. **Zone 7:** West has possible precipitation. Southern California is windy. Low pressure and precipitation fourteenth through the sixteenth. East is warm, fair, ending with possible rain. **Zone 8:** Alaska: West is cooler, cloudy, possible rain. Southwest precipitation the fourteenth through the sixteenth. Central sees some precipitation. Low pressure over southern areas the fourteenth. Warm and fair the nineteenth. East has a chance of rain. Hawaii: Rising temperatures. Chance of rain the sixteenth.

New Moon April 20–27

Zone 1: Mid-Atlantic has a chance of showers the twenty-second. New England sees warming the twenty-second. Thunderstorm potential the twentieth, twenty-fifth, and twenty-seventh. **Zone 2:** Partly cloudy, cooler the twenty-second through the twenty-fifth. Chance of showers the twenty-second. North has thunderstorms the twentieth and twenty-seventh. Southern thunderstorms the twenty-seventh. **Zone 3:** Zone has thunderstorms the nineteenth. Partly cloudy, cooler the twenty-second through the twenty-fifth. Great Lakes and northeast see thunderstorms the twentieth and twenty-seventh. Tennessee and Kentucky have thunderstorms the twenty-first through the twenty-second. Alabama sees thunderstorms the twenty-seventh. **Zone 4:** West is partly cloudy, cooler, and windy, then warmer; showers the twenty-fifth. Central thunderstorms the nineteenth. Cooler, windy the twenty-first. East is cooler, breezy to gusty, especially around the twenty-first. Rain the nineteenth and twenty-seventh. **Zone 5:** West sees thunderstorms, then partly cloudy, cooler, and windy. Becoming warmer with showers the twenty-fifth. East sees thunderstorms the nineteenth. Cooler, breezy to gusty, especially around the twenty-first. Rain the nineteenth and twenty-seventh. Central Texas thunderstorms the twenty-seventh. **Zone 6:** West has intermittent coastal showers. Windy northwest. Partly cloudy, cooler. East has possible thunderstorms. Warm, windy. Ending partly cloudy, cooler. **Zone 7:** West has intermittent coastal showers or thunderstorms. Partly cloudy, cooler. East sees possible thunderstorms. Warm, windy. Period ends partly cloudy, cooler. **Zone 8:** Alaska: West is partly cloudy, cooler, scattered thunderstorms, wind. Breezy southwest. Central and east have scattered showers or thunderstorms, windy. Warm, windy central the twenty-third. Hawaii:

Partly cloudy, then warmer with a chance of showers. Windy the twenty-third.

2nd Quarter Moon April 27–May 5

Zone 1: Mid-Atlantic mostly fair. New England windy the first; possible strong storms, wind, rain the fourth. **Zone 2:** Cold front, possible thunderstorms. Period ends fair. **Zone 3:** Stormy, windy the twenty-ninth through the first. Heavy rain over the Mississippi Valley. Low pressure over Great Lakes the fourth. Central and northeast end fair. **Zone 4:** West is mostly fair, possible showers. Possible thunderstorms the fourth. Central and east are stormy; windy the twenty-ninth through the second over Kansas. Possible heavy rain the fourth. **Zone 5:** West is mostly fair, possible showers. Possible thunderstorms the fourth. Central and east are stormy; windy the twenty-ninth through the second over Oklahoma. Possible heavy rain the fourth. **Zone 6:** West is windy, chance of rain over coastal areas. East sees some wind and showers, mostly warm and fair. Chance of thunderstorms the fourth. **Zone 7:** West is windy, chance of rain over coastal areas. East sees some wind and showers, mostly warm and fair. Chance of thunderstorms the fourth. **Zone 8:** Alaska: West is mostly fair, possible wind and storms the twenty-ninth and first. Possible storms, wind, and rain the fourth. Central and east have possible rain, heavier the second through fourth. Hawaii: Warm with possible showers. Strong storms the fourth.

Full Moon May 5–12

Zone 1: Possible showers. Thunderstorms the sixth through the ninth. Cooler, partly cloudy, fair the twelfth. **Zone 2:** Scattered showers. Cooler, partly cloudy, fair the twelfth. **Zone 3:** Cooler, fair, partly cloudy. Great Lakes high pressure. Low pressure the twelfth. **Zone 4:** Wind, storm over zone on the fifth. West sees storm system the tenth. Fair the twelfth. Central sees storm system the tenth. North central is cooler. East is cool with gusty winds, possible showers the sixth through the twelfth. **Zone 5:** Wind, storm over zone the fifth. West and central see possible thunderstorms the tenth. East is cooler, gusty winds, possible showers the eighth through the twelfth. **Zone 6:** West sees high pressure the sixth, then stormy the ninth. East is warmer the seventh. Thunderstorms the ninth. Cooler on the tenth. **Zone 7:** West sees high pressure the sixth, then stormy the ninth. East is warmer the seventh. Thunderstorms the ninth. Cooler on the tenth. **Zone 8:** Alaska: West sees thunderstorms the fifth through the ninth. Central has storms the ninth, then cooler, partly cloudy, fair. East sees storms the ninth, then fair. Hawaii: Fair with possible showers. Thunderstorms likely between the seventh and ninth.

4th Quarter Moon May 12–19

Zone 1: Partly cloudy and cooler zone. Windy storms the seventeenth. High pressure resumes. **Zone 2:** Cool, windy, and fair. Northern and central see possible windy storms the seventeenth. South is warm, ends fair. **Zone 3:** Northeast partly cloudy, cooler. West and central warmer, fair. Great Lakes high pressure. All zone sees windy storms fifteenth through the seventeenth. **Zone 4:** West is warm, fair. Strong storms sixteenth through the eighteenth, then fair. Central sees thunderstorms. East has rising temperatures. Thunderstorms, wind the thirteenth and seventeenth through the eighteenth. **Zone 5:** West is warm, fair. Strong storms sixteenth through the eighteenth, then fair. Central sees thunderstorms. East has rising temperatures. Thunderstorms, wind the thirteenth and seventeenth through the eighteenth. **Zone 6:** Pacific Northwest begins fair. Coastal areas windy, warm. Strong storms sixteenth through the eighteenth, which push eastward, then fair. **Zone 7:** Coastal areas windy, warm. Strong storms sixteenth through the eighteenth, which push eastward, then fair. **Zone 8:** Alaska: Cooler, partly cloudy, fair. A warm-up, then windy storms sixteenth through the seventeenth across the zone. Hawaii: Cooler, partly cloudy, fair. Possible thunderstorms the seventeenth.

New Moon May 19–27
Zone 1: Mid-Atlantic is cool, fair, breezy. Storms on the twenty-fifth. New England has high pressure. Thunderstorms on the twenty-third and twenty-seventh. **Zone 2:** North has thunderstorms then cool, fair, and breezy. Storm generation on twenty-fifth. South is cooler. Possible heavy precipitation the twenty-second, then unsettled. **Zone 3:** Thunderstorm potential. North and central cooler, cloudy. Possible heavy precipitation the twenty-second. Possible scattered showers or thunderstorms continue. Southwest strong thunderstorms the twenty-fourth. Great Lakes low pressure the twenty-third, then clearing the twenty-fourth. Ending clear, cool west. **Zone 4:** West has high pressure north. Warm, intense storms the twenty-third. Central sees strong storms the twentieth through the twenty-third, then scattered precipitation. Warming the twenty-fifth. East is clear, cool, possible thunderstorms the twentieth and twenty-fourth. **Zone 5:** West is warm; intense storms the twenty-third. Afterward, possible showers. Central sees strong thunderstorms the twentieth, then scattered precipitation and thunderstorms. East sees storms the twentieth, then clear, cool, possible thunderstorms the twenty-fourth. **Zone 6:** West sees thunderstorms, some intense. East is warm; possible intense storms the twentieth through the twenty-third, afterward scattered showers. **Zone 7:** West sees thunderstorms, some intense. East is warm; possible intense storms the twentieth through the twenty-third, afterward scattered showers. **Zone 8:** Alaska: West is stormy the twentieth and twenty-fourth. Possible heavy precipitation. Clear, cool southwest the twenty-sixth. Central sees possible windy storms. East is warmer, stormy. Hawaii: Warm, fair. Possible storm center (460 miles) east of Honolulu on the twentieth. Possible storm system southwest of islands the twenty-fourth.

2nd Quarter Moon May 27–June 3

Zone 1: Mid-Atlantic sees below-average temperatures, showers, thunderstorms, and gusty winds. **Zone 2:** Mid-Atlantic sees below-average temperatures, showers, thunderstorms, and gusty winds. **Zone 3:** Northeast has gusty thunderstorms. Central sees fine weather, thunderstorms the third. West is warmer, scattered thunderstorms. Southwest has strong thunderstorms. **Zone 4:** West sees rising temperatures, showers. Central and east are warm and humid with possible showers. Windy, thunderstorms the first. **Zone 5:** West sees rising temperatures, showers. Central and east are warm and humid with possible showers. Windy, thunderstorms the first. **Zone 6:** West sees rising temperatures, possible showers. Cooler, windy, stormy weather the thirty-first. Probable thunderstorms the second. East is overcast, precipitation. Warmer, local showers the second. **Zone 7:** West sees rising temperatures, possible showers. Cooler, windy, stormy weather the thirty-first. Probable thunderstorms the second. East is overcast, precipitation. Warmer, local showers the second. **Zone 8:** Alaska: West sees rising temperatures, possible showers, then becoming overcast with precipitation and wind. Brief local showers the second. Central and east see rising temperatures, possible showers. Low pressure, precipitation. Becoming fair the thirtieth. Warm, local showers the second. Hawaii: Low pressure. Precipitation. Possible thunderstorms the thirty-first.

Full Moon June 3–10

Zone 1: Potential thunderstorms or tropical system West Virginia, Virginia, North Carolina third through the sixth. Mid-Atlantic possible wind, thunderstorms ninth through the tenth. New England sees showers, thunderstorms, chance of clearing the eighth, then windy. **Zone 2:** Potential thunderstorms or tropical system West Virginia, Virginia, North Carolina third through the sixth. Mid-Atlantic increased chance of wind, thunderstorms ninth through the tenth. Mid-Atlantic possible wind, thunderstorms ninth through the tenth. South has potential thunderstorms, gusty winds. Florida begins with high pressure. **Zone 3:** Northeast is generally stormy. Potential thunderstorms or tropical system in West Virginia the third through the sixth. Strong low over Great Lakes, Michigan, Ohio the seventh. Elsewhere, seasonal temperatures, scattered thunderstorms, some severe over west on the fourth. Louisiana and Mississippi intense storms on the eighth. **Zone 4:** West is mostly warm, clear, possible showers. Central sees thunderstorms early on, then possible showers. East sees potential for wind, severe thunderstorms. Afterward, scattered showers, thunderstorms. **Zone 5:** West is mostly warm, clear, possible showers. Central sees thunderstorms early on, then possible showers. East sees potential for wind, severe thunderstorms. Afterward, scattered showers, thunderstorms. **Zone 6:** Windy, stormy, precipitation the fifth through the seventh. Afterward, warm, chance of showers. **Zone 7:** Windy, stormy, precipitation the fifth through the seventh. Afterward, warm, chance of showers. **Zone 8:** Alaska: West and central are windy, stormy, then

warm, partly cloudy, possible showers. East is warmer, possible showers, chance of stronger storms the fifth. Hawaii: Potential for strong storms, wind, and a possible tropical system runs high.

4th Quarter Moon June 10–18

Zone 1: Mid-Atlantic sees chance of showers and thunderstorms. Lunar phase ends cooler, wetter. New England is fair, windy. Chance of thunderstorms the eleventh. **Zone 2:** North is cloudy, cooler, damp. Chance of thunderstorms, wind. Cool and damp the seventeenth. Central and south are cool, cloudy, precipitation. **Zone 3:** Great Lakes and north are cooler, cloudy, showers and thunderstorms. West and central see increasing risk of severe thunderstorms. **Zone 4:** West is warm, some wind, chance of showers. Possible severe thunderstorms the fourteenth. Cooler with precipitation the seventeenth. Central sees possible showers and thunderstorms, severity increases the fourteenth. East sees possible showers. Low pressure over western Great Lakes and Minnesota. Some strong thunderstorms around Missouri and Iowa. **Zone 5:** West sees chance of showers, some wind. Possible severe thunderstorms the fourteenth on. East sees risk of severe thunderstorms the fourteenth on. **Zone 6:** West is warm, windy coast, chance of showers. Period ends fair. Inland is cloudy, some precipitation and wind. East sees gusty winds, possible showers, thunderstorms. Warm and fair the fifteenth on. **Zone 7:** West is warm, windy coast, chance of showers. Period ends fair. Inland is cloudy, some precipitation and wind. East sees gusty winds, possible showers, thunderstorms. Warm and fair the fifteenth on. **Zone 8:** Alaska: West has chance of showers, thunderstorms. Cooler, damp the seventeenth. Central sees chance of showers. Thunderstorms the fourteenth. Cooler and damp the seventeenth. East is warmer, windy. Chance of thunderstorms fourteenth through the sixteenth. Cooler and damp the seventeenth. Hawaii: Scattered showers and thunderstorms. Cooler temperatures and chance of rain end the period.

New Moon June 18–26

Zone 1: Cooler with possible showers. Potential thunderstorms, gusty winds the twenty-second through the twenty-fifth. **Zone 2:** Variable temperatures, possible showers. Potential thunderstorms, gusty winds twenty-second through the twenty-fifth. **Zone 3:** Cooler, possible precipitation. Strong thunderstorms west to east the twenty-first. Northeast potential thunderstorms, gusty winds the twenty-second through the twenty-fourth. Western Great Lakes to Gulf Coast see strong thunderstorms, heavy rain the twenty-fourth. **Zone 4:** West sees below-average temperatures. Wind, chance of precipitation increases. Strong thunderstorms the twenty-fifth. Central is cooler, possible rain. Increasing wind the twenty-first. Potential strong thunderstorms, heavy rain the twenty-fifth. Central and Southern Mississippi Valley sees low pressure the eighteenth. East has thunderstorms midweek. Stronger storms the twenty-fifth. **Zone 5:** West sees below-average temperatures. Wind, chance of precipitation increases. Strong thunderstorms the twenty-fifth. Central is cooler, possible rain. Increasing wind, the twenty-first. Potential strong thunderstorms, heavy rain the twenty-fifth. Central and Southern Mississippi Valley sees low pressure the eighteenth. East has thunderstorms midweek. Stronger storms the twenty-fifth. **Zone 6:** West is cooler, some wind, chance of rain. Stronger thunderstorms, wind the twenty-first, then windy Pacific Northwest. East is cooler, possible rain, some wind. **Zone 7:** West is cooler, some wind, chance of rain. Stronger thunderstorms, wind the twenty-first, then windy Pacific Northwest, then thunderstorms decrease. East is cooler, possible rain, some wind. **Zone 8:** Alaska: West, temperatures vary. Thunderstorms, gusty winds twenty-second and twenty-fifth. Central sees variable temperatures, possible scattered showers, and thunderstorms. East sees increasing humidity, possible thunderstorms. Hawaii: A chance of showers, thunderstorms, and some wind.

Summer

Under beneficial planetary aspects, the summer for Zone 1 will generally see temperatures more on the cool side with local showers and moderate breezes. Under adverse aspects, a slowly falling barometer brings intense general rains with cooler temperatures and east winds. A warmer influence temporarily takes place in mid-July.

The general summer weather influence for Zones 2 and 3 shows an emphasis on high pressure, cooler-than-average temperatures, and breezy northwest winds. Negative influences bring overcast skies and squally storms. A damp and penetrating atmosphere is common under this influence with sudden changes to cooler weather.

The favorable influences on weather patterns for Zones 4 and 5 include fine but warm conditions. When adverse aspects are in play, the weather conditions become hot and sultry, leading to thunderstorm formation or dashing showers.

For Zones 6 and 7, warmth is a key weather condition, and under beneficial aspects, fair conditions reign. The influence of negative alignments will increase windy conditions and storminess.

Cooler temperatures are indicated for Alaska, especially over western and central areas. When adversely aspected, slowly developing low-pressure systems can bring heavy rain with lower temperatures and easterly winds. Eastern areas are generally cooler as well with potential for breezy to windy conditions accompanied by precipitation. Hawaii should expect temperatures generally below normal with local showers when under favorable alignments and stronger storms and wind with cooler temperatures when adverse alignments form.

2nd Quarter Moon June 26–July 3

Zone 1: Zone is cool, fair, partly cloudy, especially from midweek on, then windy and fair. New England sees a chance for showers around the weekend. **Zone 2:** Mid-Atlantic and central are cooler, fair, partly cloudy. South has thunderstorm potential, some strong. **Zone 3:** Low-pressure areas or fronts are indicated throughout the zone, bringing precipitation and some wind. **Zone 4:** West and central see possible thunderstorms. Fair north the first. East has strong to severe thunderstorms and wind, especially over Wisconsin-Illinois. **Zone 5:** West and central see possible thunderstorms. Fair north on the first. East is mostly stormy. **Zone 6:** West sees rising temperatures and humidity, chance of showers, especially around the second. Pacific Northwest storms the twenty-ninth. East has some wind, possible thunderstorms, then windy and fair around the first. **Zone 7:** West sees rising temperatures and humidity, chance of showers especially around the second. East sees some wind, possible thunderstorms, then windy and fair around the first. **Zone 8:** Alaska: West is windy, possible thunderstorms, then fair, cooler, and partly cloudy. Windy again the first. Central and east see possible thunderstorm, then fair, lower temperatures. Increasing humidity, warmth, possible showers over the weekend. Windy, fair the first. Hawaii: Mostly fair, partly cloudy, and cooler. Windy and fair around the first.

Full Moon July 3–9

Zone 1: Zone sees low-pressure activity or front the sixth. High pressure the eighth. New England sees some wind after sixth. **Zone 2:** Mid-Atlantic has some precipitation the sixth. Central and south have possible thunderstorms, becoming warmer and fair the ninth. **Zone 3:** West sees scattered thunderstorms, then breezy, fair the sixth. Central sees similar conditions, then possible thunderstorm, then warmer, fair. Northeast has possible thunderstorm fourth and eighth, and the Eastern Great Lakes see high pressure the eighth. **Zone 4:** West has possible thunderstorms. Central has stormy southern plains. East is warm, with thunderstorms, then fair with some wind the sixth. Scattered showers and thunderstorms the eighth. **Zone 5:** Zone has scattered showers, thunderstorms. Central sees possible storm system in Texas and Oklahoma. **Zone 6:** West has high pressure in Washington and Oregon, low pressure in Idaho. Atmospheric disturbance in coastal areas. Pacific Northwest is windy. East sees scattered showers, thunderstorms. **Zone 7:** West sees atmospheric disturbance in coastal areas. Central California sees thunderstorms or windy conditions. Elsewhere, thunderstorms. East is warmer, thunderstorms. **Zone 8:** Alaska: West sees thunderstorms, especially southwest. Central sees thunderstorms, some wind the seventh. Central and east have thunderstorms. Zone ends warmer and fair. Hawaii: Scattered showers and thunderstorms. Windy the seventh, then warm and fair.

4th Quarter Moon July 9–17

Zone 1: Fair then showers or thunderstorms twelfth to thirteenth. Breezy the thirteenth. **Zone 2:** Zone sees chance of showers the twelfth. Breezy the seventeenth. Central sees thunderstorms the tenth. South cooler, fair the thirteenth. **Zone 3:** Zone has showers and thunderstorms the tenth, strong over Michigan, Indiana, and Ohio. Temperatures decline, scattered showers. West sees increasing winds the fifteenth, storm system in Michigan the seventeenth. **Zone 4:** West is stormy then warm, fair, and breezy. Central and east have high pressure and wind, then possible showers. Warm, fair, and breezy the fifteenth. **Zone 5:** West is stormy then warm, fair, and breezy. Central and east have high pressure and wind, then possible showers. Warm, fair, and breezy the fifteenth. **Zone 6:** West is stormy, windy. Cooler, fair, and breezy the fourteenth. Coastal showers in Washington the fifteenth. The east sees possible windy thunderstorms then warm, fair, and breezy. **Zone 7:** West sees thunderstorms, gusty winds, stronger over central California and Nevada then cooler and breezy. East sees possible windy thunderstorms then warm, fair, and somewhat breezy. **Zone 8:** Alaska: West has showers and thunderstorms, especially southwest. Central and east see windy storms. Breezy the seventeenth. Hawaii: Generally warm with a chance of thunderstorms or showers.

New Moon July 17–25

Zone 1: Zone sees possible destructive windy storms eighteenth to twenty-second, then lower temperatures. **Zone 2:** North sees possible destructive windy storms the eighteenth. South has shower potential. Gusty winds, storms nineteenth and twenty-second. North and central see possible gusty winds and storms. **Zone 3:** Zone has scattered showers likely. Gusty winds and thunderstorms nineteenth and twenty-second. Storms possibly intense in Ohio-Michigan. **Zone 4:** Zone is windy, possible thunderstorms the eighteenth, then warm and dry. Central and east see severe thunderstorms. Wind and thunderstorms the twenty-first. **Zone 5:** Zone is windy, possible thunderstorms the eighteenth, then warm and dry. Central and east see severe thunderstorms. Wind and thunderstorms the twenty-first. **Zone 6:** West has showers. Warm and fair the twentieth. Storm potential the twenty-second. East has severe thunderstorms twentieth and afterward. **Zone 7:** West has showers. Warm and fair the twentieth. Storm potential the twenty-second. East has severe thunderstorms twentieth and afterward. **Zone 8:** Alaska: West sees strong to severe thunderstorms. Central has possible destructive, windy storms twentieth and twenty-second. East is warm and fair. Potential atmospheric disturbance the twenty-second. Hawaii: Warm and humid conditions interspersed with periods of severe thunderstorms, especially around the twentieth and twenty-second.

2nd Quarter Moon July 25–August 1

Zone 1: A warming period across the region precedes a drop in temperatures that results in low pressure and rain. **Zone 2:** A warming period across the region precedes a drop in temperatures that results in low pressure and rain. **Zone 3:** Northeast and

Great Lakes see a warming period then a drop in temperatures, low pressure, and rain. West is windy with showers around the first. **Zone 4:** West sees thunderstorms, strongest over northern portions the twenty-seventh. Central is warm with local thunderstorms. Then western and central zones see high pressure, increasing wind velocities the thirty-first. East has thunderstorms the twenty-seventh. Central and east are windy and showery the first. **Zone 5:** West sees low pressure in western Texas and western Oklahoma the twenty-seventh. West and central are warmer, local thunderstorms the thirtieth. Central and east see high pressure, windy the thirty-first followed by windy and showery weather. **Zone 6:** Zone sees rising temperatures and humidity the twenty-seventh, then thunderstorms. Strong storms over Idaho. **Zone 7:** Zone has rising temperatures and humidity the twenty-seventh, then thunderstorms. Strong storms, windy conditions over the Four Corners region the twenty-seventh and over California-Nevada the thirtieth. **Zone 8:** Alaska: Zone sees showers and thunderstorms. East is windy the thirtieth. Hawaii: Possible showers and thunderstorms the twenty-seventh.

Full Moon August 1–8

Zone 1: Zone is cloudy, rainy, and cooler the first to third. A strong low-pressure area or possible tropical system is indicated off the New England coast. Warm, partly cloudy the fifth. New England sees gusty winds, thunderstorms, another low-pressure area off the coast the seventh. **Zone 2:** North is cloudy, rainy, and cooler the first and third. North and central have rising temperatures, humidity, and wind the fourth. Showers or thunderstorms the sixth. South sees chance of thunderstorms, then partly cloudy, warmer, possible thunderstorms the fifth to seventh. **Zone 3:** Zone has chance of showers the third, then warm, partly cloudy. Chance of showers and thunderstorms. **Zone 4:** West and central are warm, partly cloudy, some precipitation. East is warm and dry. **Zone 5:** Generally, the zone sees warm, humid weather with local thunderstorms. **Zone 6:** The zone generally sees warm weather with a chance of showers. Pacific Northwest ends windy with a chance of thunderstorms. Eastern sections see thunderstorms around the first. **Zone 7:** The zone generally sees warm weather with a chance of showers. Pacific Northwest ends windy with a chance of thunderstorms. Eastern sections see thunderstorms around the first. **Zone 8:** Alaska: West is cloudy, cooler, rainy, then warmer, partly cloudy. Central and east are warm and dry, then a chance of cloudy and showery conditions. West and east see gusty winds and thunderstorms the seventh. Hawaii: Cloudy, cooler, rainy then warmer and more humid. Windy, chance of thunderstorms the seventh.

4th Quarter Moon August 8–16

Zone 1: New England sees increasing temperatures, cloudiness, precipitation. Low pressure and showers the ninth. Robust and windy storms the eleventh. Warm, likely showers the fifteenth. Mid-Atlantic has dashing rain the thirteenth. Windy, stormy the fifteenth. **Zone 2:** Zone sees thunderstorms. Some potentially intense over Virginia (fifteenth) and the Florida Panhandle (sixteenth). **Zone 3:** Zone is stormy, some wind the eighth. Possible severe thunderstorms Michigan through Kentucky the eighth. Southwest sees robust storms the eleventh to fourteenth. Period ends with more thunderstorm potential. **Zone 4:** West is warmer, cloudy, rainy the fourteenth. Central has robust storms for northern plains the eleventh. Warmer, cloudy, rainy the fourteenth. East is stormy the ninth with severe thunderstorms for Iowa. Robust storms the eleventh. Dashing showers the thirteenth. Warmer, cloudy, rainy the fourteenth. **Zone 5:** West is warmer, cloudy, rainy the fourteenth. Central sees increasing temperatures, thunderstorms the eleventh. Warmer, cloudy, rainy the fourteenth. East is stormy the ninth. Robust storms the eleventh. Dashing showers the thirteenth. Warmer, cloudy, rainy the fourteenth. **Zone 6:** Zone is cooler, windy, stormy the tenth and fifteenth. Coastal winds the thirteenth. **Zone 7:** Zone is cooler, windy, stormy the tenth and fifteenth. Coastal winds the thirteenth. **Zone 8:** Alaska: West is stormy and windy. Central has showers, low pressure off south central coast the ninth. Dashing rains the thirteenth. Cooler, windy, stormy the fifteenth. East is dry and windy the ninth and fourteenth. Cooler, windy, stormy the fifteenth. Hawaii: Sharp winds, warm and dry the ninth and fourteenth, possible thunderstorms. Period ends fair.

New Moon August 16–24

Zone 1: Mid-Atlantic is generally cooler with showers. Warmer with chance of showers the nineteenth. New England begins windy and stormy, then warm, humid. Possible heavy rain the twenty-second. **Zone 2:** Mid-Atlantic and central are cooler with showers. South and central are windy, possible thunderstorms the sixteenth. Central has showers the nineteenth. South has showers the twenty-third. **Zone 3:** Zone is windy. Chance of thunderstorms the sixteenth. A chance of showers the twenty-third. Northeast is cooler with some showers. **Zone 4:** West is warm, mostly fair with some chance of showers. Low pressure over Colorado and New Mexico the twenty-third. Central and east see thunderstorms the sixteenth. Possible thunderstorms and heavy rain the twenty-first to twenty-third over the Front Range and eastward to Missouri and Arkansas, then a windy event sets up over the zone. **Zone 5:** West is warm, mostly fair with some chance of showers. Low pressure over Colorado and New Mexico the twenty-third. Central and east see thunderstorms the sixteenth. Possible thunderstorms and heavy rain the twenty-first to twenty-third over the Front Range and eastward to Missouri and Arkansas, then a windy event sets up over the zone. **Zone 6:** West sees atmospheric disturbance in Pacific Northwest and potential showers over central areas the sixteenth. Possible western showers the twenty-first. Windy the twenty-fourth. East is warm, humid, with potential storms and flash flooding. **Zone 7:** West sees cold front and showers the sixteenth. Possible western showers the twenty-first, becoming windy the twenty-fourth. East is warm, humid, with potential storms and flash flooding. **Zone 8:** Alaska: West is cool, showery; west coast storms the eighteenth. A chance of heavier rain the twenty-second, then becoming windy. Central sees atmospheric disturbance the sixteenth, then possible heavy rain the twenty-second. East has windy conditions throughout with heavy rain the twenty-second. Hawaii: Possible strong storms as the period begins. A chance of heavier rain around the twenty-second.

2nd Quarter Moon August 24–30

Zone 1: Zone sees showers on the twenty-fourth. Declining temperatures, windy, thunderstorms the twenty-seventh. These storms could be powerful, perhaps even tropical in nature. **Zone 2:** Mid-Atlantic sees showers the twenty-fourth. Zone has declining temperatures, windy, possible thunderstorms the twenty-seventh. **Zone 3:** Zone is warm, fair, chance of showers the twenty-fourth. Temperatures decline, windiness increases, chance of thunderstorms the twenty-ninth. Stormy Great Lakes the twenty-ninth. **Zone 4:** West and central are warm, possible showers (twenty-fourth). Northwest has declining temperatures, increased wind velocities, possible thunderstorms the twenty-eighth. Central and east see increasing temperatures and winds, possible showers, or thunderstorms the twenty-seventh. **Zone 5:** West and central are warm, a chance of showers the twenty-fourth. All areas increasing in temperatures and winds, possible showers or thunderstorms the twenty-seventh. **Zone 6:** West begins fair with windy conditions for coastal areas starting around the twenty-seventh. Eastern areas see thunderstorm activity. **Zone 7:** The west begins fair. Windy conditions for coastal areas the twenty-seventh. Possible severe thunderstorms throughout the zone bringing rain and wind starting the twenty-sixth, especially over the Nevada area. **Zone 8:** Alaska: West sees showers the twenty-fourth. Cooler, cloudier, developing storminess over the zone the twenty-seventh. Winds pick up over eastern areas. Hawaii: Showers the twenty-fourth. Cooler, cloudier with developing storminess the twenty-seventh. The period ends with declining temperatures and windy conditions.

Full Moon August 30–September 6

Zone 1: Zone is generally fair. Mid-Atlantic sees increasing warmth, humidity, and chance of rain. Possible gusty thunderstorms over western mid-Atlantic the sixth. **Zone 2:** Mid-Atlantic sees increasing warmth, chance of rain. Thunderstorms likely over Carolinas the first. Possible gusty thunderstorms over southern and central areas the sixth. **Zone 3:** Zone is generally fair. West sees windy conditions the second. Northeast sees increasing warmth, humidity, and chance of rain. Gusty thunderstorms the sixth. **Zone 4:** West is generally warm, fair with a chance of showers. Windy with possible thunderstorms the sixth. Central is warm, sultry, some showers, then ending with winds and possible thunderstorms. East is fair, warm, sultry, possible showers. **Zone 5:** West is generally warm, fair with a chance of showers. Windy with possible thunderstorms the sixth. Central is warm, sultry, some showers, then ending fair. East is fair, warm, sultry, possible showers. **Zone 6:** Zone starting windy. Generally fair, warm, more wind along coastal areas the second. Windy, stormy coastal areas, a chance of rain over eastern sections the sixth. **Zone 7:** Zone starting windy. Generally fair, warm, more wind along coastal areas the second. Windy, stormy coastal areas, a chance of rain over eastern sections the sixth. **Zone 8:** Alaska: West sees thunderstorms the fourth. Central is fair the thirty-first. Increasing warmth, humidity, and chance of rain mid-period. Wind, possible thunderstorms the fifth. East sees wind, possible thunderstorms the second, then fair. Wind, possible thunderstorms the fifth. Hawaii: Windy, possible storms. Increasing warmth, humidity, and chance of rain mid period.

4th Quarter Moon September 6–14

Zone 1: Zone is cooler, cloudy with rain. Mid-Atlantic sees showers the thirteenth. New England is windy, possible showers ninth and thirteenth. **Zone 2:** South and central see fair conditions the eleventh, then scattered thunderstorms. South ends cool and fair. Mid-Atlantic is cooler. Chance of showers the thirteenth. **Zone 3:** Zone is fair and cooler the seventh to the eleventh, then scattered thunderstorms. Period ends cool and fair. **Zone 4:** West is fair the eighth. Southerly breezes, chance of rain the ninth. Warmer, chance of showers the thirteenth. Central is fair the eighth. South central sees southerly breezes, possible showers the ninth. Warm, fair, then gusty thunderstorms the twelfth. East is fair the eighth. Southerly winds, possible showers the ninth. Cool, fair the twelfth. **Zone 5:** West is fair the eighth. Southerly breezes, chance of rain the ninth. Central is fair the eighth. South central sees southerly breezes, possible showers the ninth. Cool and fair the twelfth, then gusty thunderstorms. East is fair, chance of showers and thunderstorms. Fair conditions the eighth. **Zone 6:** West sees rising temperatures, potential thunderstorms the eighth. Coastal showers the tenth. East sees thunderstorms the thirteenth. Warm and fair the fourteenth. **Zone 7:** West sees rising temperatures, potential thunderstorms the eighth. Coastal showers the tenth. East sees thunderstorms the thirteenth. Warm and fair the fourteenth. **Zone 8:** Alaska: West is cooler, cloudy. Warm, fair the twelfth, then scattered thunderstorms. Central is cooler and breezy. Fair the eighth. Breezy, possible showers the ninth and thirteenth. East is breezy, showery the eighth and thirteenth. Generally, southerly winds and showers. Hawaii: Generally cooler and breezy. Gusty thunderstorms the eleventh.

New Moon, September 14–22

Zone 1: Mid-Atlantic is cooler, cloudy, and wet. New England is cool, breezy. Possible tropical system or strong storms fueled by tropical moisture over the Carolinas the sixteenth and may travel up the East Coast. Showers and some wind over zone the twentieth. **Zone 2:** Mid-Atlantic is cooler, cloudy, and wet. Southern regions see showers, especially around the nineteenth. Possible tropical system or strong storms fueled by tropical moisture over the Carolinas the sixteenth may travel up the East Coast. Possible showers the nineteenth. **Zone 3:** West is fair, chance of showers seventeenth and nineteenth. East is cooler, fair, then possible showers. East sees possible showers the nineteenth. **Zone 4:** West starts windy, then showers. Period ends fair. Central is windy over the High Plains the fifteenth, then increasing warmth, chance of showers the seventeenth. Possible heavy rain the nineteenth. East is generally fair, chance of showers the seventeenth. Possible heavy rain the nineteenth. **Zone 5:** West starts windy, then showers. Period ends fair. Central sees increasing warmth, chance of showers seventeenth and nineteenth. East is generally fair, chance of showers the seventeenth. Possible heavy rain the nineteenth. **Zone 6:** Zone is generally warm, dry. Windy conditions, possible showers the sixteenth. West Coast is fair the twenty-first, possible showers over the central zone. East has shower potential mid-period, then ending fair. **Zone 7:** Zone is generally warm, dry. Windy conditions, possible showers the sixteenth. East sees increasing warmth, possible thunderstorms or showers mid-period, then ending fair. West Coast is fair the twenty-first. **Zone 8:** Alaska: West is cooler, cloudy, and wet. Possible strong atmospheric disturbance the sixteenth. Period ends cooler. Central is cool, breezy. Possible strong atmospheric disturbance the sixteenth. Period ends cooler. East is warmer, chance of rain sixteenth and nineteenth. Hawaii: Generally cooler with a chance of rain and some breezy conditions.

2nd Quarter Moon, September 22–29

Zone 1: New England is generally fair, chance of showers. Mid-Atlantic sees possible thunderstorms twenty-fourth and twenty-sixth. **Zone 2:** South sees rising temperatures, thunderstorms twenty-fifth and twenty-seventh. Central has possible thunderstorms the twenty-third. North has a chance of thunderstorms twenty-fourth and twenty-sixth. **Zone 3:** Zone sees generally rising temperatures, thunderstorms. West sees warm conditions, especially southern portions with possible thunderstorms. **Zone 4:** West sees chance of showers. Central sees rising temperatures, chance of thunderstorms. Possibly windy by end of period. East sees showers, rising temperatures, chance of thunderstorms. **Zone 5:** West sees chance of showers. Central sees rising temperatures, chance of thunderstorms. Possibly windy by end of period. East sees showers, rising temperatures, chance of thunderstorms. **Zone 6:** West is cooler. Windy, possible thunderstorms across the zone the twenty-fifth. East-southerly winds, increasing temperatures, chance of showers. Possible thunderstorms the twenty-seventh. **Zone 7:** West is cooler. Windy, possible thunderstorms across the zone the twenty-fifth. East-southerly winds, increasing temperatures, chance of showers. Possible thunderstorms the twenty-seventh. **Zone 8:** Alaska: West sees possible showers. Central is warmer, chance of showers. East is warm, chance of showers. Zone ends cloudy, chance of showers. Hawaii: Generally fair conditions for the islands.

Autumn

The New England portion of Zone 1, when under benign planetary influences, enjoys a clear and mild autumn atmosphere. Under more challenging planetary alignments, cloudiness and rain increase and temperatures become colder. The mid-Atlantic region of Zone 1 along with Zone 2 are generally mild but subject to windy storms at times.

Zone 3 along with central and eastern portions of Zones 4 and 5 are under a warm and dry influence when benevolent planetary aspects operate. Under adverse planetary alignments, stronger storms, some of them generating severe winds and hail, are likely.

The western extension of Zones 4 and 5 and eastern areas of Zones 6 and 7 are mild and pleasant with rising temperatures. When under more challenging planetary influences, temperatures rise; fog may be an issue in highlands, while windy and rainy conditions affect lowland areas. Western regions of Zones 6 and 7 are generally windy and fair under good planetary aspects. Conversely, unharmonious planetary influences bring wind and rain followed by cooler nights.

Zone 8 sees western areas with warm and fair conditions under good planetary influences. Strong storms accompanied by gusty winds are the result of the more difficult planetary alignments. Variable weather conditions are shown for the central zone, while a more clear and mild influence is at work over eastern portions. Cloudiness and precipitation increase, and temperatures drop under adverse planetary aspects. Hawaii is generally warm and pleasant, interspersed with breezy conditions and some thunderstorm activity.

Full Moon, September 29–October 6

Zone 1: Mid-Atlantic sees possible showers the thirtieth. Zone sees thunderstorms, some windy conditions, which are strongest the second. **Zone 2:** Zone is mostly warm, dry. Possible showers the thirtieth. **Zone 3:** Zone is warm, dry. East and west have possible showers the thirtieth. Thunderstorms over eastern Great Lakes the second. Warm, windy west on the third. **Zone 4:** West has thunderstorms. Central and east see possible showers, breezy to windy. West and central, the period ends warmer, atmospheric disturbance. **Zone 5:** West has thunderstorms. Central and east see possible showers, breezy to windy. Strong thunderstorms in Oklahoma the second. West and central, the period ends warmer, atmospheric disturbance. **Zone 6:** West Coast sees wind and rain push eastward the twenty-ninth to the second. Windy, possible showers the fifth. East has showers and wind, then cooler with high pressure. Possible rain the fourth. **Zone 7:** West Coast sees wind and rain push eastward the twenty-ninth to the second. Windy, possible showers the fifth. East has showers and wind, then cooler with high pressure. **Zone 8:** Alaska: West and central see showers and thunderstorms, then windy the third. East has some rain, cooler the twenty-ninth. Showers the fifth. Hawaii: Mostly fair, but possible rain early. Possible thunderstorms the second.

4th Quarter Moon, October 6–14

Zone 1: Mid-Atlantic sees some showers and thunderstorms. Possible heavy rain the tenth, then cloudy, windy. New England sees possible showers, thunderstorms the seventh and tenth, then cloudy, windy. **Zone 2:** Showers, thunderstorms Florida to northeast. North and central see potential heavy rain the tenth, then becoming humid, cloudy, windy. **Zone 3:** West sees possible thunderstorms, warmer. Southwest sees possible heavy rain the tenth. Possible thunderstorms, wind the fourteenth. Zone sees showers the ninth. Northeast has thunderstorms and more storms the twelfth. **Zone 4:** Zone is warmer, scattered showers, thunderstorms. Possible strong storms seventh and tenth. Cloudy, windy the thirteenth. **Zone 5:** Zone is warmer, scattered showers, thunderstorms. Possible strong storms seventh and tenth. Cloudy, windy the thirteenth. **Zone 6:** Possible showers, thunderstorms, which push eastward the eighth. Windy, showers or thunderstorms the eleventh, which push eastward. **Zone 7:** Possible showers, thunderstorms, which push eastward the eighth. Windy, showers or thunderstorms the eleventh, which push eastward. **Zone 8:** Alaska: West sees showers, thunderstorm, then warmer. Central has possible showers. Potential thunderstorms the twelfth. East has possible showers, then clear and mild. Hawaii: Strong storms the seventh, then fair, warm, and dry. Possible tropical system about five hundred miles east of the islands the eleventh.

New Moon, October 14–21

Zone 1: Mid-Atlantic possible showers the fifteenth. Possible stronger storms, wind eighteenth to the twentieth. New England is warm, fair the fifteenth. Windy, stormy the eighteenth. **Zone 2:** South is warmer, possible showers the fifteenth. North and central see possible storms the fifteenth. Zone is windy with thunderstorms the eighteenth to twentieth. **Zone 3:** West sees potential showers the fifteenth, then stronger storms the twentieth. East is warm, cloudy, possible showers. Northeast sees potential thunderstorms, wind the eighteenth to twentieth. **Zone 4:** West has possible showers the nineteenth. Central is windy, thunderstorms the twentieth. East sees chance of thunderstorms fifteenth and twenty-first. Western Great Lakes see low pressure the nineteenth. **Zone 5:** West has possible showers the nineteenth. Central is windy, thunderstorms the twentieth. East sees chance of thunderstorms fifteenth and twenty-first. **Zone 6:** West is windy, possible storms fourteenth to the seventeenth. Chance of rain for coast the eighteenth. Strong storms for West

Coast the twentieth. East has southerly winds, possible showers. Strong thunderstorm potential in southern Arizona the fifteenth. Strong storms the twentieth. **Zone 7:** West is windy, possible storms fourteenth to the seventeenth. Chance of rain for coast the eighteenth. Strong storms for West Coast the twentieth. East has southerly winds, possible showers. Strong thunderstorm potential in southern Arizona the fifteenth. Strong storms the twentieth. **Zone 8:** Alaska: West sees possible showers, thunderstorms, and windy conditions fourteenth to seventeenth. Stronger storms the twentieth. Central has storm potential the fifteenth and twentieth. East starts warm and fair. Potential strong storms the eighteenth. Hawaii: The period begins with thunderstorm potential, becoming more intense by the eighteenth.

2nd Quarter Moon, October 21–28
Zone 1: Mid-Atlantic is cooler, some rain. New England is cool, thunderstorms. **Zone 2:** Mid-Atlantic is cooler, some rain. South is gusty, thunderstorms the twenty-third to twenty-fifth. **Zone 3:** South has showers likely the twenty-second on. Great Lakes sees shower potential twenty-second to twenty-fifth. West is windy the twenty-fifth to twenty-seventh. **Zone 4:** West is cooler, fair, increasing chance of rain. Central is warm, fair, cooler, increasing chance of rain. East has showers the twenty-second and twenty-eighth. Windy the twenty-fifth to twenty-seventh. **Zone 5:** West is cooler, fair, increasing chance of rain. Central is warm, fair, cooler, increasing chance of rain. East is windy the twenty-fifth to twenty-seventh. **Zone 6:** West is warm, fair. Possible coastal rain the twenty-fourth. East is cool, fair. Zone sees possible strong storms the twenty-seventh. **Zone 7:** West is warm, fair. Possible coastal rain the twenty-fourth. East is cool, fair. Zone sees possible strong storms the twenty-seventh. **Zone 8:** Alaska: Zone sees showers twenty-second and twenty-third. Central has

cooler temperatures, possible precipitation. Southwest is cooler, possible rain and gusty thunderstorms. West has showers the twenty-eighth. Hawaii: Fair but increasing thunderstorm activity. Decreasing temperatures throughout the period.

Full Moon, October 28–November 5

Zone 1: Mid-Atlantic sees possible heavy rain the second to third. New England is warm, breezy, possible gusty thunderstorms twenty-ninth to thirty-first. Possible heavy rain the first. **Zone 2:** Zone sees fair conditions, cooler temperatures. Mid-Atlantic and central have possible heavy rain the second. South sees thunderstorms the second. **Zone 3:** Great Lakes and east have potential thunderstorms the second. South has showers the fourth. **Zone 4:** West and central see possible violent thunderstorms the twenty-ninth, which push eastward. West is clear and cool, then possible heavy precipitation the second. Windy, stormy the fourth. Central and east see declining temperatures, possible rain after the fourth. **Zone 5:** West and central see possible violent thunderstorms the twenty-ninth, which push eastward. West is clear and cool, then possible heavy precipitation the second. Windy, stormy the fourth. Central and east see declining temperatures, possible rain after the fourth. **Zone 6:** West coastal areas see strong fronts, wind, rain. East has clear skies, cooler. Possible rain the third, then temperatures fall after the fourth. **Zone 7:** West coastal areas see strong fronts, wind, rain. East has clear skies, cooler. Possible rain the third, then temperatures fall after the fourth. **Zone 8:** Alaska: West is warm, breezy, then cool and fair the thirty-first. Possible heavy rain for far west on the second. Northern coast is windy, stormy. Central is mostly fair, breezy, possible thunderstorms the twenty-ninth. East has thunderstorm potential the twenty-ninth, first, and fourth, otherwise fair but windy weather. Hawaii: Possible thunderstorms, gusty winds the twenty-ninth, then warm, breezy, some storminess the second.

4th Quarter Moon, November 5–13

Zone 1: Zone sees southerly winds, higher temperatures, rainfall. Mid-Atlantic sees possible showers the eleventh. New England sees rising temperatures, cloudy, some rain, occasionally breezy. **Zone 2:** Zone sees southerly winds predominate, higher temperatures, rainfall. Showers the eleventh. **Zone 3:** Zone has southerly winds, higher temperatures, rainfall. Great Lakes, central, and south are warm, fair, and breezy. Southern showers possible the eleventh. **Zone 4:** West is warm, fair, and breezy; possible showers the eighth. Strong gusty thunderstorms the eleventh. Central is cloudy, chance of rain the eighth, then gusty, thunderstorms stronger afterward. East is warm, fair, and breezy, possible showers and thunderstorms the tenth. **Zone 5:** West is warm, fair, and breezy; possible showers the eighth. Strong gusty thunderstorms the eleventh. Central is cloudy, chance of rain the eighth, then gusty, thunderstorms stronger afterward. East is warm, fair, and breezy, possible showers and thunderstorms the tenth. **Zone 6:** Rain, high wind, which push eastward around the tenth. **Zone 7:** Lower temperatures, rain, wind for coastal areas, which then transit eastward around the tenth. **Zone 8:** Alaska: West is fair, breezy, chance of showers and thunderstorms the eleventh. Central is breezy, moderate temperatures. Gusty winds, thunderstorms the twelfth. East is stormy, then colder temperatures, gusty winds, and thunderstorms the thirteenth. Hawaii: Thunderstorms, then lower temperatures, windy conditions, and an increase in thunderstorms after the eighth.

New Moon, November 13–20

Zone 1: Zone sees some wind, possible thunderstorms. Temperatures increase, possible heavy rain the nineteenth. Warmer, fair the twentieth. **Zone 2:** North and central see possible showers the eighteenth. Possible heavier rain from the nineteenth on. South has gusty winds, thunderstorms the thirteenth. **Zone 3:** South has some wind, possible thunderstorms. Strongest on the seventeenth, then ending warm, fair. Great Lakes and east see gusty winds, thunderstorms the thirteenth. **Zone 4:** West has rising temperatures, potentially heavy rain the nineteenth. Central is warm, fair. Heavy rain the nineteenth. Western Great Lakes have thunderstorm potential the fourteenth. East sees severe thunderstorms the seventeenth. **Zone 5:** West has rising temperatures, potentially heavy rain the nineteenth. Central is warm, fair. Heavy rain the nineteenth. Western Great Lakes have thunderstorm potential the fourteenth. East sees severe thunderstorms the seventeenth. **Zone 6:** Western area has chance of showers. Gusty winds and potential thunderstorms the eighteenth. East has gusty winds, thunderstorms the fourteenth. Increasing temperatures, atmospheric disturbance, and potential for heavy rain seventeenth and nineteenth. **Zone 7:** Western area has chance of showers. Gusty winds and potential thunderstorms the eighteenth. East has gusty winds, thunderstorms the fourteenth. Increasing temperatures, atmospheric disturbance, and potential for heavy rain seventeenth and nineteenth. **Zone 8:** Alaska: West has showers interspersed with gusty winds and thunderstorms. Central sees rise in humidity, showers. Warmer, atmospheric disturbance the seventeenth. East sees energetic storms, gusty winds the thirteenth and between the seventeenth and nineteenth. Hawaii: Generally fair. However, windy conditions, possible thunderstorms thirteenth to fifteenth.

2nd Quarter Moon, November 20–27

Zone 1: Zone is warm, fair, chance of rain the twenty-second, then cloudy, cooler, some precipitation. Strong thunderstorms push eastward. Mid-Atlantic has precipitation the twenty-seventh. **Zone 2:** Mid-Atlantic is warm, fair. Zone is warmer, showers the twenty-second. Stronger thunderstorms the twenty-fifth. Possible showers the twenty-seventh. **Zone 3:** West is warm, fair, temperatures increase, possible thunderstorms push eastward through zone the twenty-second. West is fair, moderate winds the twenty-fifth. Central sees thunderstorms the twenty-second, otherwise fair with moderate winds. **Zone 4:** West is warmer, chance of rain. Cooler, strong thunderstorms the twenty-second. Cool, fair the twenty-sixth, then cloudy, precipitation. Central is warm, fair. East is warm, fair, chance of thunderstorms the twenty-second. **Zone 5:** West is warmer, chance of rain. Cooler, strong thunderstorms the twenty-second. Cool, fair the twenty-sixth, then cloudy, precipitation. Central is warm, fair. East is warm, fair, chance of thunderstorms the twenty-second. **Zone 6:** West is stormy, cooler temperatures. East is generally cool, cloudy, and rainy. **Zone 7:** West is stormy, cooler temperatures. East is generally cool, cloudy, and rainy. **Zone 8:** Alaska: West has warmer temperatures. Chance of showers, strong thunderstorms after the twenty-first. West sees precipitation on west coast the twenty-sixth. Central and east see lower temperatures, wind, precipitation, and storms. East is cool, high pressure, some wind the twenty-fourth. Hawaii: Cooler, fair. Strong thunderstorms the twenty-fourth. Afterward, some wind, possible thunderstorms the twenty-sixth.

Full Moon, November 27–December 5
Zone 1: Mid-Atlantic has lower temperatures, cloudy, rainy. New England is cooler with rainy conditions, then warm, dry. **Zone 2:** East Coast front brings precipitation along the coast. North has lower temperatures, cloudy, rainy. Central sees possible rain. Central and south are warm, cloudy the thirtieth, then a chance of rain on the third. **Zone 3:** South has rain, wind the first to third. East is warm, cloudy the thirtieth. Rainy the third. **Zone 4:** West is cloudy, rainy, then a brief warm-up. Windy, rainy weather the first. Central sees wind, rain the first. East sees possible severe thunderstorms around the western Great Lakes. Stormy conditions the second. **Zone 5:** West is cloudy, rainy, then a brief warm-up. Windy, rainy weather on the first. Central has rainy weather the twenty-seventh, then wind and rain potential the

first. East sees stormy conditions on the second. **Zone 6:** West is cloudy, rainy then fair (thirtieth). Wind, rain conditions, lower temperatures the first. Wind, rain the fourth. East is rainy, then becoming fair, lower temperatures on the second. A chance of rain the fourth. **Zone 7:** West is cloudy, rainy then fair (thirtieth). Wind, rain conditions, lower temperatures the first. Wind, rain the fourth. East is rainy, then becoming fair, lower temperatures on the second. A chance of rain the fourth. **Zone 8:** Alaska: West is predominately cloudy, rainy with a couple of fair days. East is like west with stronger atmospheric disturbance the thirtieth. Hawaii: A chance of rain. Generally cool and dry. Possible showers the third.

4th Quarter Moon, December 5–12

Zone 1: Mid-Atlantic is cool, fair, then southerly winds, increased rainfall. New England is fair, possible showers. Chance of showers and thunderstorms the twelfth. **Zone 2:** North is cool, fair, then southerly winds, increased rainfall. South sees rising temperatures, some wind. **Zone 3:** West has increasing temperatures, possible showers. Strong thunderstorms the eleventh, which may move over central and eastern areas. East sees rise in temperatures, some wind. Eastern Great Lakes have potential low pressure the ninth. **Zone 4:** West has southerly winds, precipitation. Central is warmer, cloudy, brief showers. East is warmer, possible thundershowers. Severe around the eleventh. **Zone 5:** West has southerly winds, precipitation. Central is warmer, cloudy, brief showers. East is warmer, possible thundershowers. Severe around the eleventh. **Zone 6:** West is generally fair. Possible gusty thunderstorms the eleventh. East sees increasing moisture, resulting in precipitation. Period ends fair. **Zone 7:** West is generally fair. Possible gusty thunderstorms the eleventh. East sees increasing moisture, resulting in precipitation. Period ends fair. **Zone 8:** Alaska: West is generally fair, then rainfall. Stormy the eleventh, especially over the Aleutian Islands. Central is warmer, cloudy, brief showers, then stormier by the twelfth. East is fair. Slight chance of rain the ninth. Hawaii: Generally fair, chance of rain. Temperatures decline the tenth, with possible showers or thunderstorms.

New Moon, December 12–19

Zone 1: Mid-Atlantic is warmer, precipitation especially by sixteenth. New England sees increasing chance of rain, then fair. **Zone 2:** Rising temperatures. Precipitation, especially around the sixteenth. South sees windy conditions or gusty thunderstorms. **Zone 3:** Zone, generally, sees acute westerly to southwesterly winds, possible thunderstorms. West and south have possible severe, windy storms the sixteenth, then warm and dry. North is windy and rainy the sixteenth. **Zone 4:** West is generally rainy, then colder, windy after the thirteenth. Low pressure the seventeenth. Central has lower temperatures, cloudy, rainy. Windy the fifteenth. East is windy, then severe storms the sixteenth. Warm, dry the eighteenth. **Zone 5:** West is generally rainy. Strong winds the fifteenth. Central sees lower temperatures, cloudy, some possible heavy rain, especially over Texas and Oklahoma. East is windy, then severe storms the sixteenth. Warm, dry the eighteenth. **Zone 6:** West, major storm system affects coast, then generally rainy. East is generally rainy. Windy the fifteenth. **Zone 7:** West, major storm system affects coast, then generally rainy. East is generally rainy. Windy the fifteenth. **Zone 8:** Alaska: Zone is mostly rainy. West and central have wind the fifteenth. West and east see strong, windy storms the seventeenth. Hawaii: Generally rainy. Acute winds, especially around the fifteenth.

2nd Quarter Moon, December 19–26

Zone 1: Mid-Atlantic cold fronts generate showers. New England is fair, increasing temperatures. Strong cold front or low pressure, precipitation, wind the twenty-first. Continuing cold and unsettled. **Zone 2:** Zone has possible thunderstorms the nineteenth.

North has possible showers. South is fair. Chance of rain the twenty-fourth. **Zone 3:** Zone is generally cool, fair. Possible showers the twentieth. South sees slight chance of showers. West has a chance of showers the twenty-third. Rising temperatures, fair the twenty-fifth. **Zone 4:** West is generally fair, then rising temperatures, thunderstorms, especially around the twenty-second. Central and east see intense winter storms, especially around the twenty-second. Possible strong Christmas storm bringing wind and precipitation. **Zone 5:** West is generally fair, then rising temperatures, thunderstorms, especially around the twenty-second. Central and east see intense winter storms, especially around the twenty-second. Possible strong Christmas storm bringing wind and precipitation. **Zone 6:** West sees possible showers, then fair. East sees rising temperatures, fair with a slight chance of thunderstorms. **Zone 7:** West sees possible showers, then fair. East sees rising temperatures, fair with a slight chance of thunderstorms. **Zone 8:** Alaska: West and central are generally fair and dry. Winter storm potential west on the twenty-second. East has rising temperatures, then precipitation and lower temperatures. Increasing temperatures and fair conditions the twenty-fifth. Hawaii: Unsettled conditions bring the chance of rain and windy conditions.

Full Moon, December 26–January 3, 2024

Zone 1: Mid-Atlantic sees low pressure, cloudy, rainy, chilly then zone is cold and fair. **Zone 2:** Zone has strong thunderstorms, sharp winds the twenty-seventh. North and central are cloudy, rainy, chilly the thirty-first. South is warm, breezy the twenty-ninth, then low pressure, rain, and colder temperatures. **Zone 3:** Zone is warm, breezy the twenty-ninth. Cloudy, rainy, and colder the thirty-first. **Zone 4:** West is generally warm, pleasant with an invigorating atmosphere, minimal chance of rain. Central and east see thunderstorms, sharp winds the twenty-seventh, then showers the thirtieth. Period ends with a front that triggers showers throughout zone. **Zone 5:** West is generally warm, pleasant with an invigorating atmosphere, minimal chance of rain. Central and east see thunderstorms, sharp winds the twenty-seventh, then showers the thirtieth. Period ends with a front that triggers showers throughout zone. **Zone 6:** West is warmer, pleasant. Precipitation over coastal areas the thirty-first. East is warm, pleasant, chance of showers the twenty-eighth. **Zone 7:** West is warmer, pleasant. Precipitation over coastal areas the thirty-first. East is warm, pleasant, chance of showers the twenty-eighth. **Zone 8:** Alaska: West has potential thunderstorms, sharp winds the twenty-seventh, then warmer and breezy the twenty-ninth. Cloudy, chilly with rain the thirty-first then cold and fair. Central and east see rising temperatures, squally storms the twenty-seventh then chance of showers. Hawaii: Generally warm. Stormy conditions and sharp winds are shown around the twenty-seventh. Period ends fair with declining temperatures.

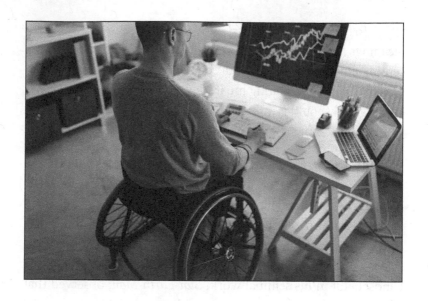

Economic Forecast for 2023

Christeen Skinner

Active investors will surely find navigating the planetary currents of 2023 challenging. In 2023, the Moon spends several days each month "out of bounds": a factor likely to contribute to wild fluctuation in prices. "Out of bounds" means that declination exceeds that of the Sun, whose maximum at the summer and winter solstice is either 23' 27° north or south. An "out of bounds" Moon brings great waves of emotion, which, in the trading world, leads to great highs and lows in prices. In 2023, Mars, too, reaches out-of-bounds status, adding to the probability of traders and investors experiencing a wild ride.

Astrologers study previous alignments and positions of the planets to make forecasts based on the probability of history repeating. Today, they face fresh challenges with the discovery of new planetary bodies. Whereas astrologers of long ago developed meanings for the visible fixed stars, astrologers of the twenty-first century are learning more about the influence of black holes, quasars, and more. Integrating lunar phases with this new material is exciting and should improve forecasting.

The Sun

There is a recognized rhythm or pulse to solar activity. These cycles are numbered, and in 2023, we should be amidst Cycle 25. Yet the length of a solar cycle can vary between nine and fourteen years. Maximum solar activity is expected in 2025 but could arrive earlier with recent estimates suggesting it could arrive in 2024—or even possibly 2023. The great researcher Theodor Landscheidt in his seminal work, *Sun-Earth-Man*, observed that when sunspot activity is at maxima, then so, too, is commercial activity (Landscheidt, 1989, n.p.).

In 2020, a major alignment in Capricorn placed many of the known planets on one side of the Sun. Though the distribution of the planets around the Sun has since altered, several slow-moving planetary bodies remain on one side of the Sun. This suggests a "pull" on our special star that influences its cycles, perhaps even speeding climate change and affecting global economies.

"Old" Planets

Until 1781, the known solar system ended with Saturn. It is unsurprising that, astrologically speaking, Saturn is the "planet of boundaries" and that the planet "discovered" in 1781, Uranus, is considered to be the "disruptor or tearer down of all structures and ideas that are thought-limiting." If Saturn represents tradition and continuity, then Uranus represents freedom, future thinking, and discontinuity. Certainly, Uranus's discovery was exciting. Once added to horoscopes, astrologers quickly determined it to be the "planet of shocks and surprises." Uranus brings deviation from the norm and—at times—financial mayhem. (Witness the 2008 September Full Moon when Uranus aligned with the Moon. Lehman Brothers collapsed and the world experienced financial shock.)

Astrologers were faced with decoding the influence of Neptune in 1846 when its orbit was identified. Neptune at times appears to have a negligible effect, but at other times brings confusion: prices and indices have inflated when the Moon is aligned with this planet only to collapse later.

In 1930, when astronomers determined the presence of Pluto, astrologers again ran research projects, concluding that Pluto, too, had influence. Pluto is viewed as god of the underworld but also of wealth—and of commodities, especially rare earth metals. Indeed, amongst other factors, the Venus-Pluto cycle correlates with a rhythm in the gold price.

In the last few decades, the orbits of more planets or, more accurately, minor planets and asteroids have been calculated. Financial astrologers are comparing and scrutinizing the orbits of these and slowly reaching a consensus as to the "effect" or influence of these planetary bodies.

Financial astrologers have long noted that the ingress (entry of a planet into a new sign) of slower-moving planets has coincided with obvious ripples and altered direction in global financial markets. For example: Pluto's most recent ingress (Capricorn in 2008) coincided with the global financial crash whilst Neptune's (Pisces ingress, 2011) coincided with the credit rating downgrade of America's sovereign debt; Neptune is associated with loss).

Uranus's eighty-four-year ingresses also appear to have influence. As viewed from Earth, Uranus made entry into Taurus twice (in May 2018 and March 2019). Between the two dates, Uranus retrograded back into fire-sign Aries. This suggested the probability of unexpectedly extreme turbulence—as proved to be the case. The Dow Jones experienced its worst Christmas Eve (2018) on record. In typical Uranus (surprise) fashion, it rebounded by the next December.

With several planetary bodies making ingress in 2023, there is a high probability of sea changes in global financial affairs bringing extreme turbulence to global markets.

Dominating the ingress list is Pluto's Aquarius ingress on March 23. Pluto's influence is to "pull the rug." It exposes all that is rotten or toxic, requiring complete overhaul or repair before successful rebuild. At the global financial crisis in 2007, it was subprime mortgages and the banking sector (Capricorn-related areas) that were most affected.

In 2023, attention will be on endeavours linked to the sign of Aquarius. These include mutual funds and cooperative banking together with the reinsurance industry. Those born under Aquarius are often involved in group activities where there is shared interest—very often political. Just who is funding which political groups—and how—will surely come under scrutiny. As Pluto is the planet most associated with power, we should expect news stories exposing corruption and malign influence in the sectors listed. To be clear, just as the banking sector suffered in 2007–2008, with some banks failing entirely, we should anticipate the collapse of some (but not all) hedge funds, bond markets, insurance giants, and cooperative ventures.

Just as important are the declination cycles of the Moon and planets. In January 2023, Jupiter moves from south to north declination. (A similar pattern can be found in 2010–2011, when indices made a fast recovery following the global financial crash but offered a roller coaster ride to investors in the process.)

As it does at each of these crossings, Jupiter will be moving through Aries as it crosses from south to north. It is perhaps unsurprising that when Jupiter made a similar move in 2010–2011, many new and pioneering companies came into existence. These businesses were formed by those who had lost their posi-

tions in the aftermath of the global financial crash. In 2023, it is likely to be those who were displaced as a result of the pandemic whose entrepreneurial talents will surface, and it is entirely possible that these start-ups—as with many of those incorporated in 2011—will realize quick profit.

Again, as in 2011, in 2023, Jupiter moves first through Aries and on into Taurus. Sectors associated with these two signs should show signs of development. Though it may be a little too late to invest in the Aries sector (which rules all things sharp and includes armaments), the Taurus sector should be given due consideration,

"New" Planets

The so-called "new" or dwarf planets or planetoids have been in orbit for millennia. They are only "new" in the sense that they are recently discovered.

Sedna's Gemini Ingress 2023

Sedna spends more than half a century in each sign. It moved into Taurus in the mid-'60s: a period recognized as being a time of political, social, and economic upheaval. In Inuit culture, one of Sedna's myths is that she was a very hungry baby who threatened the lives of her parents. They tried to drown her, but she survived to live as a sea goddess. It may be that Sedna's Gemini ingress creates financial waves that will threaten even the most stable of financial vessels.

The last Sedna ingress—in the mid-'60s—coincided with the development of hire purchase and other credit agreements, which grew at such speed that they threatened existing financial systems. Certainly, prior to this ingress, the emphasis was on "saving first and buying later." Mortgages were not readily available. The reverse became the norm after this ingress: people bought first and paid—with interest—later. Financial systems were overwhelmed by demand for credit and expanded exponentially to cope with the demand.

As Sedna moves to Gemini, systems may be overwhelmed by an expanding foreign exchange system that incorporates cryptocurrencies. Foreign exchange dealers will surely experience a wild, wild ride.

Sedna's Gemini ingress from September 2023, coupled with Pluto's Aquarius (another air sign) ingress adds to the probability of the birth or emergence of many new financial ideas—some of which may be so complex that they are understood by few.

Ixion

Ixion is another of the "newly discovered" planets. Ixion doesn't make ingress in 2023 but, as it is still in early degrees of Capricorn (it made this ingress in 2020–2021), it will likely be a contributing factor in bringing rough financial seas. Whilst much was made of the extraordinary stellium in Capricorn in January 2020, and which presaged the extraordinary challenges of 2020–2021, it was also true through this period that Bitcoin, Ethereum, and a host of other digital currencies gained influence. Dwarf planet

Ixion has gained a somewhat negative reputation. It has prominence in the charts of those who display obvious rebelliousness or who are associated with chaos and apparent unthinkingness, and who have little respect for tradition or even the law.

In the chart for the March New Moon, which coincides with the equinox, Mercury (planet of commerce) and Ixion are within a degree of right angle to one another. Disruption to trade seems inevitable, and it is not inconceivable that this will manifest as severe disturbance on currency exchanges and impact international bank trade.

Haumea Ingress 2023

Haumea made its first crossing into Scorpio on November 13, 2022, and through 2023 hovers on the boundary of Libra-Scorpio.

Just as the world will be adjusting to Ixion's recent ingress, so, too, we must learn to work with Haumea operating at Scorpio rather than Libra frequency. Initial studies indicate Haumea is linked to "abundance or lack thereof" (Kientz, 2015, n.p.). It is more than a little interesting that it is prominently placed in the charts of those who show philanthropic tendency. Philanthropy requires that there must be need before the giver gives. It is a form of alliance.

As Haumea passes through Scorpio—one of the four signs most associated with finance and where the accent is on partnership, shared responsibility, and deep, deep commitment—we should expect to see the polarization of "haves and have-nots." In the months when Haumea is in sharp aspect to the New, quarter, or Full Moon positions, this division will likely be marked. We should also expect threats to dissolve or break off inequitable agreements—with considerable consequence on stock markets across the world. This may be particularly apparent at the solar eclipse in October when Haumea conjoins Mars—then traveling through the sign it "rules": Scorpio.

Eris

Another key dwarf planet is Eris, which has a similar nature to Pluto but with an orbit over twice as long. Eris does not make an ingress in 2023 but is included in this study as, whilst moving slowly through Aries, it is holding long-term right-angle to Pluto (travelling through another of the cardinal signs, Capricorn). So far, this square aspect has coincided with the menace of—and sometimes actual—trade war. Looking ahead to the lunar phases of 2023, we find this square has prominence on several occasions. The Moon could be considered the "trigger," bringing with it the potential for weeks of chaotic commerce.

Tempests

As must now surely be clear, the ingresses of Pluto, Sedna, Ixion, and Haumea—all within months of one another—suggest threatening crosscurrents that destabilize the safest of financial vessels. Storms will likely be tempestuous. The financial rhythms will undoubtedly emerge a few years later, when each of these planets is firmly transiting the "new" sign and will require navigational skills quite different to those employed in the past. We will each need new financial lifeboats and may need to learn a new financial language. Just as derivatives were gaining increased popularity as Sedna made ingress in 1966, new terminology is likely to emerge with each ingress.

Eclipses

It is not difficult to conclude that 2023 will be a year of acutely fluctuating fortunes. Yet despite the financial rocks (ingresses) that lie ahead, it may not be a wholly "bad" year for inactive investors, i.e., those who choose to "hold" and so do not make frequent trades. Certainly, if investors might reflect back on years with similar eclipse activity, they will surely be encouraged to stay their trading hands. Eclipses repeat every nineteen years, and these investors, reviewing 2004, would see that the Dow Jones Index rose over 3 percent and the S&P was at 9 percent. So, whilst the planetary formations around the eclipses of 2023 suggest difficulty, indices could still rise.

The solar eclipse on April 20 occurs just before the Sun makes Taurus ingress. At 29° Aries, this special New Moon is within a few degrees of Jupiter (23° Aries) and at first glance appears to have benign influence. However, we must note that it is also within orb of the square aspect between Eris and Pluto and that Jupiter will then be in north declination. These factors together represent a potentially terrific force that could manifest as Earth movement (volcanic activity, etc.) or, at the level of human emotion, in volatile trading or war.

The path of exactitude of this eclipse begins off the west coast of Australia and carries through to Papua New Guinea. It will be partly visible from New Zealand through to Kuala Lumpur. It would not be abnormal for there to be shifts in political thinking through these areas and for this to lead to new trading arrangements.

This eclipse—with the Sun and Moon conjoining the lunar north node—is part of Saros Cycle 7, a series of eclipses that began in October 1103 (Brady, 1999, 317). The most striking feature of the initial eclipse chart of this series is Pluto's position on the Venus-Mars midpoint. Astrologers look to the first in any series of eclipses as offering a "genetic code" that lasts through the entire series. Venus and Mars may be thought of as the "relationship" pairing, and Pluto's presence at this midpoint suggests deep-rooted passions.

The most recent solar eclipse of this series took place in 2005 when tech sector investment deals rose by 75 percent to $340 billion. It seems reasonable to anticipate a similar trend in 2023 and that the greatest trading news will come from the Southern Hemisphere.

It should also be noted that with asteroid Hygeia—then travelling through Aquarius—prominently placed through Australia in

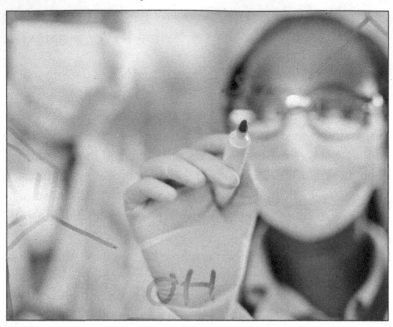

the geodetic chart for this eclipse, health issues on that continent will make headline news. One possibility is that it will be break-throughs by researchers (Aquarius) in Australia that leads to the development of new drugs to combat disease or further decoding of the human genome. It would surely be worthwhile researching the initial public offerings (IPOs) to be listed on the Sydney Stock exchange in the first quarter of 2023. Obviously much depends on the actual time and date of the offering, but companies coming to market following this eclipse could do very well indeed.

This eclipse is followed just two weeks later by a lunar eclipse on May 5 with the Sun and Moon at 14° Taurus-Scorpio respec-tively and with Mars at 13° Cancer—the degree held by the Sun in the chart for the US. A lunar eclipse across this finance-associated Taurus-Scorpio axis suggests the likelihood of strong market reac-tion. Activating the Sun in the chart for the US draws attention to the financial affairs of that nation and to the US dollar.

Mundane Astrology

There are charts or horoscopes for countries. Though the land we know as America existed long before independence was declared, there is acknowledged sensitivity to the zodiacal positions held by the planets in July 1776. Pluto is only now returning to the position held in that chart.

Not every country has been in existence long enough to experience its Pluto return. William the Conqueror was crowned King of England on Christmas Day in 1066. It is fascinating to note that Pluto returned to this area of the zodiac in 1801, when the present-day chart for the United Kingdom came into being. It is not unreasonable to suppose that the United States will experience some form of rejuvenation as Pluto returns to its 1776 position: 27° Capricorn. We should expect this to have singular impact on America's wealth—effecting the value of the US dollar against a basket of other currencies.

The horoscope for the solar eclipse on October 14 shows Mars at 1° Scorpio conjoining Haumea at 0° of that same sign. As was noted earlier, research suggests Haumea is a powerful force—at times bringing abundance and at other times lack. The extreme nature of this minor planet and its proximity to Mars in Scorpio suggests sharp divides between "haves and have-nots" that could so easily lead to war. Added to this, Eris—in Mars-ruled Aries—is exactly conjoined to the north node and still in square to Pluto, increasing the potential for confrontation.

The central path of this October solar eclipse runs from Brazil through Colombia, Mexico, and the US and will be partly visible through much of South America and Canada: areas which might be susceptible to earth movement and increased friction at both the trading and military level.

This solar eclipse is part of the Saros south node Cycle 7, which, like the north version, carries a Pluto overtone: this time linked with just Mars (without the Venus influence as at the April eclipse). Mars and Pluto are the rulers of Scorpio: a sign associated with high finance and collaboration. Financial astrologers expect to see mergers and alliances made quickly (Mars and Pluto represent fast furnace heat). But yes, this planetary combination can also be seen as a "fighting force," accenting the possibility of violent disruption (war), currency turmoil, or both.

Any eclipse accenting the Taurus-Scorpio axis puts focus on finance. With Mars, the energizer, in Scorpio (a sign that it rules and in which it is thought to work especially well), it is reasonable to expect aggressive commercial activity. Mars will be exact on the midheaven in Havana, Cuba, at the solar eclipse, whilst Neptune will be on the ascendant in New York at the lunar eclipse as Venus sets in Miami.

These planetary pictures suggest intense financial activity along the Eastern Seaboard of the United States, possibly, but not exclusively, including severe hurricanes causing devastation and privation to citizens and leading eventually to massive losses on Wall Street when insurance costs are finally calculated. Yet natural calamity is not the only possibility. The Venus-Neptune link must surely include the transfer of "drug money" or fraud on a fantastic scale.

First Quarter

Haumea makes Scorpio ingress in the fourth quarter of 2022, likely bringing turbulence that develops markedly by the Full Moon on January 6. Jupiter, which has a track record for bringing storms as well as excitement, will then be in 150° relationship to Haumea, potentially prompting panic as storms become tempests—especially with Haumea at right angle to Pluto. A strong possibility is that bond markets will come under significant pressure. Indeed, before Pluto crosses into Aquarius, there may be indicators of collapse in this sector.

The potential for fast-flowing financial currents is increased given that between the January 2023 Full and New Moons, Jupiter moves from south to north declination. These declination crossings, together with the Moon's out-of-bounds position, indicates the potential for extreme reaction manifesting as volatility.

Financial astrologers noted that the 2020 conjunction of Jupiter and Saturn was the first in a series spanning over two centuries that would each occur in air signs. Aquarius is thought of as futuristic and scientific. It was expected that the first of these cycles would see businesses working in the fields of artificial intelligence, robotics, and space age technology quickly advance. The two planets conjoined in 2020 at 1° Aquarius—the exact degree of the New Moon on January 21, 2023. Investors should be on alert for a growth spurt in companies launched since December 2020. This New Moon could see these move to their next stage—possibly moving toward IPO.

The phase (angular relationship or aspect) between Jupiter and Saturn yields clues as to how the cycle has developed. In this first quarter of 2023, the two planets are moving first toward the benign 30° angle and then to 45°: the division of a circle by eight. The latter is viewed as a critical phase when, commercially, the desire to expand is restricted—usually by fear of rising costs and the threat of inflation. (We should note that inflation is unlikely to be a serious issue until Neptune moves into Aries in 2026).

It is not only the "hard" aspect between Jupiter and Saturn that indicates potential trading difficulty in this first quarter of the year. We know that an ingress coincides with alteration in global financial rhythm and should expect this to be felt again in March as Saturn moves into Pisces. By the last quarter Moon on March 14, Jupiter and Saturn will be 45° apart: as set out above, an acknowledged critical point in the cycle. By then, Mars, the energizer, will be out of bounds—another cosmic clue for out-of-the-ordinary trading behaviour and volatility.

This is followed by a New Moon on March 20 at the equinox. This is a special New Moon in that it is on the world axis: the first degree of a cardinal sign. In this chart, Venus conjoins the north node. We should expect to hear news of a major proposed merger or alliance that has global implications. This would doubtless send indices higher. Yet just a week later, as the Sun reaches 8° Aries, this deal could hit the rocks.

The critical actor here is that as this merger reaches the final stage before announcement, Jupiter, too, crosses 8° Aries. Not all degrees of the zodiac are equal, and it can be shown that planets have been transiting this degree at highly eventful periods in financial history. Jupiter's transit of 8° Aries takes place at the last quarter Moon on February 13, coinciding with the conjunction of the Sun and Saturn and the Moon's passage through Scorpio. This is unlikely to be a happy day for markets generally and should be viewed as "writing on the wall" ahead of likely decline at the end of March.

Currency markets, too, are likely to experience turmoil in this quarter. The New Moon on February 20 finds Jupiter at the exact midpoint between Vesta (the trader's asteroid) and Chiron (the corrector). By the last quarter Moon on March 14, Jupiter is exactly conjoined with Vesta and Saturn (Saturn will have made Pisces ingress). The expertise of foreign exchange traders will doubtless be tested to the full—notably where the "new" cryptocurrencies are concerned. It seems likely that a dramatic fall in their value could come around March 15 and echo again in the days following the second quarter Moon on March 28.

Second Quarter

Jupiter and Haumea, at opposite ends of the zodiac, make ingress (Jupiter moving into Taurus whilst Haumea moves back into Libra) this quarter. This suggests considerable potential for increasingly large financial waves, most likely driven by the threat of war.

The New and Full Moons of April through early June are the first for over two hundred years to include Pluto in Aquarius, so no one living today has experience of this dynamic. These conditions will likely lead to erratic behaviour as humankind adjusts to this new vibration. Of course, this does not have to be negative. There is high probability of panic, however, which in turn would surely lead to huge swings in market values.

There is particular potential for negative reaction at the Full Moon on April 6, when Chiron is within a few degrees of the solar position. This planetoid is often prominently placed at times of market correction. Accepting that the various ingresses of 2023 point to turbulence, it is not unreasonable to suppose that indices will fall should traders deduce further difficulties ahead. This may be particularly true in the Far East. Study of the Hang Seng Index shows it to turn downward when Saturn is moving through a mutable sign. Saturn will have entered mutable Pisces in March.

The possibility of negative reaction is increased by Mars "out of bounds" in Cancer: a status that is maintained through the solar eclipse on April 20. A maverick Mars in a sign noted for husbandry is indicative of investors withdrawing from markets and turning to what they perceive to be safe havens (property, gold, silver, etc.). Haumea opposes the degree of the eclipse while Neptune lies at right angle to the Galactic Center. Might this represent a sudden financial slope that takes all by surprise and exaggerates again the gulf between those who have and those who have not?

By the solar eclipse, Venus, too, is out of bounds: yet another factor pointing to unusual behaviour. Aside from the potential for breakdown in alliances, it might also be that "unholy" alliances are formed: factors that contribute to market mayhem.

It is not unusual for there to be a change in trend at the halfway point between equinox and solstice. In 2023, on May 5, there is a Full Moon—in this case also a lunar eclipse, with the Sun in orb of Uranus within twenty-four hours of the event. Venus, the solar ruler of this Taurus-Scorpio lunation, reaches maximum declination and Jupiter, the "exaggerator," is by then in Venus-ruled Taurus. This planetary picture suggests sudden and extreme moves—and should bring a particularly wild ride to those trading in Venus-ruled copper. We must note, too, that Mars will be in near exact opposition to Pluto, adding to the argument that not only might there be "warmongering," but that there will be significantly high levels of market activity.

The planetary picture is not much improved by the Taurus New Moon on May 19. In this chart, Jupiter in Taurus is square to Pluto—usually indicative of a wealth crisis—whilst the lunation itself is within 150° (quincunx) Haumea: the total picture contributing to a scene of wild fluctuation in prices, inferring perilous conditions for the day trader.

The value of precious metals, gems, and jewels will surely gain value around the June solstice. Reaction to this chart, with Ixion opposing the Sun (itself in mutual reception with the Moon and so requiring us to think also of Moon opposing Ixion) may be extreme, prompting many to turn to what they perceive to be the safer havens of gold, silver, and other precious commodities. The potential for this reaction is further enhanced by Vesta moving to conjoin Sedna with both in trine to Ceres.

Third Quarter

In 2023, it will be a quarter of a century since the Russian ruble crisis of 1998, and few present-day currency traders will have this earlier experience. Turmoil in currency markets is to be expected in this third quarter of 2023. Clues as to how challenging these markets will be should be apparent at the New Moon on July 17 when the lunation is within orb of opposition to Pluto—itself within orb of the US's Pluto return. The value of the US dollar could be severely impacted.

Just a few days later, on July 23, both Venus and Chiron arrive at retrograde stations. Both turn retrograde in fire signs with Chiron stationing at the critical 19° of cardinal sign Aries. As has been noted, the 19° of cardinal signs is often occupied at times of financial crisis: in this instance, likely to mark a correction.

Venus stations on the Neptune-Pluto midpoint and in hard aspect to the degree held by the Sun on July 4, 1776. This may not be the easiest of days for the US dollar, which could come under extreme pressure.

Pluto squares the lunar nodes at the Full Moon on August 1. Coincidentally, Jupiter (think extremes) in Taurus squares the Leo-Aquarius Full Moon, holding degrees accentuated in 2021 when Saturn and Uranus came to the last quarter phase of their cycle, suggesting major difficulty. It is entirely possible that the true cost of dealing with the pandemic of 2020–2021 will be apparent and perhaps even magnified by Jupiter's position.

There are two Full Moons in August 2023. The second, on the second-to-last day of the month, aligns with Saturn in Pisces. As noted earlier, this is not the easiest of placements for Asian markets, which will likely experience downturn.

Haumea and Ceres are in exact conjunction at 29° Libra at the New Moon on September 14. This suggests a picture of "earth in upheaval," the upside of which providing fertile ground on which young companies thrive. With Uranus in trine to the lunation, there is scope for companies offering support to infrastructure projects—including those involved in space industries—to show significant gain.

Fourth Quarter

Eclipses are each part of a sequence against which the planetary background is ever-changing. The Libra solar eclipse on October 14 is made special by virtue of Jupiter's opposition to Ceres, which simultaneously squares Hygiea. Though we know there to be at least forty-two asteroids orbiting between Mars and Jupiter, Ceres and Hygiea hold prominence. Each can be shown to correlate with cycles involving soil (Ceres) and health (Hygeia).

Accelerated climate change has been of major concern for several decades. In this quarter of the year, expect for there to be clamor for businesses and countries to be legally bound (Jupiter) to make alteration to their sourcing and general systems.

This theme should be heard even more loudly at the Full Moon just two weeks after the solar eclipse. This lunation at 11° Taurus-Scorpio shares a similar degree to the recent Saturn-Uranus last quarter phase. Enforcement of agreements reached at the COP26 conference in November 2021 and threat of harsh penalties for those businesses and countries that have since reneged should be headline news.

This is a continuing theme at both the New Moon with stellium in Scorpio on November 13 when ultimatums are given, and at the Full Moon on November 27 when Ceres, then in Sagittarius (legal matters) forms right angle to Saturn in Pisces. Attention may then be on the world's oceans and a major cleanup operation. Obviously, it will be necessary to check the fundamentals of companies working in this area, but it could yet be that investing in this area yields positive results.

The December 2023 lunations are no less interesting, but this time feature Ixion: the dwarf planet associated with lawlessness and chaos. Ixion opposes the trader's asteroid, Vesta, at the December 12 New Moon: once again drawing attention to currency markets and, most probably, difficulties with cryptocurrencies.

Pluto's retrograde return to Capricorn in this last quarter of 2023 could bring a last gasp by "traditional" banks and systems as they attempt to avoid inevitable reset. With Mercury retrograde within conjunction of the Galactic Center, however, there may be many who wish to return to what they perceive to be the safer havens of precious metals (gold, etc.). It should be apparent though that there can be no return to "old" ways of working given that Ixion in Capricorn is aligned with the Full Moon on December 26.

In Summary

There is high probability of Asian market indices turning downward as Saturn moves into Pisces in 2023. If the past is indeed indicative of the future, then the eclipse alignments of 2023 are positive for Western market indices, which should fare relatively well. A volatile year in forex markets—particularly within the crypto arena is probable. Blockchain technology will affect every area of human endeavour by 2023, and investors would surely be well advised to learn more about developments in this area.

References

Brady, Bernadette. *Predictive Astrology: The Eagle and the Lark.* York
    Beach, ME: Samuel Weiser, 1999.
Kientz, Sue. *More Plutos.* Indianapolis, IN: Dog Ear Publishing, 2015.
Landscheidt, Theodor. *Sun-Earth-Man.* The Urania Turst, 1989.

New and Full Moon Forecasts for 2023

Sally Cragin

Recently, my youngest child, who is on the cusp of adolescence, took an interest in the phases of the Moon. I got them (Jet is female but prefers "they/them" pronouns) a Moon sign calendar. Sometime in the summer, they began to put glass jars of water on the windowsill as the Moon waxed toward full.

"I'm making Moon juice!" Jet declared happily, adding crystals to their liquids.

We should all make "Moon juice" as best we are able as the Moon makes her wonderfully predictable path across the night skies. Consider this: the earth takes one day to make a rotation, but the Moon takes 29.5 days, which is about the same amount of time it takes to revolve around the earth. (The earth rotates at about 1,000 miles per hour, whereas the Moon's rotational speed clocks in at about 10 miles per hour. A fast runner could easily outpace the Moon!)

Luna's slow and stately—mostly nighttime—waltz means the same side of the Moon is always turned toward us. So when the Moon is full, we are seeing the same craters, mariae, and other lunar features month after month. As a matter of fact, when the Moon is full, it beams an impressive amount of light our way. Have you ever tried to read by the light of the Full Moon? It can be done.

However, the phases we see more of are the crescent and quarter phases as the Moon goes from new to first quarter, to full to last quarter, back to new. Did you ever notice how a crescent Moon doesn't seem quite as bright as a Full Moon? Sure, the phase has much less of the Moon's surface illuminated but, in fact, the Moon during first or last quarter has only one-sixth the amount of brightness of a Full Moon. During a Full Moon, the rays of the sun bounce off the full face of the Moon, thus making a more radiant celestial object.

However, you should be able to see the craters and pitted surface of the Moon during that crescent phase. "The man in the moon" is usually depicted as a quarter Moon—the man in profile. However, most of the ancients, particularly the Greeks, always saw the Moon as feminine. The Moon symbolizes Artemis, goddess of the hunt, and if women are more tuned in to the Moon—look no futher than our biology plus etymology. "Mene" means the moon as well as the lunar month, thus the word *menstrual*.

As you read these forecasts, consider skipping ahead. All twelve signs are mentioned during every New and Full Moon entry, along with other astrological events of interest. And now, let's raise a cup of Moon juice and toast the new year: 2023!

Friday, January 6, Full Moon in Cancer

The Cancer Moon brings out the desire to be *Gemültlichkeit* ("cozy," as the Germans say). This water sign Full Moon suggests home entertainment is the way to go this weekend. Baking and massage are appealing activities. So is finding ways to make your house more comfortable. (Hammock in the office? Foot roller under your desk?) Cancer really needs to be with others right now—but others they respect, not those whom they must "explain" themselves to (retrograde Mercury, opposing your sun in Capricorn). Scorpio, Leo, Taurus, Virgo, Gemini, and Pisces: deepening intimacy will delight you—pursue! Aries, Capricorn, Aquarius, Libra, and Sagittarius: others may find your tone brusque no matter how careful you are. Use soft tones.

Saturday, January 21, New Moon in Aquarius

The next two days are excellent for combining unexpected idea elements, particularly notions involved with human resources, mass marketing, and innovation. The bright lights shine more brightly during this New Moon, and Aquarius is having excellent astrological energy for the next lunar month. Water carriers: ask for what you want—demand it when necessary (particularly those born after February 12). Libra, Gemini, Sagittarius, Capricorn, Pisces, and Aries: keep communication general but optimistic; others will respond. Leo, Virgo, Cancer, Taurus, and Scorpio: if you're being misinterpreted, you're in tune with the Moon. Have a laugh instead of building a grudge.

Sunday, February 5, Full Moon in Leo

"Shoulder to Shoulder Around the Fire Moon" (Wishram Tribe, Columbia River, Washington). Find someone to snuggle up to as the Moon and Jupiter are in sync—generous females will be repaid in spades. Leo Moons favor parties and frivolity, also children's activities. When's the last time you played cards or a board game? Socially minded Leo could be excited about a project that began in mid-January. You could be feeling "poor me" for no particular reason. Resolve any irritation by reaching out to those who adore you; Leo can be soothed by fellowship always. Gemini, Cancer, Virgo, Libra, Sagittarius, and Aries: Make connections you couldn't make late in the week—follow through Monday to Wednesday. Aquarius, Taurus, Scorpio, Capricorn, and Pisces: you may feel you're being dissed when actually there's a real mistake in communication—possibly by yourselves. Forgive and move on.

Monday, February 20, New Moon in Pisces

A fresh start for all, especially artists and those who work with special-needs children, adults, and seniors or those who are incarcerated (this includes mental illness, which is definitely imprisoning). Visual arts are favored and some folks, particularly musically minded Pisces, could "see behind the frame" of an image. Follow your gut, fishies—that will keep you safe. Wandering down memory lane can be a consolation for Scorpio, Cancer, Aquarius, Capricorn, Taurus, and Aries (nostalgia is not usually an interest for them). Virgo, Gemini, Sagittarius, Libra, and Leo: you may need to dig deeper to get the whole story from folks who are evasive.

Tuesday, March 7, Full Moon in Virgo

"Moon of the Whispering Wind" (Hopi Tribe, Arizona). The Moon is at odds with Mars (in Gemini), so male-female conversation could bring mistrust. Female-female and male-male interaction (romantic or platonic) could be satisfying and detail-oriented. Virgo: the next few days could find you at the center of everyone else's circle. If it brings you joy to "fix" their problem, jump in. Otherwise, smile diplomatically and walk backward out of the room. Taurus, Capricorn, Cancer, Leo, Libra, and Scorpio: focus on a health matter—whether it's removing some item from your diet or resting a muscle that's overworked (could include the tongue). Pisces, Gemini, Sagittarius, Aries, and Aquarius: if others are crazy fussy, they're in tune with the Moon. Let them fizz and sputter—they may save you time and trouble by stepping up.

Tuesday, March 21, New Moon in Aries

Spring equinox is "Happy New Year" for those of us who enjoy astrology, and this new year has a lot of delicious fire sign action. With Jupiter also continuing in Aries, rams born April 4 through the 10 have a boost of good luck in the next several weeks. And all rams should ask for what they need and initiate new relationships. Be bold! Aquarius, Pisces, Taurus, Gemini, Leo, and Sagittarius: moving forward is inevitable—don't hang on to the "old stuff" (relationships, patterns) that no longer work. Fresh starts for you! Libra, Cancer, Capricorn, Virgo, and Scorpio: let others say their piece—you may think your issues aren't being taken seriously if you speak first.

Thursday, April 6, Full Moon in Libra

"Moon of the Big Leaves" (Apache, Southern Plains). On the one hand, Libra Moons are excellent for seeing both sides. On the other hand, this Moon plus contrasting astrological movements (Mars making an awkward angle in Cancer) could add up to indecisiveness or a triumph of fuzzy thinking for all. However, for Libra, Mars could give you just enough juice to defy the gods, the odds, and the naysayers. Stick close to water sign friends, who are enjoying smooth passage this month. Aquarius, Gemini, Leo, Virgo, Scorpio, and Sagittarius: say it twice, say it nice, and stick to your guns. Cancer, Capricorn, Aries, Pisces, and Taurus: You may all feel a seismic shift during this Full Moon. Are you moving in the right direction? Wait until the Moon is waning, when that answer is more distinct.

Thursday, April 20, New Moon in Aries

Break out the sun lotion, remember to wear a hat outside, and take on projects that can be done quickly. It's the ram's time to shine.

Aries: from now through mid-May, the planets are arranged to show you in a highly favorable light. Take a gamble and improve your occupation or living space. Sagittarius, Leo, Taurus, Gemini, Pisces, and Aquarius: listen to your gut instinct—lingering over a problem that's not resolving brings no reward. Move forward and move quickly. Cancer, Libra, Capricorn, Virgo, and Scorpio: agitation could bowl you over—making you seem more irked than you are. Choose confidants carefully.

Friday, May 5, Full Moon in Scorpio
This Moon favors sex, spies, probate, and ill-gotten gains—in short, if your life resembles a John le Carré novel, you're in tune with the Moon! Spring flings are all around: these could range from real romantic interests to a fleeting infatuation with a warm-weather fashion that isn't usually your thing. (Apart from prisoners and Department of Public Works folks, how many of us do look fab in orange?) Scorpio: get a mission—don't bother about permission, pretend there's no supervision, and forge forward! Pisces, Cancer, Libra, Virgo, Capricorn, and Sagittarius: looking beneath the surface will be difficult but necessary—especially if workmates are in the habit of "assuming" you know everything you need to. Taurus, Aquarius, Leo, Gemini, and Aries: others may presume you're gullible. Make sure you're not.

Friday, May 19, New Moon in Taurus
The Moon, Venus, and Mars are in sync, which could make for spiciness on the romance front—especially if home cooking is involved. Taurus Moons are excellent for being possessive or calculating net worth or purchasing luxuries, particularly scarves and necklaces. Taurus: you may feel rushed—particularly by fire sign folks you know—but this is good in the long run for you. Virgo, Capricorn, Gemini, Aries, Pisces, and Cancer: be conservative, but be elegant—you'll be convincing to a new audience. Scorpio, Leo, Aquarius, Libra, and Sagittarius: others may think

you're more decided than you are. Be clear so you don't miss out on the fun field trip.

Saturday, June 3, Full Moon in Sagittarius

The Potawatomi Tribe called this the "Moon of the Turtle." Are you feeling slow? Or that you'd just as soon take a long journey on your own? Sagittarius Moons are about "getting out of Dodge" and crossing more than a few mountains. Sagittarius: you're the center of the circle—and as much as you need your independence, others may be vocal about needing *you*. Virgo, Gemini, Pisces, Cancer, or Taurus: try not to take everything seriously. Sagittarius Moons bring humor, ranging from meringue-pie-in-face to philosophical irony. Sagittarius, Leo, Aries, Scorpio, Libra, Capricorn, and Aquarius: find a different way, shake up the usual, try a different path home. The astrological elements reward the adventurous!

Sunday, June 18, New Moon in Gemini

Venus and Mars are in harmony in Leo, so love is a fiery force. Gemini Moons help us all to see both sides, and flexibility of

mind is a key to success. New Moons are about "tentative" steps and cautious optimism, although Gemini should be full steam ahead—and the chattier you are, the better. Libra, Aquarius, Taurus, Aries, Cancer, and Leo: you may be drawn to a different sort of friend—folks who aren't your usual "type" could be irresistible. Sagittarius, Pisces, Virgo, Scorpio, and Capricorn: these signs are in transition. Your usual insights may be blunted—and you'll be irked at folks you perceive as "two-faced." Be patient with yourselves.

Monday, July 3, Full Moon in Capricorn

"Moon When the Buffalo Bellow" (Omaha Tribe, central Nebraska). An excellent period for dealing with home improvement, long-term finance, and improving structures. Yes, the holiday is imminent, but work now could pay off with a delightful late-season holiday. However, folks inclined to stubbornness in your circle might indeed need to bellow—especially if you try to rush them. Capricorn—make time for long-term plans. Your wisdom and stick-to-itiveness are valued by many folks. Don't waste your time with the "fair weather" crew. Taurus, Virgo, Aquarius, Sagittarius, Pisces, Scorpio: deepen all the connections that bring you joy or advancement. Libra, Aries, Cancer, Leo, and Gemini: it's too easy to misspeak or be misunderstood. Proofread your text—and tighten your tongue!

Monday, July 17, New Moon in Cancer

Relationships that begin now could turn into "instimacy" (instant + intimacy), which is enjoyable but sometimes…well, short-lived. However, folks with deep feelings may find themselves enjoying being an important player in another's life. Cancer: usually this describes you—your compassion for the downtrodden and needy. However, please use this New Moon period as a time to recharge and isolate. Think of this as a natural "molting" time when your crab shell needs time to harden. Pisces, Scorpio, Leo,

Virgo, Gemini, and Taurus: take time to make your home more delightful or your relationships with parents (or quasi-parental mentors) deeper. Libra, Aries, Capricorn, Aquarius, and Sagittarius: enjoy the long summer days and try not to rush the "next big thing." The lunar phase would prefer you kick back.

Tuesday, August 1, Full Moon in Aquarius

This is the first Full Moon in a "blue Moon" month. The Passamaquoddy Tribe called this Moon the "Feather Shedding Moon," and given the airy preoccupations of the water carrier, the image is astute. Aquarius Moons are about discarding old ideas and timeworn patterns and looking for innovation. This Full Moon brings opportunities for professional advancement, although retrograde Venus suggests that "getting fit" or "deepening love opportunities" could be thwarted. Aquarius: this is no time to be diffident—demand what you need and understand your emotions may bubble over. Three days from now, ask yourself if you're better off. You should be. Libra, Gemini, Capricorn, Sagittarius, Pisces, Aries: wild, improbable schemes bring delight (or

wild companions will). Taurus, Leo, Scorpio, Virgo, and Cancer: it will be easy to misread another's vagueness for disapproval or lack of interest. You are probably incorrect to presume.

Wednesday, August 16, New Moon in Leo

There's a good time to be had—but an effort will need to be made to find it. If you haven't had a "summer vacation," now's the time to get back to the food or pastimes that delighted you as a child. It's an excellent day for new clothes or a new look (particularly hairstyle). Leo: this is your month, and Venus and the sun are in sync. Is someone trying to cut you a break? Give them time to reach out! Aries, Sagittarius, Virgo, Cancer, Libra, Gemini: looking good matters—make an effort with your presentation. Taurus, Scorpio, Aquarius, Capricorn, and Pisces: be modest with financial outlays. Don't be taken in.

Wednesday, August 30, Full Moon in Pisces

This is the "blue Moon," the second Full Moon in the month. For the Cherokee Tribe in the Carolinas, it was the "Drying Up Moon." Generally, Pisces Moons are superb for buying shoes, learning a dance step, visiting folks in prison (which can also mean spending time with folks imprisoned by circumstance, including mental illness or incapacity). But the Cherokee have it right—if you're feeling a surfeit of emotions, aim for "drying up" feelings that make you feel helpless. Pisces: consider turning off your electronic devices because you are the belle, or the beau, of the ball. And you know how difficult too much attention can be. Scorpio, Cancer, Aries, Taurus, Aquarius, and Capricorn: spend money on art or items that improve your environment—or that help with your spirituality. Virgo, Libra, Gemini, Sagittarius, and Leo: others may be more sensitive than you think. Go slow.

Thursday, September 14, New Moon in Virgo

Now that Jupiter is retrograding in Taurus (since September 4), that feeling of "bountifulness" may be diminished for some folks, particularly Scorpio. This New Moon puts the focus on your health as well as what's going on in the workplace. Starting new practices or habits is favored, as is working alone (versus on a team—that was earlier in the week). Virgo: your willingness to work even harder is a theme—but may not be noticed as you'd like. Make your brilliant brain use this lunar time to streamline your strategies. Taurus, Capricorn, Leo, Cancer, Libra, and Scorpio: your aesthetic sense is heightened; make improvements in areas relating to nutrition and skill-building. Pisces, Gemini, Sagittarius, Aries, and Aquarius: you may think your tone is neutral, but others may detect judginess.

Friday, September 29, Full Moon in Aries

"Moon of Full Harvest" (Hopi Tribe, Arizona). Mars and the Moon are at odds, so arguments or grumbling could be a theme. Look for projects you can do quickly, and if outdoor cooking is your thing, the astrological gods have three letters for you: BBQ. Aries: the spotlight is on you. Ask for what you want, and as much as you enjoy doing so much *on your own*—others really want to ease your burden. Sagittarius, Leo, Taurus, Gemini, Aquarius, and Pisces: problems could resolve on projects that have taken center stage for the last two weeks. Libra, Capricorn, Cancer, Virgo, and Scorpio: it is too easy for you to be irked by others' childishness. Take a step back.

Saturday, October 14, New Moon in Libra

If you've got something to communicate to a partner, the words come tumbling out. A fine day for appreciating or acquiring art or items that come in pairs. (Gloves? Winter's coming.) Libra: you may have had "an embarrassment of riches" in the past six weeks—but now, things are quiet. Review those opportunities or relationships. What can you gamble on? Aquarius, Gemini, Virgo, Leo, Scorpio, and Sagittarius: all the signs point to partnership— a new one. Has someone shown up who's your new "go-to" savior? Aries, Cancer, Capricorn, Pisces, and Taurus: speaking awkwardly could come easily—you're just trying to be frank, and others are thinking it's "blame game" time. Who needs to be reassured in your circle?

Saturday, October 28, Full Moon in Taurus

Taurus Moons, particularly the waxing and full varieties, augur well for acquisitions of all kinds: investments, paintings, jewelry (necklaces)—even singing lessons. However, just as we saw in September, the Full Moon is at odds with Mars again, so romantic pairings could be difficult—too easy to misunderstand one another. Taurus: you know how people always say, "Well, what are you doing for you? Why are you doing so much for others?" Ignore and continue to take charge exactly as you please. The astrology says, "Forward march." Virgo, Capricorn, Gemini, Aries, Pisces, and Cancer: pursue luxury in the form of experiences that make you feel like a superstar. Scorpio, Leo, Aquarius, Libra, and Sagittarius: others will think you're more committed or decided than you are.

Monday, November 13, New Moon in Scorpio

Mars and the Moon are in Scorpio: secrets are the theme. If you've got a James or Jane Bond side to your nature, you might find drama where there's only comedy (e.g., don't take others' change of direction as a serious matter). Scorpio: from mid-October through November, you can do anything—especially big leaps forward for career or socializing. Your charisma is at a two-and-a-half-year high. Have fun! Cancer, Pisces, Sagittarius, Capricorn, Libra, and Virgo: being efficient comes easily—focusing on one or two things the wiser course. Taurus, Aquarius, Leo, Aries, and Gemini: your tongue is a blunt instrument, and it will be easy to misspeak, mis-text, or mis-email. Others may see you as more severe than you are.

Monday, November 27, Full Moon in Gemini

"Freezing River Maker Moon" (Abenaki Tribe, Maine). The Abenaki may have found this Full Moon a time of climactic transition, but Gemini means we'll all say a lot more than we intended. Superb day for meetings and collaborations (seriously, plan these). Gemini: you can get your own way—just don't focus on the people who aren't meeting your eyes. Stick with those who "get" your energy level. Aquarius, Libra, Taurus, Aries, Cancer, and Leo: fellowship brings satisfaction, particularly among folks bursting with ideas *and* follow-through. Yes, that's an unlikely combination, so keep standards high. Virgo, Scorpio, Sagittarius, Capricorn, and Pisces: others' talkativeness—or gossiping—might rile you up. Hold off on vital communication for a day, especially if you need to cool off.

Tuesday, December 12, New Moon in Sagittarius

Mars is also in Sagittarius. This is a super time to plan—or embark on—a long trip or educational opportunity. And if you're not traveling, restlessness could beset you. However, tomorrow,

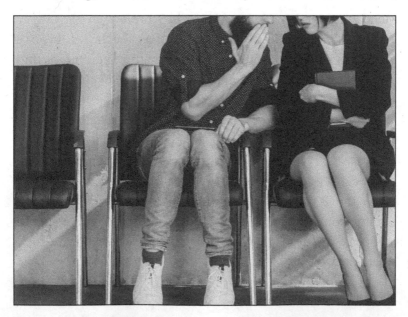

Mercury is retrograde (until January 1), so double-check your communications. Sagittarius may be called upon to adjudicate a situation—this could be as simple as giving feedback to a colleague or separating spitting cats. Aries, Leo, Libra, Scorpio, Capricorn, and Aquarius: friendship is worth working on—get back in touch with folks, especially those you think of as "rebels." Pisces, Gemini, Virgo, Cancer, and Taurus: if you're trying to do things "by the book," you may need to break the spine (e.g., loosen up).

Tuesday, December 26, Full Moon in Cancer

This is the "Small Spirits Moon" (Anishnaabe, Chippewa, and Ojibwe, Great Lakes). Wintry Full Moons are so high in the sky that it's worth staying up to see them if you live in North America. This is an excellent time for enjoying baked goods or getting the dishes and bowls you think would give your kitchen an elegant new look. Cancer: you may feel you need "alone" time, but this Moon suggests that companionship heals. Pisces, Scorpio, Leo, Virgo, Gemini, and Taurus: your insights into others are deep—but you don't have to tell everyone "chapter and verse" on your thoughts. Libra, Capricorn, Aries, Aquarius, and Sagittarius: social awkwardness could be a "thing" for you. A word to the wise: dress up, so if you stumble on the stairs, it looks like dancing!

Reference

Snowder, Brad. "Native American Moons." Western Washington University Physics & Astronomy Department. Western Washington University. Updated February 16, 2021. https://www.wwu.edu/astro101/indianmoons.shtml.

2023
Moon Sign Book
Articles

The Moon and the Elements

Bernadette Evans

Have you ever wondered why you feel a certain way on some days? All of a sudden you throw all your plans out the window and do something completely different from what you'd arranged! Suddenly you're going on an unexpected road trip. Or a friend you haven't spoken to in a while pops into your mind and you pick up the phone to see how they're doing. Maybe you woke up and feel like cooking or tidying up your home, or you jump out of bed, inspired and ready to put some plans into action! Your subconscious is tapping into the energy of the Moon.

There are four elements in astrology: fire, earth, air, and water. Every planet in the chart is in a particular sign, which is ruled by an element. The Moon represents our emotions as well as what nurtures us and makes us feel safe and secure. The Moon moves quickly through the sky and the zodiac, completing its journey approximately every 28–29 days. Then she begins her voyage all over again. The astrological signs are paired with one of the four elements. The Moon acts differently in each element and each one has a distinctive feel and wants to express itself in its own way. By paying attention to what sign the Moon is in on a particular day, you can tap into the sign and its element and work with it in a conscious manner.

The Moon in a Fire Sign

When the Moon travels through a fire sign, you can expect to feel more energized. Fire is hot, energetic, impulsive, passionate, and determined. You can be excited, ready to take a leap and just go for it. You may also feel more generous and want to share your joy and bounty with others. When the Moon is in a fire sign, you're more apt to take a chance on something. You feel brave and courageous and a part of you wants to be seen, to be noticed. It can also be dramatic and burn you if you're not careful. Let's look at the signs that are ruled by fire.

When the Moon flies through the sign of Aries, you could use this energy to start a new venture! You feel inspired and enthusiastic about your ideas and are eager to get started. Your passion for a project or even the spark of an idea can help you begin, but if you don't keep adding fuel to the fire, you could run out of steam. When the Moon is in Aries, you could be quick at initiating things but have a hard time finishing what you began. Try and persevere if you're able, or delegate the rest of the job to someone who can run with it. Exercise is a great way to move fiery energy through your body. Any exercise that makes you feel alive and excited would feel fantastic.

When the Moon is in the sign of Leo, you could feel more playful. You may feel like you're in a buddy movie and all you need is a supporting player, aka an admirer, to accompany you on the ride for some fun and adventure. You're living in the moment and want to be noticed and celebrated. There's a need to express yourself and say, "Here I am, world!" Getting the attention of others feels like a balm. You want to express yourself by creating something, whether it's poetry, pottery, or telling a good joke. You need to say, "Look at me; see what I can do." When the Moon is in Leo, you can feel more generous and supportive, wanting to give your friends a helping hand.

When the Moon rides through the sign of Sagittarius, you feel like you're fired up and want to travel and explore. It could be the exploration of a new subject. You want to immerse yourself in learning something spiritual or mystical, or anything with a psychological framework. If you do decide to delve into a subject, it will be something that fascinates and inspires you. Maybe you feel the open road is calling your name. When the Moon is in Sagittarius, you could feel pulled in a few directions, as there are so many things to do, learn, and soak up. You feel like you're on a quest to discover something big! Optimism and enthusiasm stoke your fire while you endlessly move and search for more.

The Moon in an Earth Sign

You can feel the shift when the Moon meanders through an earth sign. There's a desire to build something substantial. It's a good day to get things done. It's really all about planning, making lists, organizing, doing chores, and working on projects. The adage slow and steady wins the race is fitting when speaking about earth energy. You want to get your hands dirty, to build something. It's about perseverance and doggedness, wanting a tangible result after all the effort. It's a great time to deal with the practicalities of life. Organizing parties, closets, and checkbooks can be easier when the Moon is in an earth sign. Getting in touch with your body, being stable and grounded helps you be present. You may take on a lot of responsibility when the Moon is in an earth sign. Remember to balance work with play and have some fun.

When the Moon is in the sign of Taurus, it has a sensual feeling. Touching and being touched is a nice use of this energy and feels fabulous. Going for a massage or any bodywork would be beneficial. Spend some time in nature by strolling through a forest or a park, or go out into your garden and feel the dirt between your fingers. There's a desire to build something, to leave a legacy, to have something to show for your hard work. Taurus is ruled by Venus, so if you make money from your efforts, that's a bonus. Venus is also about beauty and art, so sitting down to doodle, make jewelry, paint, sing, or any other artistic pursuit would bring its own rewards.

When the Moon is in the sign of Virgo, you may bolt out of bed to get started on that to-do list. Making lists and checking them off feels satisfying when the Moon makes its home here for a few days. Be conscious of taking on too many projects at once. It's easy to get bogged down with too many details and think you're not doing a good job. Let go of the need to be perfect and just get the job done. You may have an urge to clean the house—go for it. You

can accomplish a lot when you follow the energy, tap into it, and use it constructively. Making nutritious meals to nurture yourself and others would be perfect, as Virgo is concerned with health matters. Studying up on a modality related to health concerns could be helpful. You never know when this information will come in handy.

When the Moon is in the sign of Capricorn, there's more of a structured feel to the day. Again, you might want a list, but it's all about business. How can you create more business or further your career? You need to contact the right people who can help you advance. There's a more serious "get to work" vibe when the Moon is in the sign of the goat. It's about putting one foot in front of the other and then doing it again and again. Career, money, advancement, and prestige take center stage. Capricorn energy is very dedicated and focused, so remember to schedule a coffee break during the day. It will all get finished, so don't push yourself too hard.

The Moon in an Air Sign

When the Moon is in an air sign, the energy shifts gears—it's quicker. It's about communication and connection. It's time to call up a friend to catch up. Since air is so fast, you may rush in with questions without waiting for a response. Remember to take a breath, slow down, and listen to what's being said. You could write in a journal, give a lecture, sing—anything where you let your voice be heard in the most authentic way you can. Be curious, reading and studying a subject that captures your interest. Turn inward, listen to your intuition, let it guide you, and make a vision board of your hopes and dreams.

Working with the Moon in Gemini is easy and complicated at the same time. You could wake up and have a million great ideas, but if you don't write them down or do something with them, they could just evaporate. That's the thing with Gemini—you can easily get distracted. Pay close attention to your thoughts, and carry a notebook to write down all your ideas or use your phone to record a voice memo. You're like a wordsmith, collecting information and sharing it with others. When the Moon is in Gemini, you should have no problem entertaining yourself; pick up a crossword puzzle or a sudoku puzzle to play with. There's so much information on the internet and social media that discovering new ideas is not the problem; it's learning when to shut it off. You may get information overload, and that's when you might want to do something physical to shut off the noise and get out of your head.

Friendships and relationships take center stage when the Moon travels through Libra. Call up a friend and go for a coffee or just gab on the phone. This is the time when you're drawn to be with others. Sharing stories, learning what's happening in their lives— it's what makes the world go 'round. When the Moon is in Libra, you crave harmony above all else. You want fairness and balance and go out of your way putting others' wants and needs before your own. Remember, relationships are about an equal amount of give and take. I'm not saying you want to keep score, but pay attention if the scales seem unbalanced in any way. You might want to add some beautiful touches to your home at this time, a few special items that add a homey quality to your surroundings.

Freedom and excitement are calling your name when the Moon lands in Aquarius. The air has an electric quality to it, and you're up for anything new and bizarre. If it's got a bit of a weird or odd slant to it, all the better; it's like it has your name written all over it. Socializing with groups, specifically the people closest to you, the ones who understand you, is part of the function of the Aquarian Moon. You could rebel and be argumentative for the fun of it or just because. A good use of this energy is to enjoy hanging out with friends or visit someplace you've never been before and explore.

The Moon in a Water Sign

Feelings abound when the Moon swims through a water sign. Your psychic antenna is tuned in to the frequencies of the watery Moon. Your sensitivity and emotions are amplified so much that you can't distinguish if what you're feeling actually belongs to you or to someone else. Water absorbs, and you can easily absorb other people's feelings and energy. Learning to create good boundaries is vital to your health during this time. When the Moon is in a water sign, you may want to have some time alone to meditate or just sit quietly, turning inward. A watery Moon can bring your creativity to the surface. Listening to music can get your juices flowing and help your creativity. Tuning in to your body at this time is also great, either with meditation, yoga, qigong, swimming, or any exercise where you are bringing awareness to your activities.

When the Moon is in Cancer, spending time at home can look inviting. Having some time to yourself to retreat, rest, and rejuvenate is important for you to restore your energy sources. Whatever nurtures you is the perfect thing to do with the Cancer

Moon. It could be cooking a favourite recipe that is comforting and nourishing. Maybe it's curling up in a corner with your herbal tea and a good book or watching a favourite sentimental movie. You just want to slow things down and bring them down a notch—some quiet and solitude looks good about now.

The Scorpio Moon could bring up some intense feelings. Passions may run hot when the Moon is here. You could channel that heat by expressing it through dance or any physical activity, such as running, martial arts, or boxing. Another great outlet is sexual expression. Sexual expression is physical intimacy, but it's also creation in all its forms. There are times when you want to know more about life and the secrets that it holds. Spend time exploring a subject where you find out more about human nature. Digging below the surface is one of the ways to tap into this energy. Another avenue is to be hypnotized. Some insights may be uncovered when you're in a trance, and you never know where they could lead you. Think of the Scorpio Moon as a treasure hunt: so many things to explore and discover.

When the Moon is in the sign of the two fishes, Pisces, there is a dreaminess to this time. The veil is thinner, and you could get more intuitive hits during this time. Which makes this a fantastic time to write in a journal and see what messages come through after you meditate. It's also the perfect time to play with tarot cards or any other divination tool that grabs you. You may want to think about keeping a dream journal by your bed to record your dreams; you never know what insights you'll receive. Feelings of empathy and compassion may surface, as you want to help those in need. Ultimately, you want to connect with a higher power, whether you're meditating, praying, or attending a spiritual or religious gathering.

Final Thoughts

Have fun playing with the Moon and the elements. Keep a journal and pay attention to how you're feeling when the Moon transits a specific sign. Figure out your own particular way of communicating with the Moon. You'll soon see a relationship building between the two of you. Above all, enjoy riding the lunar waves.

Yoga, the Sun, the Moon, and You

Jilly Shipway

Hatha yoga is the physical yoga system that unites the complimentary *ha* (sun) and *tha* (moon) energies within our own body. Yoga teaches us to look inward and discover mirrored within ourselves the entire solar system. Through our yoga practice, we learn how to locate the sun and moon within our own body and so connect with a deep source of inner wisdom, which makes decision-making easier. With yoga's help, we become more intuitive and able to make leaps of faith, even when circumstances aren't entirely favourable.

Modern astronomers have confirmed what the ancient yogis discovered through meditation, that "most of the elements of our bodies were formed in stars over the course of billions of years and multiple star lifetimes" (Lotzof, 2018). When you consider that we are literally made of stardust, it makes perfect sense that through our yoga practice we are able to locate the sun and moon within our body.

Once you have learned to tune in to the sun and moon energies in your body, you will find it compliments your outward astrology practice. For example, although the astrological forecast might be inauspicious, for you this might be a good time, and by being able to reference your own inner constellation of thoughts, feelings, physical sensations, etc., you will intuitively know whether this is a good time for a certain activity or not. As a creative person, I have always loved the buzzy energy of the full moon, whereas my friend gets anxious around the full moon and is always glad when the moon starts to wane. We both practice yoga, so we are in tune with our inner reactions to the moon's cycles, and we can respond to them by using our yoga practice to stay happy and balanced.

Many of us turn to astrology to find answers to the big (and small) questions of life: Is this a good day to start a venture? Will this person fit in with my team at work? Should I buy electronic equipment on this day? Am I romantically compatible with this person? Although we can use our astrological knowledge to nudge our life in a favorable direction, there are many things that are beyond our control. So, although we can do our best to align our plans with the stars, sometimes the stars have other plans for us! Your yoga practice can support you on those inauspicious days, when despite your best efforts, life happens! Yoga can help you to access your own "inner astrologer" intuitively, and this can complement your outward-looking practice of astrology.

Practicing the physical yoga postures (*asanas*) anchors us in our body, which is, of course, made up of the earth element. In a shamanistic way, many of the asanas are named after animals, birds, or natural elements, such as the lion pose, cat pose, dog pose, eagle pose, mountain pose, and tree pose. By practicing these earth-inspired poses, we come back to the experience of our body in the present moment and connect with the natural world around us, even as we open ourselves to heavenly wisdom.

Below are four yoga techniques that will help you to connect with the cosmic wisdom within you, balance your sun and moon energies, and ground you in the present moment here on this beautiful planet earth in your amazing human body!

Standing like a Tree

In this exercise, we connect with the earth element. It's an excellent way of creating stability, grounding oneself, and creating the resilience to cope with a world that is in a state of constant flux.

I always use this exercise at the start of my own home yoga practice, before I teach a class, and any time when I feel thrown off course by life's events and need to ground myself. It's a great way of calming a troubled mind and allowing your innate wisdom to surface and show you the way forward. And it only takes a few minutes to do.

Stand tall. Feet are parallel and about hip-width apart. Imagine that there's a string attached to the crown of your head, pulling you skyward, and a weight attached to your tailbone, pulling it down toward the earth.

Be aware of the contact your feet are making with the earth and imagine that, like a tree, roots are growing from the soles of your feet and extending way down into the earth. Feel the stability that your roots give you.

On each inhale, imagine that you are drawing energy up through your roots, into the soles of your feet, up through your legs, and into your body. On each exhale, imagine that you are letting go of anything you do not wish to hold on to, down through your feet and back into the earth, where it is composted.

Now, be aware of the space surrounding your body and feel yourself expanding into that space. Imagine that every pore in your body is breathing and being energized and rejuvenated with each breath.

Then, consciously place yourself in a circle of safety and protection, silently affirming, "I surround myself with love and light, and I am safe."

When you are ready, let go of the image of the tree. Resolve to take this sense of stability and spaciousness into the next activity that you do today.

Locate Your Inner Sun

The following exercise is energizing and boosts your mood. It's also empowering, so it's a good one to do on days when you're facing a challenge and need a confidence boost.

Find yourself a comfortable position, either sitting or lying down. Be aware of your spine and make sure that your body is arranged symmetrically around this midline.

Notice how your body is feeling, consciously letting go of any tension and relaxing. Be aware of the natural ebb and flow of your breath.

Now, imagine that you are able to locate the sun within your body. Scan your body and see if you can find the spot where it feels like the sun is residing. When you've found that sweet spot, rest your awareness there. If you can't decide exactly where the sun is located, then picture a sun at the solar plexus, as that will work well for the next part of this exercise.

Now, with each inhale, imagine that you are breathing into your sun and the sun is glowing a little brighter. And with each exhale, imagine you are breathing out from your sun and healing rays of sunlight are radiating around your body.

Now, let go of following the breath, and repeat this affirmation three times: "I am the Sun at the center of my life." This is a powerful affirmation and particularly recommended for people who tend to neglect their own needs and always put others first.

Notice how you are feeling now at the end of this exercise. Take this warm, sunny optimism into the next activity you do today.

Sun and Moon Breathing

The following exercise will help you to become familiar with the energizing, solar quality of the inhalation and the relaxing, lunar quality of the exhalation. It also calms and quiets an agitated mind, allowing you to hear the quiet voice of your inner wisdom.

The skilled yoga practitioner learns to use the breath to energize or relax their system. The inhalation is energizing and associated with sun energy. The exhalation is relaxing and associated with moon energy. The inhalation is like the waxing moon. The exhalation is like the waning moon. All yoga breathing techniques (*pranayama*) begin with mindful breathing.

Find yourself a comfortable position lying on your back. Bend both knees; both feet are on the floor, about hip-width apart. If you wish, for comfort, place a slim cushion under your head. You might want to set a timer for between five and fifteen minutes.

Rest your hands on your belly. Sink your awareness down into the belly, which is a center of intuition and deep knowing. Notice how your belly rises and falls with each in- and out-breath. Allow your breathing to be natural and easy. You don't need to impose a pattern on your breathing, simply allow it to come and go, to ebb and flow.

Now, on each inhalation, silently affirm, *energize*, and feel your body expanding and taking in sun energy. On each exhalation, affirm, *relax*, and feel your body letting go and relaxing. Inhale, energize, exhale, relax.

When you are ready, let go of following the breath and silently repeat this affirmation three times: "The Sun within energizes me; the Moon within relaxes me." Then let go of the affirmation.

Notice how you are feeling now and take this balanced energy into the next thing you do today.

Meditation Questions

Sometimes in life we are faced with a challenge or dilemma that seems impossible to solve. We find ourselves stumped! To resolve the problem, we might seek guidance from an astrologer, counselor, or wise friend. Although it's good to share a problem and seek a fresh perspective, we should also remember to consult our own inner wisdom too, as otherwise we deny ourselves free advice from a source that knows us inside out!

Even if you don't think you're that wise, I'm here to tell you that you are! Within you there's an infinite source of wisdom, and your yoga practice can help you reconnect with it. Yoga has a myriad of ways to help you to relax, and it is in these states of deep relaxation that you open yourself to hearing the wise voice of guidance from within.

In yoga, we use meditation questions as a way of posing a question to our subconscious—and the Universal Consciousness (if that is meaningful for you)—and asking for a solution to a particular problem. You can pose a question at the start of a yoga session, whilst you are staying in a yoga pose, during a meditation or relaxation session, or just before you go to sleep at night.

Once you've posed the question, let it go and trust that your subconscious and the Universal Consciousness will come up with an answer. You might ask, "Should I accept this job offer?" or "Should I buy this house?" or "Should I take this relationship to the next level?" Whatever you ask, no need to strive too hard to find an answer. Simply be open to receiving the answer when the time is right. I often find that an answer will float into my mind during a yoga session, when I'm relaxing or meditating, or even sometimes in a dream.

Yoga to Unite Heaven and Earth

In this article, we've explored the idea that regardless of whether a day is auspicious or inauspicious, yoga is always there to reconnect you with your cosmic consciousness, which in turn will reveal the way to make a bad day better! Our yoga practice teaches us that the rhythms of the natural world are also our own rhythms. As in the heavens, so here on earth. The ultimate aim of yoga is self-realization (*samadhi*), which is a state of bliss where you experience a sense of union with the whole cosmos. May the stars within you guide your way home.

Resources

Marchant, Jo. *The Human Cosmos: A Secret History of the Stars*. Edinburgh: Canongate Books Ltd., 2020.

Shipway, Jilly. *Yoga by the Stars*. MN: Llewellyn Publications, 2020.

———. *Yoga Through the Year*. Woodbury, MN: Llewellyn Publications, 2019.

Reference

Lotzof, Kerry. "Are We Really Made of Stardust?" The Natural History Museum. Accessed February 28, 2022. http://www.nhm.ac.uk /discover/are-we-really-made-of-stardust.html?gclid=EAIaIQobCh MI2dif1cP_3wIVyr3tCh3x8gMAEAAYASAAEgLFGvD_BwE.

Nature on Its Own Terms

Lupa

> *For the animal shall not be measured by man. In a world older and
> more complete than ours they move finished and complete.*
> —Henry Beston, *The Outermost House*

Over my lifetime, my explorations have wandered here and there, but they have always centered on the natural world. First it was the animals that called to me, inviting me to rediscover my love of the forests, fields, and waterways they called home. Later on they introduced me to a whole host of other beings that shared these ecosystems: the plants and fungi, lichens and slime molds, and so many microscopic beings that they seemed nearly uncountable. Not that I was meant to count them, of course. Their existence is not dependent upon whether humanity has categorized and named them; that is a practice that primarily benefits us and our understanding of the natural world.

As I have deepened my renewed connection with the natural world that was first forged in childhood, my relationship to and understanding of nature has evolved. I grew up in mainstream American society, which places humans above nature. Our economic system sees nature only as resources to exploit; our culture, heavily influenced by Christianity, exhorts our supposed God-given superiority over the rest of the world. Ask most Americans where we stand in the order of things, and they'll say things like "top of the food chain" and "better than the animals." Growing up in a small Midwestern town without a lot of outside influence, I never thought to challenge these assumptions, and I carried them with me for years after I moved away.

When I went to graduate school for my master's degree in counseling psychology, I focused in particular on ecopsychology, which explores our relationship with the rest of nature. During this time I was introduced to the concept of deep ecology, so named by Norwegian philosopher Arne Næss in a 1973 paper. Rather than seeing humanity as being the pinnacle of all creation, deep ecology instead places us within the community of nature, one of many vibrant and diverse species of animal sharing this planet. From this new vantage point, we begin to see other beings not as resources to be used or lesser beings to exploit but our neighbors and relations.

Sure, this seems obvious on the surface. But even those of us who consider ourselves to be nature-crunchy environmentalists often still have a lot of biases and attitudes that stem from mainstream American culture. I'd like to discuss a few specific ways in which this often manifests itself within this country.

You Are Not a Disney Princess

Let me talk for a moment about something that primarily concerns wild animals. I have seen, on more than one occasion, a starry-eyed person talk about how when they were meditating in the woods all the wild animals gathered around them like they were Snow White singing a Disney song. I admit I'm pretty skeptical of these claims; although sitting still for a while can make some wild animals a little less wary; they'd likely check out any large predatory animal that had settled down for a bit. And it's likely that any watchful animals ran away the moment the meditator got up and began moving around again.

We assume that a wild animal not immediately running away means that the animal is "friendly" and wants to interact with us. It's a rather selfish viewpoint, really, because it makes the encounter all about us and how special we supposedly are, rather than it being a random, brief interaction between two species in the same moment in space and time. And when we actively seek these encounters, particularly when we want them to be up close and personal, it puts everyone involved at risk.

Where did this need to connect come from? In spite of our increasingly urbanized, human-centered lifestyles, inside of us there's still a need to connect with nonhuman beings. Edward O. Wilson calls this deep instinctual drive "biophilia." And when we do make those connections, we feel better on a variety of levels. We've been so incredibly isolated that we're desperate for any attention from other beings that we can get. Unfortunately, we don't always consider the long-term effects of our activities.

For example, a lot of people deliberately feed wild mammals, whose behavior is different from that of birds (see the end of the article for details.) This is often so that they can see them more easily and even "befriend" them. This can be small critters like raccoons and opossums, or even megafauna like deer and bears. It happens in backyards all across the United States, as well as in state and federal parks (including, most famously, Yellowstone National Park) in spite of regulations prohibiting feeding the animals. I have also seen numerous examples of completely untrained people "adopting" injured wildlife; instead of taking them to a professional rehabber who will prepare the animals to be released back into the wild once healed, the finders decide to keep the animals as pets, robbing them of any chance of a normal, wild life. Even when they do release them, the animals have been handled improperly and have no fear of humans any more.

Sure, it may seem like a magic moment when your favorite deer walks up to you and gently eats corn out of your hand. Maybe you feel virtuous when a raccoon gets fatter and fatter on the leftovers of your meals left outside for it to feast on. But this only benefits *us* in the long run. Much of what we feed wildlife isn't good for them and can make them sick or even malnourished. Encouraging animals to congregate at one feeding site over and over again in larger-than-natural numbers increases the spread of disease and leads to more wildlife dying slow, agonizing deaths from infections and other sicknesses. Too much food can lead to overpopulation, which again breeds disease and can also cause some of the animals to have painful slow deaths from starvation. The animals' dependency on humans as food sources and their

lack of fear can combine to make them much more aggressive in seeking handouts, to the point where numerous people have been bitten, scratched, or gored. These aggressive animals usually end up euthanized because they present a danger to people. Thus it is that our selfish need to be the center of an animal's attention leads to its demise.

Harmful Narratives

There's another way in which our biases can wreak havoc on the lives of wild beings. This is the tendency to denote certain species as "good" or "bad"—not based on anything ecological, but subjective human values. These do vary from culture to culture, but again I'll be focusing on mainstream American culture.

Let's look at a common scenario in a birding group I'm in, where people share photos they've taken out in the field. Photos of great blue herons catching fish and frogs are met with oohs and ahhs pretty universally. However, someone shared a picture of a great blue heron that had caught and was about to eat a juvenile red-winged blackbird, which ended up with a number of people saying it was an inappropriate picture, that it was horrible, that they didn't want to see that sort of thing, and so forth. Even though fish, frogs, and young birds are all a natural part of a heron's diet, the blackbird was given more subjective value than the cold-blooded creatures.

Sure, the group members may have had some bias toward our avian neighbors because it's a birders' group. But it also betrays a common bias in our culture overall: we value cute and cuddly looking animals over less attractive ones, and we usually value warm-blooded animals over cold-blooded. We even have preferences for vertebrates over invertebrates. And anything that might even remotely inconvenience us is automatically shunted into the "bad" category, even if the individual animal is just out somewhere living its life without causing trouble—hence why some people kill snakes and spiders simply for existing, and why some farmers shoot coyotes on sight no matter how far away from livestock they may be.

Yet the extirpation of unwanted species has frequently caused massive ecological upsets. The loss of wolves, bears, and other large predators from an ecosystem almost invariably leads to overpopulation of large prey animals like deer and elk, as well as an increase in diseases like chronic wasting disease in their numbers. Some people advocate for eradicating all mosquitoes everywhere, not realizing just how crucial a food source they are for animals ranging from salmon to swallows and other birds.

The valuing of certain plants over others has also caused deep upsets. Look at how the lawn has become the gold standard of yard care all across America, even in deserts and other places inappropriate for grass of any sort. Over 40 million acres of lawns exist here, and they guzzle down nearly nine billion gallons of fresh water every day. Yet any plant that encroaches upon this monoculture of fescue is seen as a weed, whether a non-native plant like a dandelion or plantain, or any of a variety of species native to that area. Tons of herbicides are used to keep anything that isn't grass out, with massive ecological impacts across the board.

The same goes for gardens and farms. We privilege any plant that we want to have there, while we wage war on the ones we reject. While a certain amount of weeding is needed to grow food, and invasive non-native species need to be removed to restore an ecosystem's balance, these things can be done without applying moral values and biases to whether the plant is inherently "good" or "bad" just because it's not what we wanted in that spot.

Righting the Balance

All of the examples above place the human being over all others, whether as controllers of nature or as the audience that nature is supposed to entertain and enlighten. So what is the antidote?

First, we must question all of our assumptions about our relationship to the rest of nature, even if it's not comfortable to do so. This can include examining how the idea that we are superior to nature manifests in many ways in our society, for example the seemingly casual way in which landowners, developers, and massive corporations decide to bulldoze and destroy entire ecosystems for "natural resources" or to build houses, strip malls, and resorts without any thought toward the beings that lived there already. We also need to figure out whether the well-intended good deeds we try to enact toward wildlife and other beings are truly beneficial to them or just make us feel better.

Even with all this thought and discussion, there will never be universal answers of how best to be a part of the community of nature. One person's answer may include as plant-based a lifestyle as possible while living in a condo in a green building in an urban area. Another may choose to buy land and restore it to as natural a habitat as possible, other than a portion set aside for a big permaculture garden and a few humanely raised animals for meat and milk.

What's most important, I think, is that we each embody to the best of our abilities that deep ecological idea that we are neither better than nor separate from the rest of nature. We need to let that lens affect our vision of the world and, by extension, our actions. Even if we cannot achieve the sort of "purity of action" that our ideals suggest, just striving as far as we realistically can is a good goal in and of itself.

So what might that look like? Let's start with the concept of deep ecology; one of its tenets is that humans are just one species in a planetwide community of other animals, as well as plants, fungi, microbes, and other living beings. How might we make our decisions, using all our many tools, resources, and knowledge, if we considered the impact on other beings as well as humans? What would our actions look like if, instead of the assumption that we are better than nature and that it only exists for us, we acted from a place of compassion, empathy, and care toward all life? The individual responses may vary, but the collective change would be astounding.

Let's also look at nature literacy: how much a given person knows about the nature around them. People who feed wild mammals and entice them to come close have poor nature literacy compared to someone who professionally rehabilitates wildlife to be released back into nature. The former people think they know about nature, but they only have a surface understanding of the fact that just about any wild animal can be enticed with food if the right sort of food is offered. The rehabilitator, on the other hand, has to understand a wider variety of factors surrounding even a single animal. In order to properly care for an abandoned baby deer, for example, they have to know that does routinely leave fawns alone in hiding for hours at a time, and that a fawn with crinkled, drooping ears is dehydrated and likely has been abandoned or orphaned. They need to know how to feed the fawn properly so that they are not malnourished and how to house the fawn as it gets larger and more potentially dangerous. They need to know signs of any communicable diseases the fawn could spread to other animals and symptoms of congenital defects that could make the fawn less likely to survive in the wild. They must know when the fawn is old enough to be released and where the best place might be. Most importantly, they need to be able to handle this animal day in and day out for weeks or even months in such a way that the fawn does not lose its natural fear of humans.

If we took the time to really observe nature and learn its cycles, and to educate ourselves about the animals, plants and other living beings and *their* needs and boundaries, we would be doing something much more valuable than giving them handouts of inappropriate food. We would be learning about their world—a

world we now have a skewed view of due to our perception that we are separate or superior. We would be able to approach them on their terms, not just ours.

And that just might make us learn to be better neighbors to them all.

Note

I specifically say wild mammals because their behavior is different from wild birds. Birds, the little dinosaurs that they are, tend to be less likely to lose their fear of us or become dependent on us. Birds that visit feeders are usually species that are used to their food sources, like insects or berries, being seasonal and therefore temporary, so they travel around a lot more to various feeding areas. Waterfowl are an exception; ducks and geese very quickly get dependent on humans feeding them and can run into the same problems as mammals.

Florilegia: Creating Your Personal Moon Book

Melissa Tipton

Have you ever happened upon a book passage that perfectly illustrates a concept you were *just* thinking about, and it oh-so-helpfully supplies the right little nugget of information to propel you along your path of understanding? This is one of my favorite forms of synchronicity, or meaningful coincidence, and I love that tingly goosebumps feeling it imparts—the sense that the world is conspiring to help me grow. It's no surprise, then, that I love the practice of florilegia, which is the gathering of different passages around a single theme and collecting them in a special book. The name translates literally to the "gathering of flowers."

A number of medieval florilegia have survived, compiled by early Christian monks, and it's fascinating to see which passages from a mixture of religious and secular sources were chosen to be painstakingly copied by hand, sometimes accompanied by intricate illustrations and elaborate initials. It's worth Googling a particularly striking example from the turn of the fourteenth century, the *Rothschild Canticles*, which can be viewed in its entirety online, down to the fantastical creatures frolicking in the margins and the full-page illuminations, still alive with breathtaking color.

A Lunar Take on Florilegia

The practice of florilegia continues to hold value for expanding your self-awareness and gaining traction on your goals, and one way that I've chosen to adapt the practice to these ends is through the creation of what I call a "Moon florilegium." To make your own, you'll need a book in which to compile your findings, and it can be as simple or as fancy as you like. While not required, you might find it helpful to select a book that allows you to insert additional pages as needed. From there, you'll choose a method of dividing up the book so you know where to place your entries. My version, which I'll outline below, is divided by Moon signs (e.g., Moon in Virgo, Moon in Pisces, etc.), but you could also divide your florilegium by Moon phases, sticking simply with the New Moon and Full Moon, or getting more granular by listing out each distinct phase: New Moon, waxing crescent, first quarter, waxing gibbous, Full Moon, waning gibbous, last quarter, and waning crescent. Clearly label each section, and feel free to illustrate or incorporate collage elements to the pages to lend extra flair to your book.

Regardless of the categorization method you use, the basic idea is this: During each Moon phase or sign, you'll make note of things that capture your attention, and for our purposes, we're going to expand beyond written texts as possible sources. In your Moon florilegium you can compile passages from books, a description of a captivating image, a song lyric, something a friend says to you, a message from a tarot card you pulled that day, a memorable dream, a snippet from your daily horoscope, and so forth.

If you'd like to arrange your florilegium according to Moon signs, divide your pages up by the signs of the zodiac: Aries, Taurus, Gemini, Cancer, Leo, Virgo, Libra, Scorpio, Sagittarius, Capricorn, Aquarius, and Pisces. And even if you don't organize your book by signs, you can still add a little notation next to each entry, such as an astrological glyph indicating which sign the Moon was in at the time, just in case you want that information later. (And the reverse can be done if you arrange your book by signs: Add a little Moon symbol to notate which phase the Moon was in for each entry in case that's useful to you later.) You'll need a calendar, app, or Google to check which sign or phase the Moon is in before adding material to your florilegium so you can file it under the proper category.

What's the point of doing this? Well, I've found that I'm drawn to different things as the Moon travels through the signs and phases, and it can be quite eye opening to look back over time and see common themes emerging in my florilegium. I might notice that when the Moon is in Aries, I'm attracted to quotes, songs, and tips that motivate me to get a jump on any projects that have been relegated to the back burner for far too long. You can also look to where Aries is in your natal chart to see if this offers additional clues. For instance, in my chart Aries is in the fifth house, which, among other things, relates to creative projects, so it makes even more sense why my energy would be oriented toward moving projects forward during this time. And knowing this, I can plan ahead for the next Moon-in-Aries phase, scheduling the start of an important project to capitalize on my natural creative flow.

You might also make a note of any supports that were particularly effective for you during a sign or phase. For instance, maybe you used passionflower essence when the Moon was in Cancer, and you found that it dramatically soothed your anxiety. This is great information to have! Add it to your Moon-in-Cancer section for future reference. And just like in the example above, you could also check to see where Cancer falls in your natal chart to see if that provides further insights. Maybe it's in your first house, which relates to the image you present to the world. Your florilegium entries might uncover that when the Moon is in Cancer, you struggle with heightened anxiety around what people think of you. Knowing this, you now have options as to how you support yourself, such as remembering to use that anxiety-soothing passionflower essence or not hosting a live workshop until the Moon has exited Cancer and you're naturally feeling less self-critical.

If you find the natal chart angle helpful, you might choose to add a note next to each Moon sign in your florilegium indicating which house this sign rules for you, perhaps jotting down a few keywords for each house. Here's a list to get you started:

- First house: what you present to the world, persona, self-image
- Second house: what you value, your resources and money, self-worth
- Third house: learning, communication, siblings and extended family
- Fourth house: parents, home, family patterns, your foundations
- Fifth house: children, creativity, desires, pleasure, self-expression
- Sixth house: work and coworkers, physical health, pets, your routines
- Seventh house: committed partnerships (romantic, platonic, business), legal stuff

- Eighth house: death, sex, mental health, other people's resources (like wills and loans)
- Ninth house: things that expand your mind (travel, education, spiritual teachings, etc.)
- Tenth house: career, public roles, reputation, recognition
- Eleventh house: community, your goals and dreams, good fortune
- Twelfth house: your hidden life, karma to be worked out, loss, healing

Weaving Together Your Inner Threads

Perhaps one of the most useful benefits of keeping a Moon florilegium is that it weaves together what might otherwise be scattered threads, and I've learned that this lends power to my choices and actions. For example, I began noticing that around the Full Moon I was drawn to things that helped me look at reality in mindbending ways. I found myself listening to a podcast on quantum physics, and in particular, the many-worlds interpretation that suggests timelines branch at each quantum event. Rather than

possibility A happening and canceling out possibility B, *both* are simultaneously occurring, each existing in their own branch of the universe. I jotted down a few snippets from that podcast in my florilegium. Then, later that day, a friend mentioned a concept she'd just learned about in her Human Design community called "timeline jumping," and into my Moon book it went. Finally, as I was scrolling through Netflix, I saw a trailer for the show *Russian Doll*, which stars Natasha Lyonne caught in a bizarre time loop. Think *Groundhog Day* in New York City but with more chain-smoking and a shocking way to die every time. The trailer lingered in my mind, so I wrote about it in my florilegium.

Reading this summary of entries after the fact, the obvious connections smacked me right in the face, but in the midst of going about the rest of my life, I didn't notice how strongly I was orbiting around the concept of the squishiness of time. But once I did, I was inspired to work this into my spiritual and goal-setting practices. Through a handful of experiments, I discovered that the Full Moon is a great phase for me to work on projects or initiate mindset shifts that bend the ordinary constraints of time, which might allow me to finish a project way sooner than I would've expected or make radical jumps in my personal growth. It's a time when I'm less likely to resign myself to thoughts like, "Well, I guess that's just the way things are," and instead, I'm open to creatively pushing boundaries and ditching limited thinking in service of more expansive living.

I could also capitalize on this energy by scheduling my therapy session around the Full Moon, because I'll be more likely to make quantum leaps in self-awareness and the shifting of patterns. Or perhaps I'll task batch stuff that ordinarily leaves me feeling bogged down, struggling with the sensation that it's taking forever and a day to finish. During the Full Moon phase, I often find myself motoring right along, crossing things off my to-do list like a boss, so it's great to take advantage of this to complete tasks that might otherwise feel like a grind during a different phase. It's also fun to schedule hangouts with philosophically minded friends so we can tumble, headfirst, down the rabbit hole of weird concepts and trippy possibilities. I've had more than a few successful creative ideas come through thanks to these mind-expanding conversations around the Full Moon!

Learning to map your own internal ebbs and flows through the organizing, synthesizing power of florilegia allows you to tap into your innate power phases, while going easy on yourself if you're trying to do something during an ill-suited time and it's not working as well as you'd like. Rather than beat yourself up in the latter case, you can flip through your florilegium to see if there are any tips or clues that can help you make better use of this time. In the moment, I'm always convinced that I'll remember this stuff when I need it, but when I flip through my florilegium later, without fail, I find little wisdom nuggets that I'd totally forgotten about but that end up being *just* what I needed that day.

The Art of Bibliomancy

You can also use your florilegium for bibliomancy, or the art of divination with books. Place your hands on your florilegium, close your eyes, and take a few moments to calm and center yourself, connecting with your book. Then, ask your question and flip open the book to a random page, letting your eyes fall to a particular entry. If you assume that whatever guidance you need is contained within this material, how does it speak to your question? Are you inspired to think about things in a different way or take another action than you normally would? The more you use your florilegium, just like any divination tool, the more attuned you become to it, and the more useful its responses will be.

Another way to use your Moon florilegium for divination is to pair the book with your tarot or oracle cards by using the book as a surface upon which to do your readings, allowing the book's

Moon-aligned energy to enhance your awareness so you can tap into deeper threads of meaning. You can do readings specific to the Moon's current phase or sign (for example, "What's most important for me to know right now while the Moon is in Scorpio?") by opening the florilegium to the related section and using the book as your portable divination surface.

Tailoring Astrology to Your Inner Tides

When I was first learning astrology, I discovered that my Moon florilegium was a great way to personalize general astrological information, which then made it *much* easier to remember. Given that studying astrology is a bit like learning a whole new language, I was happy to take whatever help I could get! By categorizing information within your florilegium by Moon signs, you start to get a clearer sense of the "flavor" of each sign for you personally. Rather than trying to memorize a list of general associations, you're gradually building a picture of how *you* experience each sign. If you like, you can write some of the traditional sign correspondences at the top of each section in your florilegium, which will allow you to compare your lived experience to the conventional wisdom.

For instance, you might do some research and learn that the Moon in Gemini is related to communication, processing and exchanging information, learning, and making connections with others, so you write those keywords at the top of your Moon-in-Gemini section. Over time, you collect material for this section by noticing what grabs your attention—quotes, song lyrics, powerful dreams, etc.—when the Moon is in Gemini, and you notice that you're really drawn to stuff about *public* speaking in particular.

Maybe you find yourself Googling how to do more effective Facebook live videos, and in one of the trainings you watch, a quote really grabs you, so you record it in your Moon florilegium. That night, you have a dream where you're trying to talk over

your high school's loudspeaker, but the microphone isn't working and you wake up feeling incomplete. When you look back over your Moon-in-Gemini entries, you see the theme of meaningful communication in the public sphere, and then you realize, "Oh, right! Gemini is in the tenth house in my natal chart." The tenth house relates to, among other things, your reputation and public roles, so this emphasis on communication in the public arena makes sense for you, and it helps you learn not only the qualities of Gemini but also the characteristics of the tenth house. Knowing this, you might schedule public-facing events while the Moon is in Gemini, capitalizing on your naturally outward-flowing, communicative energy during this phase.

If you're thinking, wow, this seems like a lot of work, keeping track of the Moon's signs and phases—well, it can be somewhat intensive. And that's kind of the point. Keeping a Moon florilegium is an act of committing to tracking the Moon's comings and goings, which in turn puts you in touch with your *microcosmic* ebbs and flows and how they interact with the *macrocosmic* tides. By engaging in this practice of compiling and using your florilegium, you're valuing the forces above and below, within and without that don't operate strictly according to linear time.

In the busyness of daily life, it's easy to become overly fixated on what's next and where we're headed, crossing off "just one more thing" from our to-do list, yet never feeling like we're progressing fast enough. A Moon florilegium reminds us that in addition to linear processes, we operate through cyclical flows as well. For me, this relieves the steam valve of pressure around being ceaselessly productive, because the Moon is a powerful symbol of the proper times to move and groove and the natural phases for rest and incubation. *Both* are valuable. As you learn to attune more deeply to your unique expression of these cycles, your life unfolds with more ease and fluid power.

Dancing with the Shadow: Chiron's Role in Astrology

Dallas Jennifer Cobb

Dubbed a minor planet, a Centaur, or a comet, Chiron is an often-misunderstood astronomical and astrological body. Commonly referred to as "the wounded healer" in astrology, Chiron is bantered about in a negative and limited way, implying that where Chiron lies in the natal chart is where we always try to heal others but never attend to ourselves.

Moving beyond simple stereotypes, let us look at the depth and breadth of Chiron's archetypal meaning. Informed by the story of Chiron's first sighting, the astrology of the moment of discovery, and the classical mythology and storytelling about Chiron, we can come to understand much more than the simple stereotype. By painting a brighter and more detailed picture of Chiron and the role this Centaur plays in astrology, we can understand how Chiron's archetypal meaning speaks to the psyche and the need to do our work of healing. When we embrace the wider and more meaningful context of the mysterious nature of Chiron, we can open up "what's in the darkness" and reveal it to light.

Add an understanding of "the shadow" (a concept from depth psychology), a variety of techniques to work with "shadow" material, and a look at what Chiron in each house portends, and you will have lots of information and understanding to take back to your own chart and the charts of friends, family, and clients. With one possible interpretation of what Chiron's placement, by house, in the natal chart could mean, we can better help ourselves and others understand where we "dance with our shadow" and where we need to focus our energy to facilitate deep healing.

Because astrology relies on the interpretation of archetypes— and there are many, many different ways any symbol can be interpreted—the following information is intended to inspire the reader to engage in the discussion and potentially deepen their understanding of Chiron beyond the simple stereotype. To further facilitate an in-depth knowledge, and the myriad interpretations, of Chiron as an archetype, a list of resources is included at the end of the article for a deeper dive into Chiron's meaning.

Classical Mythology

In classical mytholgy, Chiron's mother, Philyra, a sea nymph, was sweet, pure, and lovely. One day, gaining unwanted predatory attention from Kronos (also known as Saturn by the Romans), she was pursued and ran away. Kronos chased her. In an attempt to escape him, Philyra turned herself into a horse so she could run faster. To catch her, Kronos also turned himeslf into a horse, caught Philyra, and sexually assaulted her. Yikes.

Conceived as a result of the violence, Chiron was born half-man and half-horse. Shocked by his appearance and disgusted by the product of the attack, Philyra rejected Chiron and abandoned him at birth. Perhaps the sight of him reminded her of the violation.

Chiron was raised by Apollo and Artemis from whom he learned many things—myriad ways to fight and many, many ways to heal. Widely educated, Chiron eventually became a healer, doctor, teacher, philosopher, and astrologer. He was known as a wise man despite his young age. As a result of the breadth of his knowledge, Chiron was consulted by demigods who sought his wisdom and teachings to aid them on their quests.

Because he was half-man and half-horse, Chiron commonly hung out with the Centaurs, other half-man, half-horse beings. But unlike the often-violent Centaurs, Chiron was known for his wisdom and healing abilities. He sought to help, not harm, others. And while he is considered a Centaur, Chiron's origins are different from the Centaurs who were born of the Centaur race. Chiron was a combination of human and horse, a result of the magic and shape-shifting at play at the moment of his conception.

Mythically, Chiron was an immortal. But when he was wounded by a poison arrow while "horsing" around with the Centaurs, Chiron was unable to heal himself. He was a doctor yet could not heal himself. He was a teacher and was eventually wounded by his student Heracles.

The wound festered and oozed. Even though Chiron could counsel, guide, and help others on their quests, he couldn't solve the conundrum that he faced. These dynamics contribute to the stereotype of Chiron as "the wounded healer."

Because Chiron was in agony and was unable to heal himself, his suffering was ongoing. Exhausted, he begged Zeus for mortality, and it was eventually granted. Chiron became mortal and exchanged places with Prometheus. When Chiron eventually died, Zeus granted him a place of honor in the stars, in the constellation of Sagittarius. Much later, the minor planet discovered in the stars was dubbed Chiron.

The Astronomy and Astrology of Chiron's Discovery

Just beyond the asteroid belt are a number of items that are dubbed Centaurs. Discovered at 3 degrees 8 minutes Taurus on November 1, 1977, Chiron was originally called "Object Kowal," named after the astronomer Charles Kowal who found it. Later the name of this Centaur was changed to "2060 Chiron."

The astrological chart cast at the time of the discovery of Chiron is fascinating. It shows all of the planets sitting above the horizon line, corresponding to "daylight" placement, except Chiron, which was below the horizen line. Alone, in the dark, even Chiron's physical position at the time of discovery intimates the association with "shadow" material. Add the square Chiron makes with Mars in the discovery chart, and astrologers have come to describe a Chiron-Mars square as a "stuck position," or when "our drives and instinctual urges may have been deeply conditioned by our understanding of the wounding process involved in asserting ourselves" (Astro Healer). The placement and aspects in the discovery chart incite many astrologers to interpret Chiron as a planet that deals with "what lays below," the "difficult material," and "what we fight against making peace with" within ourselves.

Later, when we look at the specific placement of Chiron, by house, in a natal chart, we can theorize about the specific nature of "the shadow," or the wound that cannot be healed, for that chart.

Archetypes Associated with Chiron

There are many archetypes associated with Chiron, not just "the wounded healer." Upon discovery, Charles Kowal dubbed Chiron a "maverick" because of its unique orbit pattern (White, 2018). A maverick is someone or something that is independent-minded or unorthodox, one who can break free of the matrix as Chiron does in its orbital pattern.

In space, Chiron sits between the inner and outer planets. Its orbit crosses that of Saturn and sits just inside Uranus's orbit. The unusual back and forth pattern and location between inner and outer planets bestows Chiron the archetype of being a messenger, a link, door, bridge, key, or passageway. Psychologically, the movement between inner and outer planets suggests the movement between conscious and unconscious psychology. Chiron's traditional association with holistic healing, teaching, guiding, and mentoring makes Chiron archetypally a guide to the deep inner work, the turning point, and the "hero's journey."

And, because he was rejected and abandoned by his mother, Chiron has come to symbolize our inner attachment wounds, where we struggle to feel worthy, attached, loved, and a sense of belonging. So while the poisoned arrow wound became Chiron's downfall, it was the early rejection and abandonment by his mother that really formed his deepest, most painful wound.

Compounding these archetypes, Chiron has become symbolic of where in our lives we experience shame, fear, rejection, or

abandonment and how our lack of recognition of those wounds allows relatively minor wounds (like the poisoned arrow) to fester and become toxic.

Consciously choosing Chiron as a guide, we can explore our inner terrain, undertake our own quest, become our own shaman or spirit guide, and engage the necessary inner awareness for healing and transformation. Ultimately, we can comprehend the wound that we are often unaware of and consciously engage these parts of ourself, bringing what is referred to in psychology as our "shadow" into the light.

What Is the Shadow?

Two early pioneers in psychiatry and psychology, Sigmund Freud and Carl Jung, used the term *shadow* to mean aspects of ourselves that lay hidden from our conscious mind. Whether it is the long-term effects of trauma or abuse, epigenetics passed down through our biological inheritance, the collective subconscious of the human race that is contained within each of us, cultural trauma (such as the societal experience of war), or the dark matter of our daily lives that gets pushed down, compartmentalized, and forgotten, our "shadow" is the part of the psyche that we can't consciously identify and don't understand. Yet we act it out.

Whether he was studying astrology, exploring archetypes, or practicing psychoanalysis, Carl Jung was fascinated by "the shadow." He wrote extensively about the shadow and introduced many techniques for exploring it. Jung referred to "the shadow self" and states "the shadow personifies everything that the subject refuses to acknowledge about himself and yet is always thrusting itself upon him directly or indirectly" (Jung, vol. 9, part 1, 1959, 284).

He also wrote that even though the shadow is the part of the self that is hidden and repressed, often due to guilt, its "ultimate ramifications reach back into the realm of our animal ancestors and so comprise the whole historical aspect of the unconscious" (Jung, vol. 9, part 2, 1959, 266).

In order to heal the unconscious patterns of projection, it makes sense to identify and then bring the shadow to light.

Illuminating the Shadow

Not to be undertaken lightly, early shadow work is something that is often best done with the help of a therapist, guide, or counselor because of the volatility of stored emotion that may arise and the need to work through it in a safe and healing manner. Thankfully, Jung reminds us that the shadow "does not consist only of morally reprehensible tendencies, but also displays a number of good qualities, such as normal instincts, appropriate reactions, realistic insights, creative impulses, etc." (Jung, vol. 9, part 2, 1959, 266). It is possible that in the process of illuminating the painful aspects of shadow, positive aspects of character may also be revealed. While uncovering anger, fear, and obsessions, we may also discover we possess strength, resilience, tenacity, and endurance.

Illuminating the shadow can uncover wounds from early childhood life, compounded family dynamics, overarching cultural traumas, and personal historical wounds. When choosing to undertake shadow work, we can be aided by a multitude of tools and helpers: self-help groups, individual counseling, group therapy, therapeutic written work, journaling, and meditation can help one come to know their shadow. Supports such as rehab programs, healing retreats, somatic therapy, release work, and building therapeutic relationships can also support us in processing these repressed wounds, as can daily practices such as the use of affirmations, gratitude lists, journaling, prayer, and meditation.

Not just psychological tools, the cognitive tools of studying archetypes, mythology, and astrology and engaging in psychoeducation can help support the unearthing and healing of shadow material.

Astrology and the Shadow

The shadow can be approached through many facets of astrology. Evolutionary astrologers rely on understanding the karmic axis, Pluto and its polarity point, plus the meaning of the south and north Node placements to understand the shadow. There is widespread astrological reference to Uranus as the awakener and the pivotal role that Chiron plays in identifying our shadow material.

If you are inspired to use astrology to delve into the shadow to further heal and transform yourself, consider the role of Chiron through the houses as a place to start, and consult any one of the resources below to learn more about Chiron.

Chiron Through the Houses

We all fear rejection, and where Chiron sits in the chart can be seen as where we specifically fear rejection of or for something. The following quick and dirty overview is paraphrased from Tom Jacobs's series of videos on Chiron through the houses and signs (Jacobs, "Chiron Overview by Tom Jacobs"). Be sure to check him

out for specific information on your Chiron house and sign place-ments (Jacobs, "Natal Chiron in the 1st House"):

With Chiron in the… We fear rejection of…

- First house: My body, my personality, how I show up. I have a fear of existing.
- Second house: My money or lack of money, my values, my resources, how I use time, how I live life on my own terms.
- Third house: My communication, speaking, writing, learn-ing, speaking up or out, and publishing.
- Fourth house: My inner emotional foundation, how I deal with my emotions, my sense of belonging, my family.
- Fifth house: My creativity, my personal expression, taking up space, individuality, my opinion.
- Sixth house: My daily routine, how I get things done, power imbalance, hierarchy, being a team player, owning my vulnerability.
- Seventh house: One-on-one relationships with the "other," feeling un/worthy in one-on-one relationships, including love and dating.
- Eighth house: Vulnerability, the deepest psychological trust and mistrust.
- Ninth house: My beliefs, religion, worldviews, expression, and how I "think big."
- Tenth house: The world of work, ambition, being part of the world, accomplishments and acclamation, being seen.
- Eleventh house: Groups, community, what kind of world you want to live in, the neighbourhood.
- Twelfth house: The collective, humanity, the psyche, mysti-cism, and magic.

Into the Light

As with all healing, there is no quick fix for the shadow. The human psyche is vast and complex, and research reveals new understandings of the psyche daily. Understanding that we have a shadow, and becoming aware of how our shadow manifests, is great groundwork. Being curious about how you project your shadow is also revealing.

If you do shadow work, go gently. Know you are not alone. There are many resources and tools, both psychological and astrological, to help you to dance with your shadow and reveal it to light. Go slowly, steadily, and with great self-compassion, and enjoy the Chiron journey of shadow dancing.

Astrologers on Chiron

For different perspectives on Chiron, check out these books:

Chiron, 2012, and the Aquarian Age: The Key and How to Use It by Tom Jacobs

Chiron and the Healing Journey: An Astrological and Psychologiacl Perspective by Melanie Reinhart

Chiron: Healing Body & Soul by Martin Lass

Chiron: Rainbow Bridge Between the Inner and Outer Planets by Barbara Hand Clow

Chiron: The Wisdom of a Deeply Open Heart by Adam Gainsburg

Essence and Application, A View from Chiron by Zane Stein

The Chiron Effect: Healing Our Core Wounds through Astrology, Empathy, and Self-Forgiveness by Lisa Tahir

And online resources:

The Astrology Podcast in which Chris Brennan interviews Melanie Reinhart: https://theastrologypodcast.com/2020/09/16/the-astrology-of-chiron-with-melanie-reinhart/

"Chiron & Friends," a site maintained by Zane Stein: https://www.zanestein.com/chiron_a.htm

References

Astro Healer. "Chiron in Aspect to Mars." Astro Healer by Tina Rahimi. WordPress. Accessed August 14, 2021. https://www.astrohealer.com/chiron-mars-aspects/.

Beauman, Jennifer. "Psychological Projection: Dealing with Undesirable Emotions." Everyday Health. November 15, 2017. https://www.everydayhealth.com/emotional-health/psychological-projection-dealing-with-undesirable-emotions/.

Jung, Carl G. *The Archetypes and the Collective Unconscious*. Vol. 9, part 1 of The Collective Works of C. G. Jung. Edited and translated by Gerhard Adler and R. F. C. Hull. Princeton, NJ: Princeton University Press, 1959.

————. *Aion: Researches into the Phenomenoly of the Self*. Vol. 9, part 2 of The Collective Works of C. G. Jung. Edited and translated by Gerhard Adler and R. F. C. Hull. Princeton, NJ: Princeton University Press, 1959.

Jacobs, Tom. "Chiron." YouTube playlist, 33 vidoes. Updated September 17, 2020, https://www.youtube.com/playlist?list=PLwgpizgPjVsTn6hehfQEAnlOiosG4jYV3.

White, Maya. "Chiron the Maverick." Maya White. September 11, 2018. https://www.mayawhite.com/chiron-the-maverick/.

An Introduction to Lunar Incense

Charlie Rainbow Wolf

Have you ever been walking through a flower garden or forest and the scents around you have been so memorable that they went straight up your nose and into your soul? Maybe you've sat around a campfire with the heady fragrance of spring hanging in the air or the promise of the coming autumn. Perhaps you've wanted to bottle that and take it home so you can relive those memories through the smells. After all, the sense of smell is said to be the strongest of the five senses.

For years now, smoke has been my thing. I've worked with herbs (both fresh and dried) and blended incense for special occasions (both magical and mundane). It all has a purpose, and when I add the herbs to the fire, the smoke becomes alive.

Lunar-Ruled Plants

There are hundreds—if not thousands—of lunar-ruled plants according to astrology, some of them having more than one ruler. It can be a bit confusing, and I don't want to just provide a long list of botanical names, so I'm going to start with some of the more familiar Moon-ruled plants. Should your list be slightly different, don't worry. Astrology and gardening are both artforms.

A general rule for lunar-ruled plants is they will be quite high in water content. Think about it; the Moon pulls the tides, and it is also the astrological ruler of Cancer—one of the three water signs (the other two being Pisces and Scorpio). Plants that grow next to the water's edge are also usually ruled by the Moon. Finally, look at the shape of the plant; many Moon-ruled plants will be shaped like one of the lunar phases.

A lot of lunar-ruled plants are those that you would eat, such as lettuce or cabbage or watercress. Succulents are often ruled by the Moon, as are many fruits because of their high water content. Obviously some of these are not going to make a very sweet-scented incense! This narrows the field a bit. Look at the flowers and herbs that echo the scents and mood desired from the incense—that will make a very good start.

Some of my favorite lunar incenses include camphor, chamomile, gardenia, jasmine, melissa, moonwort, myrrh, peony, sandalwood, and wild rose. Many of these are easily grown here at The Keep. Those I cannot grow—myrrh, for example—I purchase from a reputable online supplier.

Camphor

I have a big southernwood camphor (*Artemisia abrotanum*, also known as southern wormwood, garden sagebrush, sitherwood, and old man, to name a few) growing next to the back door on the south side of the house. It's a woody perennial shrub about two feet tall and four feet in diameter. It smells of camphor and is very easy to grow—this one is several years old, and I've pretty much just ignored it!

I planted this because—like most other wormwoods—its volatile oil is high in absinthol, which is meant to deter insects (and why I placed it next to the back door). Sachets of southernwood can be used in the same way as lavender to keep moths away from closets and other areas where clothing is stored. Southernwood does not lose its scent when dried. The best time to harvest it is late summer, ensuring it is dried thoroughly before putting it away to prolong storage.

Southernwood is a favored addition to my incense pot when working outside. Not only does it add that wonderful woody scent, but it assists the smoke in deterring insects from entering the area. It makes a good addition to incense burned outdoors for that very reason.

Chamomile

Chamomile is hit or miss here. Some years it does well and returns; other years I have to plant it fresh. I grow the Roman chamomile (*Chamaemelum nobile*, also called English chamomile and camomile). It's a low-growing plant; each hairy stem produces one daisylike flower. It's the flowers that are used most often.

I put chamomile in the herb garden to try to encourage it to grow as a useful ground cover. It's a perennial in USDA zones 4–9 and likes partially shaded areas. It's quite drought tolerant and is a good companion plant in the vegetable garden. Like camphor, the strong scent of the flowers is said to help keep unwanted bugs away.

Chamomile is also associated with the Sun, but I have no issues attributing it also to lunar energies because of its relaxing properties (Cunningham, 2013, n.p.). It adds a sweet and somewhat fruity scent to loose incense blends. I also have steeped it for a soothing tea and included it in dream pillows to help promote restful sleep.

Melissa

Melissa (*Melissa officinalis*, also known as lemon balm) is a member of the mint family. It has to be disciplined or it will become invasive! Having said that, it is an easy to grow perennial, and it is one of the herbs that can be grown in a pot on a windowsill. It's happiest in USDA zones 3–7 and in a soil that is neutral to slightly acidic.

I have lemon balm in two areas of the garden simply because it spread before I could stop it! It's a very useful herb in many different ways. Like chamomile, it makes a soothing, relaxing tea, and it's said to be a calming herb—one that promotes restful sleep and aids digestion.

Added to an incense blend, lemon balm brings soothing influences but also a quality of protection. It helps to keep the bugs away but softens the ambiance, as opposed to stimulating it like southernwood camphor does. In fact, burning the two together

isn't a bad idea; it embraces the best of both worlds, and the scent is woody, earthy, and sweet.

Peony

Peony is an old-fashioned garden favorite. I know someone who, in their thirties, bought their first home from an octogenarian, and the first thing they did was get rid of the "penny bushes" because they were too "old." Now in their sixties, that same person is a peony aficionado! Here, we grow peonies next to the witch hazel in the area of the yarden (yard + garden = yarden) devoted to my late mother, who loved them. There are many colors of peonies in both single and double petals, but they all belong to the *Paeoniaceae* family. Peonies are native to North America, Europe, and Asia and grow well in USDA zones 4–8, as they need the winter's chill to survive.

Peonies might seem an odd choice for an incense flower, but its petals offer a deep, sweet scent. Peony is associated with protection, which might be one reason for its old-fashioned popularity. Dried peony petals used as confetti invite stability and security. I've seen bundles of dried peonies hung over doorways. In an incense blend, the peony petals will offer the same qualities.

Pick peony flowers as they just start to open. Rinse the petals well—ants are attracted to their sweetness. Discard any that are blackened or wilted, and dry them thoroughly before storing. I was taught the traditional time for picking peonies for protection is nighttime.

Wild Rose

I've got such a soft spot for wild roses and include them in the yarden as frequently as possible. There are many different varieties of wild roses—although a more appropriate term is *species rose*, meaning that it grew without assisted pollination or special environments. There are two categories: deciduous shrubs or climbing roses.

The rose is often associated with Venus—the only planet named after a goddess rather than a god—as well as the Moon. Throughout literature it is a symbol of love. Its link with strong emotions is what makes it a lunar plant as well as a Venusian one. Most wild roses are shades of pink, but there are red ones and white ones too. All wild roses have five petals. It's possible that cultivated roses will only have five petals, but no true wild roses will have more.

Wild roses grow in the wild, but it's possible to purchase cultivars to grow in flower beds or pots. We grow the *Rosa rugosa*, an imported wild rose, because all parts of the plant are useful. It's large, sweet-scented, and showy, and the petals are edible.

When blended with incense, rose adds a heady perfume, similar to peony. Like peony, it is protective. Rose also brings luck, particularly when it comes to romance, but it's not isolated to just love spells. The love that rose embodies is deep, not just the ego-based love that comes through lust and desire; it also reflects the bond between child and mother or between good friends. In the Christian faith, rose is said to represent Mary, mother of Christ.

Harvesting for Incense

It's important to choose the right time to harvest the incense, for this helps it to stay fresh longer. A general rule of thumb is on a slightly overcast day after the dew has gone but before the Sun's heat has intensified. Pick only the freshest of petals and leaves, and try to avoid those that are wilted, older, or might be imperfect in some way. A small blemish now could turn into a big problem once the plants have been dried and stored. Watch for leaves that are wilted, older, or imperfect in some way on their leaves or flowers.

Storing the Flora

Before the harvest is stored, it is essential that it is dried properly. If stalks have been picked as well as the leaves and flowers, it is easy to tie them in a loose bundle and hang them to dry. I've done this outside on breezy days, and I've also done it inside, covering the bundles in brown paper bags before hanging on a hook in the laundry room. My favored way is to place the harvested plant material between two screen windows and store them horizontally where the air can get to them, flipping them occasionally until the herbs and flowers have dried. A food dehydrator is another way. They're dry when they're crunchy!

If the herbs have been gathered by their stalks, they can be bundled into incense sticks. You may have seen white sage bundled this way. Other herbs can be tied the same way. Use cotton string or another natural material—manmade fibers don't burn clean. Start at one end wrapping the bundle. When the end is reached, come back down to the beginning, so the bundle has been double wrapped with the string. Tie it securely. Store in a dark and dry place until used.

Incense Burning

To burn an incense stick, simply light the end! It's wise to have a heatproof dish on hand, though. I put sand in the bottom of my incense pots; this way, if the entire stick has not been burned, it can be stubbed out and relit at another time. If the entire stick is being used, then the dish makes a suitable receptacle for the short end once it's too hot to hold.

My go-to is loose incense, and I place a lighted charcoal briquette on top of the sand in the pot. These briquettes are easily available from metaphysical shops and online retailers. Once the briquette is glowing, I add the dried herbs.

This is where the fun starts, because what is burned is entirely a matter of preference. Some people choose to burn a single-note incense—white sage, for example—while others (myself included) choose to blend their incense. I always start out with a blend of common sage, cedar, and something seasonal (lilac

in spring, for example), and then to that I add one or two other herbs or resins.

Full Moon Incense

The ingredients for this Full Moon Incense are easy to grow, and if that's impractical, they're also easily obtained. There's no hard-and-fast rule; it's a matter of preference. However, I do find this makes a pleasant and powerful incense and is a wonderful way to mark the fullness of Grandmother Moon.

- 1 cinnamon stick
- 1 pinch dried rose petals
- 1 pinch dried lavender
- 2 pinches dried sage (common or white; I use common)
- 2 pinches dried melissa
- 1 pinch juniper berries

Gently crush all ingredients using a pestle and mortar. Blend well, then store somewhere dark and dry until ready to use. I have mine in glass jars in an armoire.

New Moon Incense

Like the Full Moon Incense above, these ingredients are easily grown or obtained from an herbal supply shop or even the grocery store. I've given rough guides to quantities, but I believe that incense is a personal journey and should be crafted to personal tastes. This incense is strong yet soothing—perfect for the start of a new lunar cycle.

- 2 pinches dried lavender
- 2 pinches dried sage
- 2 pinches dried chamomile
- 2 pinches dried melissa

Prepare and store as per the Full Moon blend above.

A Few Words of Caution

While incense is not considered dangerous, there are some measures that should be followed to ensure safety. At the end of the day, this is fire, and it will burn. Make sure the bowl is heatproof, and place it on a trivet or other heatproof surface, making double sure things don't get too hot. Don't place the lit incense next to curtains or tablecloths that could dangle into it, and if burning outside, bear in mind the breeze, and use a large enough container that no sparks might escape and ignite something.

Also with regard to safety, choose the herbs carefully. Just because something is herbal and organic does not mean that it is harmless. Research carefully, and if there's any doubt at all as to whether something is safe to take internally, it's best not to include it in an incense blend.

Conclusion

Lunar incense blends don't have to be limited to just lunar-ruled herbs and resins. Adding them to favorite mixes or seasonal combinations works just fine to include the Moon's energy. Another factor to keep in mind is these herbs still have the same therapeutic properties even if they are being burned as incense rather than taken internally—the smoke permeates as it burns, and some of it will still be inhaled. I frequently use burning herbal blends in my incense pot as a treatment, but I do not recommend doing this unsupervised by medical personnel.

Incense is definitely one of those situations where there *can* be too much of a good thing; limit the scents to four to six inclusions, and usually the result won't be overpowering. Of course, what is pleasing to one person may be too much or not enough for someone else. Don't be afraid to experiment; many good things came out of happy mistakes!

Further Reading

Centaury for Virgo, Rock Rose for Pisces by Debbie Sellwood, Polair Publishing, 2007.

Culpeper's Color Herbal by Nicholas Culpeper, edited by David Potterton, Sterling Publishing, 1987.

Cunningham's Encyclopedia of Magical Herbs by Scott Cunningham, Llewellyn Publications, 1985.

Making Your Own Incense by Tina Sams and Maryanne Schwartz, edited by Arden Moore, Storey Books, 1999.

The Complete Book of Incense, Oils & Brews by Scott Cunningham, Llewellyn Publications, 2008.

The Complete Incense Book by Susanne Fischer-Rizzi, Sterling Publishing, 1988.

The Psychic Explorer by Jonathan Cainer and Carl Rider, Simon & Schuster, 1988.

Reference

Cunningham, Scott. *Cunningham's Encyclopedia of Magical Herbs*. Woodbury, MN: Llewellyn Publications, 2013.

About the Contributors

Pam Ciampi was a professional astrologer from 1975 until her passing in 2019. She served as president of the San Diego Astrological Society and was President Emeritus of the San Diego Chapter of NCGR. Pam was the author of the Weekly Forecasts for Llewellyn's best-selling *Daily Planetary Guide* since 2007. Her latest contribution was an astrological gardening guide titled *Gardening by the Light of the Moon*. In its fourth printed edition, it is now available in a calendar format.

Sally Cragin is the author of *The Astrological Elements* and *Astrology on the Cusp* (both Llewellyn Worldwide). These books have been translated and sold in a number of countries overseas. She serves on the Fitchburg (MA) City Council and is the only professional astrologer elected to public office in the Commonwealth. She is also the founder/director of Be PAWSitive Therapy Pets and Communication. She does readings (astrological and tarot). Visit "Sally Cragin Astrology & TaroT" on Facebook, text or call 978-320-1335, or email sallycragin@gmail.com.

Dallas Jennifer Cobb lives in a magical village on Lake Ontario. A Pagan, mother, feminist, writer, and animal lover, she enjoys a sustainable lifestyle with a balance of time and money. Widely published, she writes about what she knows: brain injury, magick, herbs, astrology, healing, recovery, and vibrant sustainability. When she isn't communing with nature she likes to correspond with like-minded beings. Reach her at: jennifer.cobb@live.com.

Vincent Decker, a native New Yorker, has been actively studying planetary influences on the weather for over thirty years. His forecast method relies on the work of the main modern and ancient contributors to the field of astrometeorology. At the same time, Vincent has incorporated many new techniques discovered from his own rewarding and fruitful study of planetary influence on weather patterns. His analyses of important past weather patterns have appeared in several astrological magazines. His forecasts and their results are available on his blog at www.theweather alternative.blogspot.com.

Shelby Deering is a lifestyle writer from Madison, Wisconsin. She specializes in writing about home décor, natural wellness, and mental health, contributing to publications like *Better Homes & Gardens*, *The Pioneer Woman*, *Naturally, Danny Seo*, and more. When she's not writing, you'll find her hiking Wisconsin's many trails, shopping flea markets, or going on road trips around the country.

Bernadette Evans has always been fascinated with astrology, tarot, and psychology. She has been a counselling astrologer for twelve years, as well as a registered counsellor with the Canadian Professional Counsellors Association. Her daily and monthly forecasts have been a mainstay on *Conscious Community Magazine*'s website for four years. As an avid learner, she's always taking classes, watching webinars, and reading to stay informed and keep growing. She is experienced as an active and accredited EFT practitioner. In her spare time, she enjoys writing, playing with tarot cards, listening to music, and watching movies. She loves getting in touch with the cycles of the Moon and the planets to feel the different energies. You can get in touch with her at bernadetteevansastrology.com or follow her on Instagram at bernadette_evans.astrologer.

Penny Kelly is a writer, teacher of intuition, author, publisher, consultant, and naturopathic physician. After purchasing Lily Hill Farm in southwest Michigan in 1987, she raised grapes for Welch Foods for a dozen years and established Lily Hill Learning Center. Today, she teaches online, posts regularly on Patreon, Bitchute, Odyssey, YouTube, Spotify, Google Podcasts, and Apple Podcasts. She is the mother of four children, has co-written twenty-three books with others, and has written twelve books of her own. Penny lives, gardens, and writes in Lawton, Michigan.

Lupa is an author, artist, and naturalist in the Pacific Northwest. She is the author of several books on nature-based Paganism, as well as the creator of the Tarot of Bones and Pocket Osteomancy divination sets. More information about Lupa and her works may be found at http://www.thegreenwolf.com.

Kim Rogers-Gallagher has been a professional astrologer, writer, and lecturer for over twenty years. Based in Florida, Kim is the author of *Astrology for the Light Side of the Brain* and *Astrology for the Light Side of the Future*. Her monthly, weekly, and daily columns appear in *Dell Horoscope* and other astrological websites. She served on the board and edited the quarterly journal for the International Society for Astrological Research and was a Steering Committee Member of AFAN (Association for Astrological Networking).

Jilly Shipway is a qualified yoga teacher with over twenty-five years of teaching experience. She is the author of *Yoga Through the Year: A Seasonal Approach to Your Practice*, *Yoga by the Stars: Practices and Meditations Inspired by the Zodiac*, and most recently, *Chakras for Creativity*. Jilly regularly contributes to various magazines and yoga publications. She lives in the UK in a small Welsh border town, surrounded by hills. When she is not teaching, writing about, or doing yoga, she loves walking in town and country and, of course, gazing at the night sky. Visit her websites at www.yogabythestars.com or www.chakrasforcreativity.com.

Christeen Skinner D.F.Astrol.S., FRSA, is director of Cityscopes London, which specialises in future-casting. She taught for the Faculty of Astrological Studies in London, was chair of the Astrological Association of Great Britain, and is a trustee of the Urania Trust.

She is chair of the advisory board for the National Council for Geocosmic Research and a director of the Alexandria iBase Library, working to preserve texts and documents. She has spoken at many major conferences (UAC, AA, NCGR and ISAR) and is author of *Exploring the Financial Universe*, *The Beginner's Guide to Financial Astrology*, and *Navigating the Financial Universe* and a regular contributor to Llewellyn publications. In 2019 she was honoured with the prestigious Charles Harvey Award for services to astrology. Christeen is a fellow of the Royal Society of Arts.

Melissa Tipton is a Jungian Witch, Structural Integrator, and founder of the Real Magic Mystery School, where she teaches online courses in Jungian Magic, a potent blend of ancient magical techniques and modern psychological insights. She's the author of *Living Reiki: Heal Yourself and Transform Your Life* and *Llewellyn's Complete Book of Reiki*. Learn more and take a free class at www .realmagic.school.

Charlie Rainbow Wolf is happiest when she is creating something, especially if it can be made from items that others have cast aside. Pottery, writing, knitting, astrology, herbs, and tarot are her deepest interests, but she happily confesses that she's easily distracted, because life offers so many wonderful things to explore. She is an advocate of organic gardening and cooking, and she lives in the Midwest with her husband and special-needs Great Danes. Follow her at www.charlierainbow.com.

Moon Sign Book **Resources**
Weekly Tips provided by Penny Kelly, Shelby Deering, and Lupa
"The Methods of the *Moon Sign Book*" by Penny Kelly
"Gardening by the Moon" by Pam Ciampi

Notes

Notes

Notes

Notes

Notes

Notes

Notes

Notes